The
Afterlife
Bible

The
Afterlife
Bible

The definitive guide to otherworldly experience

Sarah Bartlett

FIREFLY BOOKS

A FIREFLY BOOK

Published by Firefly Books Ltd. 2015

First printing

Publisher Cataloging-in-Publication Data (U.S.)

A CIP record for this title is available from the
Library of Congress

**Library and Archives Canada Cataloguing in
Publication**

A CIP record for this title is available from
Library and Archives Canada

Published in the United States by
Firefly Books (U.S.) Inc.
P.O. Box 1338, Ellicott Station
Buffalo, New York 14205

Published in Canada by
Firefly Books Ltd.
50 Staples Avenue, Unit 1
Richmond Hill, Ontario L4B 0A7

Printed in Malaysia

First published in Great Britain in 2015 by Godsfield
Press, a division of
Octopus Publishing Group Ltd,
Endeavour House,
189 Shaftesbury Avenue,
London WC2H 8JY

Commissioning Editor Liz Dean
Senior Editor Leanne Bryan
Deputy Art Director Yasia Williams-Leedham
Picture Research Manager Giulia Hetherington
Production Controller Allison Gonsalves

CONTENTS

INTRODUCTION

*There are more things in Heaven and Earth,
Horatio, than are dreamt of in your philosophy.*

Shakespeare, *Hamlet*

A renewed fascination for discovering the spiritual world has recently created controversy, curiosity, and fresh credibility in all aspects of the afterlife. There are many who claim not only to communicate with this numinous place, but to have visited its frontiers and returned to tell the tale. Even sceptics wonder at the miraculous healing powers that seem to emanate from this spiritual realm, fascinated by the accounts of those who have had some kind of experience there.

But what exactly is the afterlife? If you are reading this book, then you either already believe in its "existence" and want to know more, or are curious, ready to take a leap into the light. Throughout history, most civilizations and cultures have believed in the afterlife. Some peoples "know" their spirit guides and speak to nature spirits or have recounted tales of journeys into spiritual dimensions or contact with ancestors. Whether from a religious, esoteric, or philosophical viewpoint, more and more people are beginning to revive the belief in reincarnation, recollection of past lives, and the experience of the soul's journey.

This book outlines many of these beliefs in the afterlife, from ancient myths and religions to contemporary spiritual faiths. There is also a chapter that explains how the scientific community has taken part in the search for evidence of the afterlife, and the book also reveals the role of contemporary spiritual practices.

If you are interested in yourself, you are interested in the afterlife. With practical work and step-by-step exercises for healing and afterlife contact, this book gives you the tools you need to unlock its secrets.

Right: Beyond the apparent real world, many people have experienced realms both heavenly and awesome, or realms in which they feel at one with the universe.

PART 1

*Belief
and Truth*

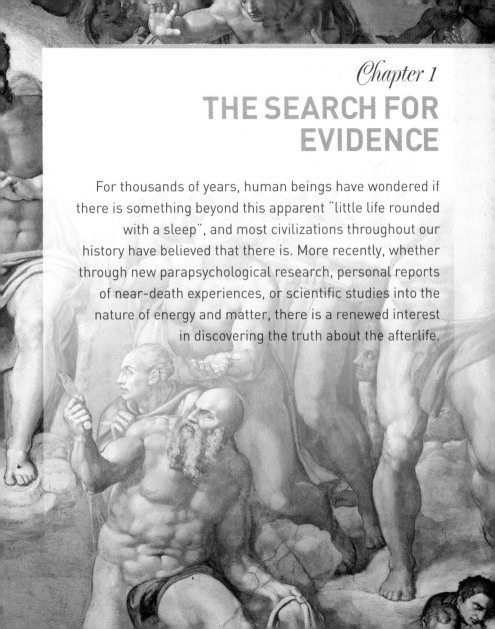

Chapter 1

THE SEARCH FOR EVIDENCE

For thousands of years, human beings have wondered if there is something beyond this apparent "little life rounded with a sleep", and most civilizations throughout our history have believed that there is. More recently, whether through new parapsychological research, personal reports of near-death experiences, or scientific studies into the nature of energy and matter, there is a renewed interest in discovering the truth about the afterlife.

WHY IS THE AFTERLIFE SIGNIFICANT?

The ancient Greek myth of Orpheus tells us of his quest to descend to the underworld to find his beloved Eurydice and take her back to the Earth.

After a successful negotiation with the god of the underworld, Hades, he returns through the narrow caves back up towards the light, with Eurydice following several steps behind him.

Hades had allowed Eurydice to return, but on one condition – that Orpheus never looked back at her while they were still in the underworld. One look, and Eurydice would vanish forever. Not hearing her

footsteps, Orpheus in a panic, did glance back to check his lover was there. As he did so, she vanished forever. Mourning his terrible loss, Orpheus revoked the love of women and, preferring young boys, was ripped to pieces by enraged nymphs. His head and lyre floated down the river to the sea, eventually landing on the shores of Lesbos, where his cult began.

This tale is a beautiful metaphor of how we ourselves might lose the ones we love because we don't trust them to be there for us. Around the time this myth was written, the pessimistic populace of ancient Greece still believed that the underworld was a terrible place; a bleak realm of eternal drudgery from which no one, not even Eurydice, could escape.

If, like Orpheus, we don't trust that what is there is actually there, or we are constantly looking for proof to fuel belief, it can only lead to disillusionment. If we keep looking for physical evidence of our soul (or, to return to the metaphor, looking for Eurydice herself), we will eventually lose touch with her. The soul doesn't hang around for ego to satisfy its requirement for physical evidence, because the soul is numinous.

But if we look from a more positive and self-empowering viewpoint of this story, we may see the light. If, unlike Orpheus,

Above: If we believe in the afterlife, if at first we see only darkness, we will soon glimpse the light.

Left: When Orpheus fled the underworld, he was tempted to look back to make sure the hand he held was that of his lover Eurydice, and not some demon.

we can trust in the unknown, then we can walk up through the dark of the underworld (paradoxically, a symbol for life itself) knowing that when we get to the doorway that leads to the light, Eurydice (our soul) will be there for us. So then, in this context, what does the afterlife mean for us? It gives us comfort, peace, and the realization that death isn't the end, bringing hope not just for ourselves, but for those we have loved and lost.

We all wonder, what will happen after I die? Some of us, the rational scientists, believe there is nothing beyond physical life, that, when death comes, it leads to oblivion – lights out forever.

The aim of this book is not only to help you find a meaning for your existence, but to encourage you to discover that belief in the afterlife goes hand in hand with a belief in the eternal essence of your own soul. Your personal soul is just a tiny part of the great World Soul, which connects everything in the universe. In fact, you are a manifestation of this universal soul. Your own soul came from this hidden world and will return again at death to the place we call the afterlife.

Right: As long as we trust in our soul being there for us, we can make our way towards the light knowing we are not alone.

For thousands and thousands of years, in every civilization, whether grand, feeble, tribal, or tyrannical, there has been belief in the continuation of the soul, just as there is a belief that without the sun we wouldn't be here at all. If we believe in our soul, and believe in the afterlife, then in this life we can confront challenges, heal our emotional wounds, calm our self-doubt and fears, and live a "whole" life loving our soul instead of denying its existence.

Belief in the afterlife helps us come to terms with the "underworld" that life is. We can then make our way towards the light, knowing that we are not alone, as long as we trust in our soul being here for us.

The quest for scientific evidence

Some people need no evidence for the existence of the soul and the afterlife to know they exist, while others might be comforted and intrigued by the findings of scientific researchers into numinous phenomena, and to hear about the experiences of people who have had their eyes opened to the afterlife. Psychic research and claims by spiritualists, channellers, mediums, shamans, and others is considered biased as the people who gather evidence of real-life cases, encounters, or tales of spiritual

visitations are usually those who are believers themselves. So in this chapter I try to explain how many people, both sceptics and believers, are trying to get to the truth of the matter.

Scientific proof helps us to construct our lives on the material plane of existence. However, because of the very nature of the "afterlife" and of the "soul" – both numinous and, therefore, not on our current reality radar screen – scientific evidence to prove the afterlife is hard to come by.

Yet there are areas within scientific research that have made some inroads into proving there is some kind of afterlife, such as parapsychological research into the supernatural or paranormal and, more recently (see page 170), psychological studies on individuals who claim to have had near-death experiences (see page 21) or out-of-body experiences (see page 30). It is this wealth of personal experience that has proved to be the most controversial yet believable, contrary to the scientific community's continued assertion that every answer is to be found in the neurological workings of the brain.

Dr Sam Parnia, of Stony Brook University, New York, is currently working with a number of hospitals worldwide on a project to investigate near-death and out-of-body experiences. He notices that people from all over the world describe the same universal experience, but the interpretation of what they see depends on their own belief system. Recent studies conducted by Dr Pim van Lommel (see page 58) and researchers from the Rijnstate Hospital in Arnhem, Holland, suggest the mind continues to exist after the death of the body.

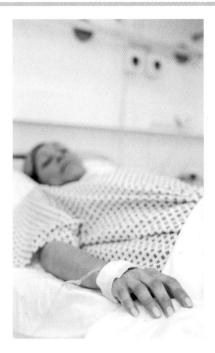

Above: Scientific research on the phenomenon of near-death experiences is being carried out in hospitals worldwide.

Left: Many people have experienced or glimpsed something otherworldly themselves.

HISTORICAL REPORTS

Since the success of the 1970s book Life After Life *by Raymond Moody, publications and the media have been overwhelmed with reports of afterlife or near-death experiences (see page 21).*

This is not just a new fashion for sensationalizing an experience, even though Moody's book did a lot to revive the idea in popular consciousness. It just so happens that our ability to communicate to the media and the world is a little easier than it was even 50 years ago.

There have been reports as far back as the 4th century BCE, when Plato recounted the story of the myth of Er (see page 204), a soldier who died on the battlefield and came back to life to recount his experiences. A tale told by the 1st-century CE historian, Plutarch, reveals how a certain man of ill repute fell from a precipice to his death only to revive three days later at his funeral. The 8th-century CE monk, the Reverend Bede, related the *Vision of Drythelm* in his *Ecclesiastical History of the English People*. Bede tells of a pious Northern family man, Drythelm, who died one evening after a severe illness but revived the next day at dawn, terrifying his mourners by sitting up abruptly on his deathbed. He related what he had seen in the otherworld to his wife and later to a monk who repeated the story to Bede.

In the 6th century, Pope Gregory the Great in his *Dialogues* told of a hermit who revived from death and testified that he had been to Hell, where he saw men dangling in fire. Just as he, too, was being dragged into the flames, an angel came to his rescue and sent him back to life with the words "leave, and consider carefully how you will live from now on".

19th-century tales include medium Mrs Conant, who revealed how, when she died from an overdose of morphine, she met her mother in Heaven, and came back to tell the tale. Swiss geologist and mountaineer, Albert Heim, survived a near-fatal accident and went on to collect 30 first-hand accounts of other survivors with similar near-death experiences.

Right: There are numerous accounts of those who have been given "a helping hand" to return to life after experiencing physical death.

EXCEPTIONAL HUMAN EXPERIENCE

Make me immortal with a kiss.

Christopher Marlowe, *Doctor Faustus*

Over the past 40 years, it is perhaps research into near-death experiences (NDEs) and out-of-body experiences (OBEs) that has come closest to signalling the presence of other worlds and/or a spiritual presence. Coined by Rhea A White, a one-time research fellow at Duke University Parapsychology Laboratory in North Carolina, exceptional human experience (EHE) is an umbrella

term that covers abnormal experiences, usually those involving spiritual or otherworldly contact.

These experiences are still, as I write, unexplained by science. They include heightened states of consciousness or awareness; transcendent or out-of-body experiences; a sense of interconnectedness to another dimension not of this universe; separation from all dimensions; and a feeling of being totally at one with the universe. There is a sense of being in a different reality or somewhere without boundaries. After having such experiences, life can become charged with meaning, and subjects report they no longer fear death. One of the most controversial of these experiences is that of the near-death experience.

Near-death experiences

Most subjects report having NDEs during major surgery, or during traumatic events such as car accidents or heart attacks. People who have claimed to have had one commonly talk of the feeling they

experience during the NDE of still having a "body", but of a different nature to the one they left behind. They glimpse the spirits of relatives and friends who have already died. They may approach some sort of barrier or border representing the limit between Earthly life and the spirit world. They are usually overwhelmed by intense feelings of joy, love, and peace. Despite this attitude, they reunite with their physical body and continue to live.

Left: Exceptional human experiences include those where people feel completely separate from any dimension.

Right: Experiencing an NDE is like approaching the border between Earthly life and the spirit world.

THE CLASSIC CHARACTERISTICS OF NDEs

- The subject passes through a tunnel of light.
- A figure of love appears, radiating light.
- Deceased relatives may appear.
- The subject is infused with a deep feeling of peace.
- Beautiful music and wondrous places are heard and seen.
- The soul undergoes a life review.
- The subject identifies ongoing life lessons.
- A choice to return or stay may be offered, or the subject is told to return to this life.

Clinical psychologist Edith Fiore recounts several reports of NDEs in her research during the 1980s. She noted that most subjects reported floating or rising into the air and viewing the scene below. At first, the subjects seem to be alone but they soon felt the presence of "spiritual guides", orbs (see page 29) or being met by deceased relatives. One case she reported was of "Roger" who "died" during a jousting match in France. He described a feeling of warmth spreading through his whole body, then he saw a white light, gradually floated away, and was able to see everything, both this world and others. Previously he had never believed in the afterlife, but during the experience the thought of returning to his body was almost repulsive, and he had no doubt of a spiritual state of existence.

Controversy

Rick Strassman, a psychiatrist who oversees the Cottonwood Research Foundation in New Mexico, theorized that a naturally occurring hallucinogenic drug known as DMT (dimethyltryptamine) helps consciousness leave the body. He theorized that when a person is approaching death or, possibly, when in a dream state, the pineal gland releases DMT, accounting for much of the imagery reported by survivors of NDEs. Yet Dr Strassman has also noted that the pineal gland first becomes visible at approximately the 49th day of foetal development, which is the same length of time that the *Tibetan Book of the Dead* states that it takes for the soul to reincarnate. Could this be a sign that the

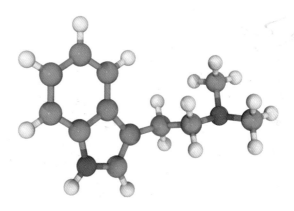

Left: During an NDE, subjects often report seeing a loved one bathed in warm light.

Right: The pineal gland releases the hallucinogenic drug, DMT, and may be the cause of an NDE.

pineal gland and the soul are in some way linked? In fact, could the appearance of the pineal gland be a sign that the soul has reincarnated into the next body?

Dr Peter Fenwick, a respected British neuropsychiatrist, has researched over three hundred NDE reports. Criticized for claiming that human consciousness can survive bodily death, he argues that it may be more than a function of the brain, and the brain and the mind are separate. He admits that no one really understands mystical experiences, but NDE survivors always reinterpret their belief system in light of the experience. He and his wife Elizabeth Fenwick reported in their studies that near-death experiences are almost always positive in nature. The Fenwicks argued that modern medical practices have devalued end-of-life experiences, and have called for a more holistic approach to death and dying. (See Chapter 5 for accounts of NDEs.)

After-death communication

Another phenomenon considered exceptional human experience involves direct communication from a deceased family member or friend. Researchers Bill and Judy Guggenheim have collected more than 3,000 first-hand reports from people who believe they have been

Above: Contact from a loved one who has recently passed over is one of the commonest experiences of after-death communication.

Right: ADC reports often include a distinct sensation that a loved one is close by.

contacted by a loved one who has passed over to the spiritual world. Their book *Hello From Heaven* documents many such experiences in which they coined the phrase after-death communication (ADC).

ADCs involve a sudden, distinct feeling that a deceased loved one is nearby, even though they cannot be seen or heard. ADCs are usually felt during the days and weeks immediately after the death, but people can have them months and even years later.

Characteristics of ADCs

Some people report hearing a voice, often the same voice of the loved one, but it is not usually audible to others. Another type of ADC is that of being touched by a loved one either as a caress, tap, stroke, kiss, or even a hug, which are considered as an expression of affection and comfort.

Sometimes the ADC occurs with a sudden whiff of fragrance of the loved one's favourite perfume, aftershave, flowers, bath oils, tobacco, and foods.

BRAIN-WAVE FREQUENCY TYPES

Neurologist Hans Berger (1873–1941) discovered in the 1920s that brain-wave frequency is divided into four main types. The first are Alpha waves, which correspond to dream states, hypnosis, and meditation. The second type, known as Beta, correspond to our wakeful, conscious and rational mind. Theta waves correspond to our emotional and feeling state of mind, Finally, Delta waves represent total unconsciousness. Alpha-waves seem most conducive to ADCs.

Above: Four types of brain-wave frequency were discovered by neurologist Hans Berger in the 1920s.

A wide variety of visual experiences may occur, ranging from a thin misty outline of the loved one to a solid body image. The vision may be of only the head and shoulders, or of a full body. The deceased typically expresses love and reassurance with a radiant smile, and is usually surrounded by a bright light. Those who died from devastating illnesses or accidents always appear healed and whole, regardless of how they died. Verbal communication between the experiencer and the deceased may also take place, but not always. Visions of the deceased loved one also include photographic or hologram-like visions. Experiences known as twilight ADCs occur while the experiencer is in an Alpha brain-wave state, usually when waking up, falling asleep or meditating. Twilight ADCs may

Right: Holograms, shadows, distorted imagery, and strange landscapes are all examples of twilight ADCs.

have some or all of the characteristics – sound, touch, visual experiences – of the ADCs described earlier.

Dream-state ADCs

Dream-state ADCs are lucid, vivid and colourful. They occur during sleep and are sometimes intense enough to wake you up. These often involve a dramatic out-of-body experience (see page 30) during which you visit a loved one in the afterlife. The environment usually contains beautiful light, landscapes, and otherworldly representations of nature and is filled with love, joy, and happiness.

ADCs by phone are also reported. The phone rings, you answer it, either in a dream or in waking life, to hear a deceased loved one giving you a message. The bereaved often report receiving a wide variety of other physical signs from their loved ones, including lights being turned on and off, mechanical objects whirring, and items being moved or turned over. This is so-called poltergeist activity. Many people ask "God" or their loved one for a sign they still exist. Many report receiving such a sign,

Left: Many subjects have reported ADCs where a deceased loved one speaks or leaves a message on the phone.

though it may take some time to arrive. Occasionally, these signs are so subtle they may be overlooked, or they may be discounted as a mere coincidence.

Orbs

Orbs are the beautiful balls of light captured in digital photographs. They can appear as wispy to brilliant white spheres of light. A growing number of people are experiencing the orb phenomenon as a spiritual or otherworldly event that occurs after the death of a loved one. When photographed by a grieving family member, orbs can give a sense of comfort during a time of loss and adjustment.

Orbs have been sighted during OBEs (see page 30) and NDEs (see page 21), the most publicized being the "brilliant orb of light" in Dr Eben Alexander's book *Proof of Heaven: A Neurosurgeon's Journey into the Afterlife*. Dr Alexander recounted that during his NDE he encountered a young woman, who accompanied him. She appeared not only in human form, but as a brilliant orb of light. She was later identified as his birth sister who had died ten years previously and was someone whom Alexander had never met.

Orbs apparently emanate from the soul and are considered to be the vehicle of consciousness in the afterlife.

OUT-OF-BODY EXPERIENCES

Commonly known as OBEs, out-of-body experiences are characterized by the feeling that one's consciousness is outside of one's body and, in many cases, able to view one's physical body from a place beyond.

OBEs are usually spontaneous, but they can be induced by either mental or mechanical means and can be either highly disturbing or deeply moving. The simplest explanation is that OBEs are exactly what the term suggests: the human consciousness separating from the human body and travelling, unhindered by any physical form, in the physical world. People who have claimed to have experienced OBEs have either willed themselves out of their bodies, been dragged out by some unknown force or suddenly realized they were outside their bodies. Some researchers believe they are hallucinations, but this requires an explanation of why so many people have the same experience. Many scientists consider the OBE as a natural phenomenon arising out of neurological processes.

Induced OBEs

There are many different ways of consciously entering into an OBE state. In one example, the mind stays awake but the body sleeps. Various methods include OBE pioneer Sylvan Muldoon's forearm trick, in which you hold the forearm perpendicularly above you in bed. As you drift off to sleep, the arm falls, to restore your mind. This deliberate attempt to stay on the edge between wakefulness and sleep induces a trance-like effect that can help to set off the sensation of an OBE.

Other methods to induce OBEs include lucid dreaming practice and deep trance and visualization work. Awareness includes imagining a cord pulling one's mind out of one's body, visualizing one's body in a different location, or projecting one's mind into the air, including the popularized Golden Dawn Body of Light Technique (see page 378).

Psychologists and scientists have used and researched extensively many other mechanical inductions of OBEs,

Right: OBEs are often reported as seeming as if one is looking down at oneself from above. .

such as magnetic stimulation of the brain, sensory deprivation, sensory overload, and brain-wave synchronization. OBEs can also be induced through hallucinogenic drugs such as ketamine.

OBE research

Most of the research into OBEs has been carried out in the scientific and experimental psychological fields. The first major study was made by Celia Green in 1968. She collected first-hand accounts of OBEs through the mainstream media. Believing the experiences to be hallucinatory, there was some question of the accounts of OBEs being genuine otherworldly experiences.

Neurological explanations suggest among other theories that OBEs are simply the stimulation of various parts

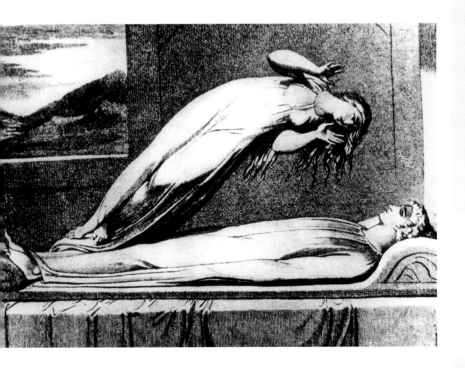

of the brain. According to English psychologist, Susan Blackmore, during OBEs sensory experience is no longer transmitted. We perceive the world only from recreated replicas that are produced in the brain. This is like the processed information of the physical world gathered during the day that occurs in our dreams.

The neurologist Olaf Blanke, the neuroscientist Michael Persinger and, more recently, the neurologist Henrik Ehrsson have all conducted studies and experiments to try to prove that there are normal neurological reasons why individuals have OBEs, as they believe the experience is triggered by a discrepancy between visual and tactile signals. However, scientists have yet to establish whether OBEs are genuine experiences or imagined ones.

Many people have argued that the OBE is some kind of dream. However, it has been pointed out that an ordinary dream does not have the important features of the subject seeming to leave the body and being conscious of perceiving things as they occur. In this sense, OBEs are better compared with lucid dreams, in

Right: Scientists have yet to establish whether OBEs are real or imagined experiences.

Right: Soul travel occurs when the soul leaves the body during sleep to visit unworldly realms.

which the sleeper knows at the time that he or she is dreaming.

In spiritual circles, OBEs are considered to be the soul's ability to leave the body at will or while sleeping, and to visit numinous or unworldly realms. In the West, the Swedish scientist and mystic Emanuel Swedenborg (see page 102) was one of the first practitioners to write extensively about OBEs as soul travel experiences in his *Spiritual Diary (1747–65)*. Since then, author and screenwriter, Michael Crichton (1942–2008), who is probably best known for his work *Jurassic Park,* also recounted how his soul travelled separately from his body in his 1988 autobiography, *Travels.*

In Eastern traditions, soul travel is accepted as part of an initiate's practice. For example, the Spiritual Master Kirpal Singh (1894–1974) founded the Ruhani Satsang (School of Spirituality or Science of the Soul) in 1948, where he taught the practice of soul travel, achieved mostly by meditation and mantra techniques. This is the basic practice of the various contemporary movements of Surat Sabd Yoga, as taught by living masters such as American Sri Gary Olsen.

American Harold Klemp, the current Spiritual Leader of Eckankar, practises and teaches Soul Travel through contemplative techniques that are known as the Spiritual Exercises of ECK (Divine Spirit).

DREAMS

Many ancient cultures, including Egyptian and Greek, believed that dreams enabled supernatural communication and that messages sent from the spirit world in dreams were to be unravelled by those who had special powers, such as oracles and shamans.

Healing temples, known as *asclepieion*, such as those found on the island of Kos, were devoted to the Greek god of medicine, Asclepius, and named after him. They were arranged so that pilgrims could spend the night in the temple and then retell their dream to the priest the next day. The priest would then prescribe them a cure, depending on the dream.

Below: At this ancient Greek temple, dreams were interpreted by priests to cure illness.

Left: Psychologist Sigmund Freud believed that dreams revealed the deepest desires of the individual.

Right: Carl Jung went on to champion and interpret dream symbolism but linked it to the world of archetypes and the collective unconscious, rather than to individual desires, as had Freud.

Ancient Chinese tradition maintained that it is your soul that creates your dreams and leaves the body to travel to other realms and meet other souls during dreams. The Chinese sages believed that in the dreaming state you are more awake than the apparent state of being awake. An ancient story tells of a monk, Chuang Chou, who dreamed he was a butterfly. He flew around from flower to flower, aware only of being a butterfly, and not of being Chuang Chou. When he awoke he was Chuang Chou, but he couldn't be sure if he was the butterfly dreaming that he was Chuang Chou, or if Chuang Chou had dreamt of being a butterfly at all.

The father of psychoanalysis, Sigmund Freud (1856–1939), wrote *The Interpretation of Dreams*, published c.1900, which marked a turning point in psychology. Freud gave enormous importance to the interpretation of dreams. He described this as the way to understand unconscious processes and believed dreams revealed the deepest wishes and desires of an individual.

The psychologist, C G Jung (1865–1961) said dreams are "the main source of all of our knowledge about symbolism". This means that the messages in dreams are expressed symbolically and must be interpreted to find their true meaning.

The famous 20th-century American psychic Edgar Cayce was able to astound people by interpreting their dreams and giving them insight into their *psyches*, lives, and even past lives. Cayce believed that dreams are actually journeys into the spirit world. He concluded that dreams are an outlet of expression for your soul, which knows both your past and your potential as a spiritual being. Cayce believed that John the Apostle's visionary experiences were at the core of the Book of Revelation. The book not only revealed his dreams, but how both prayer and reflection could add to his spiritual growth so he could eventually experience the Holy Spirit of God in physical form.

Nowadays, Spiritualists and dream analysts see dreams as a channel through which the universe provides guidance about relationships and health problems. While some dreams are there to help us release thoughts and emotions, others can be profoundly insightful in a psychological or spiritual way.

DREAM YOGA

Dream Yoga is a type of lucid dreaming practised by Tibetan Buddhists as a means of increasing their awareness on the path to enlightenment. It helps the practitioner to achieve enlightenment during sleep so that, at the time of death, he won't be trapped in the projections of his mind, and so will be enlightened and, therefore, have no need of rebirth. Once the initiate has harnessed the practice of lucid dreaming, he must then practise tasks such as visiting other realms and planes of existence, communicating with enlightened or ascended beings, meeting with beings from other realms, and shape-shifting into other forms or creatures.

Below: Dreams are nowadays interpreted both from a spiritual and psychological perspective.

SUBTLE BODY ENERGY

Invisible universal energy is believed to permeate all things and it is thought that it can be harnessed for healing. By tapping into this force field we can communicate with the spiritual world or afterlife.

Subtle energy is also called the life force, *chi* or *mana* in various Eastern religions. It was called the Odic force by chemist, geologist, metallurgist, and philosopher Baron von Reichenbach (1788–1869), and is the basic energy of human auric fields discovered in Kirlian photography.

While subtle or invisible energy is both outside ourselves and yet also flowing through us, subtle body energy is part of the system of the body itself. We have a physical structure and a spiritual structure. Our spiritual being, the subtle body, is made up of invisible energies such as meridian lines, aura and chakra systems.

These energies align with the vibrational frequencies of the universe. It is thought that by working with our own energy to align with universal energy we can contact the spiritual world (see pages 312–15 for useful meditation and visualization techniques).

In Vedantic Hinduism (the branch of Hinduism based on the Upanishads)

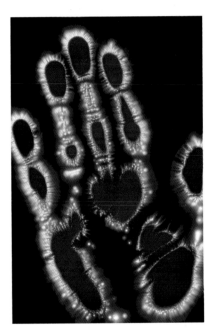

Above: Our spiritual being is made up of invisible energies that align themselves with the vibrations of the universe.

the subtle body is the vehicle of consciousness with which one passes from life to life. Members of the Theosophical Society, founded by H P Blavatsky in the 19th century, took on the Vedantic *koshas* or energies, combining this concept with Western beliefs to establish four "bodies" – etheric, astral, mental, and causal – which are the vehicle of the soul itself.

The subtle body and science

Ervin László, a Hungarian philosopher of science, coined the Sanskrit term for "space" (Akasha) to describe how the "Akashic field" connects everything at the sub-quantum level. This field, likened to the dark matter of astrophysics, conveys and conserves all information, thus linking the subtle body energy to the invisible electromagnetic forces of the universe.

Left: Subatomic particles, similar to the dark matter of astrophysics, carry invisible psychic data.

EVPs

Known as Electronic Voice Phenomena, EVPs are sounds that resemble voices that have been unintentionally recorded, and that are believed to be of paranormal origin. In an attempt to prove that contact with the dead and the existence of an afterlife is a fact, EVPs are popular devices used by practising Spiritualists.

Due to an ever-growing international interest in this progressive religion, the Spiritualist movement was prominent throughout Europe and the United States from the middle of the 19th century up until the 1930s. With a need to prove that spirit contact was genuine, new technologies of the era, including photography and voice recordings, were tested to demonstrate communication with the spirit world. The inventor of the early form of light bulb, Thomas Edison (1847–1931), was asked by *Scientific American* magazine to comment on the use of his own inventions to communicate with spirits. He replied that if the spirits were capable of subtle influences, a sensitive recording device would provide a better chance for spirit communication than the ouija boards used at the time. By the early 1920s, mediums began to use sound devices to record spiritual contact. Spiritualism declined at the end of the 20th century, but portable recording devices and modern digital technologies are still used in an attempt to communicate or record spiritual phenomena.

The National Spiritualist Association of Churches has stated that the EVP is an important modern-day development in spirit communication. An informal survey by the organization's Department of Phenomenon cites that one-third of churches conduct sessions in which participants seek to communicate with spirit entities using EVP.

Research into EVPs

Paranormal investigator, Alexander MacRae, published a report on EVPs in 2005 in the *Journal of the Society for Psychical Research*. MacRae conducted recording sessions using a device of his own design. In an attempt to

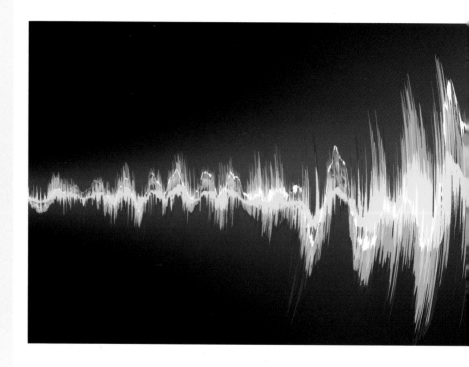

demonstrate that different individuals would interpret EVP in the recordings the same way, MacRae asked seven people to compare some selections to a list of five phrases he provided, and to choose the best match. MacRae said the results of the listening panels indicated that the selections were of paranormal origin. Portable digital voice recorders

Above: Sound devices, such as EVPs, are still used in the attempt to communicate or record spiritual phenomena.

are currently the technology of choice for EVP investigators. Enthusiasts suggest that both hearing and understanding the words in EVP is similar to learning a new language.

PAST LIVES

All streams run to the sea, but the sea is not full; to the place where the streams flow, there they flow again.

Ecclesiastes 1:4–7

There are times when we all experience a nagging feeling that we were a famous person, or someone else in a past lifetime. We have flashes of memory which seem to have nothing to do with our current life. If you are open to the idea of reincarnation (see page 68) and that perhaps you have lived other lives before and will do so again, then it is likely you have recollections from past lives.

Reincarnation has been one of the key elements of afterlife belief, although belief in reincarnation is not essential for belief in the afterlife. A current resurgence in the idea of reincarnation has also inspired the popular imagination as

Left: Many people believe in reincarnation, especially when they recall being someone else in another life.

DR IAN STEVENSON

Dr Ian Stevenson (1918–2007) was a renowned American research professor in psychiatry, investigating parapsychological phenomena such as reincarnation and exceptional human experience (see pages 20–29). Internationally recognized for his work, he uncovered evidence suggesting that memories and physical injuries can be transferred from one lifetime to another.

Travelling worldwide over a period of 40 years, he investigated 3,000 cases of children from around the world and their recollections of past lives. His meticulous research presented evidence that children had unusual abilities, illnesses, phobias, and desires for food or drugs not common to their culture. None of these could be explained by their current environment or heredity. Dr Stevenson commented that this provided the best explanation for some of the most compelling cases of past-life experience that his research team had investigated.

how best to tackle the subject. If we are to believe in reincarnation, then surely we must believe in past lives, future lives and maybe some kind of in-between life, too?

Past-life therapies

There are psychologically beneficial ways to help us come to terms with wounds left from past-life traumas and how we can prepare ourselves to deal with future lives, too. Past-life therapies are concerned with the belief in reincarnation and the concept that an individual has experienced a previous life. With past-life knowledge and help from a specialist, people can begin to understand their purpose or role in "this life", or even realize why they are locked in complexes, inhibited by specific fears, or repeating the same negative patterns in relationships.

Left: Although Buddhist teachings are about freedom from the cycle of life and death, even the Buddha remembered his past lives when he was still under the illusion of "self".

Above: Rudolph Steiner believed that cosmic forces act directly upon us in between lives.

RUDOLF STEINER

Rudolf Steiner (1861–1925), the founder of anthroposophy, an offshoot of theosophy, believed that the soul gained new insight and experience in each incarnation, and would not limit itself to one culture or race. He believed that the future and the past were constantly in conflict and that it is this tension that creates the present. Between the events of the past and those that are to come is the space for an individual's free will to make choices and thereby create their own destiny.

In essence, after death, Steiner believed, we expand into the planetary spheres. We fall asleep and the cosmic forces act directly upon us, preparing us for the next Earthly experience. Our cosmic sleep regenerates us. There comes a time when the desire to reincarnate starts to work on us. When that happens, we begin the process of going back through the planetary spheres, picking up what we need in order to fulfil our purpose in the next Earth life. The soul "germ" is carried into the embryo, forgets the whole trip and is born again on Earth.

Left: Guided imagery and visualization techniques are used in past-life regression to take the subject back to a past life.

New approaches to PLR

There are currently a growing number of past-life therapies available. The three main types are past-life regression (PLR), life-between-lives regression (LBL) and past-life readings. One of the first pioneers of LBL was the American hypnotherapist Michael Newton in the 1980s. PLR therapy has been more extensively developed since the early 1950s and has been written about by key authors such as psychologist and hypnotherapist Helen Wambach, psychiatrist Brian Weiss, and psychologist and psychotherapist Andy Tomlinson.

Past-life regression

PLR is a technique whereby therapists use guided imagery or a light state of hypnosis to activate memories of the past life of the client. PLR is often used to resolve emotional or psychological problems or activate a spiritual awakening through knowledge of that past life, or the recollection of it. Many therapists claim that PLR offers great psychological or spiritual value regardless of the validity of the memory. Most clients have past-life stories that provide clues to problems in their current life. For example, a fear of commitment or attachment in intimate relationships in a current life could be the result of being serially betrayed in a past life. A phobia of the sea or water could indicate a past-life tragedy involving drowning.

Thus, PLR therapists claim that unresolved wounds from a past life (the soul's karma) are responsible for present psychological problems but can be healed by "reframing" these recollections, as well as many other clinical methods.

Life-between-lives regression

In LBL regression, therapists use hypnosis to regress the individual to the place between two lives – to reconnect to the soul, spirit, or divine essence in the "interlife", as they call it. This technique is also called spiritual regression.

It seems many LBL clients have all had similar experiences or "memories", such as remembering the departure of the past life and how they passed through the spirit world. During their regression to their in-between life, subjects can review a past life assisted by spirit guides or evolved souls, plan their next life, and choose past-life strengths to help them improve their current life.

Dr Helen Wambach (1925–1986) was a psychologist and author of *Reliving Past Lives* and *Life Before Life*. Initially a sceptic, in 1975 she undertook a major study of past-life regressions in order to find out if there was any truth in reincarnation. With a scientific analysis on the past lives reported to her by 10,000-plus volunteers, she came up with some startling evidence in favour of reincarnation. One of her most controversial findings was that people have some choice in their current lives and that the disembodied consciousness or soul does not enter the body until near birth. Among other evidence, she found that the recall by subjects of clothing, food, housing, footwear, and so on from previous lives was better than that written in popular history books. Her subjects knew profound information about the era in which they had lived. Even when she went to find out unknown information from obscure experts, her subjects were invariably correct. Her conclusion was: "I don't believe in reincarnation – I know it!"

Past-life readings

A number of psychologists now offer past-life readings, in which, under hypnosis, the subject focuses on one past life, or concentrates on a distinct period of time in that life. Alternatively, they move through the years and decades, pausing at certain time frames and focusing on important events. Unresolved emotional issues that are carried from one life to another can be seen as either a useful guide for living in this life, or the very blockages that are holding up the individual on their current journey.

Left and above: Belief in past-lives became popular in the 1970s when John Lennon was convinced of his previous life as Napoleon, and Yoko Ono's as Josephine.

PAST LIVES OF THE FAMOUS

Many famous individuals have believed themselves to have past lives. Henry Ford (1863–1947) was convinced he was a soldier killed at the battle of Gettysburg; General George S Patton (1885–1945) believed he was the reincarnation of the great conqueror Hannibal, while John Lennon (1940–1980), the former Beatle, held that he was the reincarnation of Napoleon and that Yoko Ono had been Napoleon's wife, Josephine.

SPACE/TIME AND THE MYSTIC/PHYSICIST

The current scientific picture of our universe is one of interconnection, of mind-matter interactions, and of instant communication across vast distances. Physicists are discovering that, at the heart of all matter, there is energy, consciousness, and something quite remarkable that the mystic always knew – that everything in the universe is connected, and that the world as we see it is an illusion.

Even space, which was thought to be totally empty of atoms and molecules, contains a network of quantum energies that transmit information. This has been dubbed the Zero Point Field by the physicist Dr Hal Puthoff, who is currently attempting to harness this energy as a basis for revealing the truth about psychic phenomena. At the subatomic level, everything is interconnected, which is known as quantum entanglement, and information moves instantly across vast distances. This apparently explains how psychic phenomena work, and how people have experiences of "direct knowing".

Quantum mechanics

The convoluted jargon of quantum mechanics sounds complicated, and can be a minefield for the uninitiated, but it is simply the study of matter and energy by physicists. Current research suggests that the behaviour of matter and energy is interconnected and that the effect of the observer on the physical system being observed is part of that system. This ties with the mystical and esoteric belief that we have a major interconnection to the universe. We are part of the One, connected by the vibrant light of the universal chi, or life force – or maybe as scientists would call it, quantum energy.

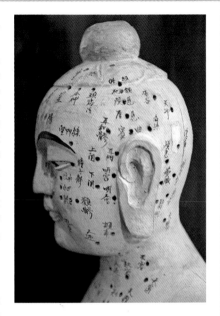

Above: Ancient Chinese sages used acupuncture to cure illnesses, based on the belief that the "ch'i" or universal energy, flowed through specific meridians of the body.

Left: Quantum entanglement moves instantly across vast distances.

There is always energy within action, and this is always changing its form. It is thought that a human action creates an invisible quantum motion of force, and these positive and negative actions and reactions flow through our conscious and unconscious world.

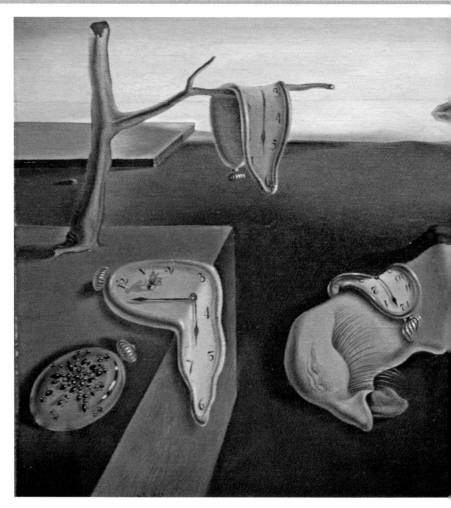

Above: Quantum physicists now believe that there are other realities, or even parallel universes that we are unable to perceive or measure.

Subatomic level

Quantum energy is also defined as a life force that connects to everything that exists in the universe, from distant stars and galaxies to microscopic atoms within your body. We are all connected at something called the subatomic level. Much like the concept of a soul, this is an instinctual energy field composed of waves of subatomic light and matter.

Since these particles, or energy packets, have been found to blink on and off and in and out of our reality, where do they go when they are not here? Quantum physics suggests that when they are not existing in our reality they are existing in other parallel universes that we are unable to perceive or measure. In fact it is this "other reality" that has been known and experienced by psychics and mediums, and anyone who has made contact with the spiritual world.

The power of light

When subjects tell of near-death experiences (see page 21), they usually talk about a welcoming, empowering, loving light source. From a physicist's point of view, light was at the start of the Big Bang and is predicted to still be there at the end of the universe, and that all forms of light are timeless.

TIME IS AN ILLUSION

Physicist Julian Barbour believes that time is an illusion. According to him, it isn't a substance, field, or particle and it can't be measured. Rather, it has been invented by mankind. Barbour's universe consists of an infinite number of "eternal nows" stretching from the Big Bang to the end of the universe. Time is merely an illusion created by human consciousness, which only sees one "now" at a time, as it moves along through the "nows" that make up its life. Somewhere in Barbour's universe, which he calls Platonia, you are being born, meeting your first lover, having your first child, and lying on your deathbed. But in this "now" you are only aware of the you that is reading this.

Barbour then theorizes that if time is an illusion, the question of an "afterlife" is entirely inappropriate. Without our notion of time, the terms "before" and "after" become meaningless. However, for all Barbour's illusory world, perhaps he is missing the point, and missing the "afterlife", which is, in fact, another dimension in which time does not exist. The very place claimed by mystics, psychics, quantum physicists, and many NDE (see page 21) and OBE (see page 30) experiencers that exists in some other form unknown to us.

Below: If, according to physicist Julian Barbour, our concept of time is an illusion, then logically the "afterlife" cannot exist.

PSYCHIC PHENOMENA

The Society for Psychical Research, founded in 1882, had the express intention of investigating Spiritualism and the afterlife, and actively studied psychic phenomena such as contact with the spirits of the dead, apparitions, clairvoyant visions, and mediumship.

Members included noted scientists such as William Crookes and philosophers Henry Sidgwick and William James, all of whom contributed to the growing belief in psychic power, later known as psi in psychological circles. Much research into ESP, telepathy, and intuition was carried out by scientists and psychologists throughout the 20th century. In the 1930s, botanist J B Rhine (1895–1980) and his wife Louisa developed psychic research into a form of experimental psychology. To avoid psychic associations with mediums, ghosts, and spirits, they dubbed it parapsychology.

According to contemporary mystics, quantum physicists, and psychic researchers there at last seems to be an agreement that a field of invisible energy is immanent, flowing through all things and accessible at any moment. Known in spiritual circles as "cosmic consciousness", this is considered by the spiritual community to be the source of all psychic phenomena.

Parapsychology

In the 1970s, parapsychology became a popular scientific study. The influx of Eastern philosophies and spiritual teachers from Asia and their claims of abilities produced by meditational states led to research on altered states of consciousness by American psychologist Dr Charles Tart. The American Society for Psychical Research conducted experiments in out-of-body experiences (see page 30), while physicist Russell Targ coined the term "remote viewing" in 1974, a phenomenon whereby an individual can consciously observe any other person or object in any part of the world via astral projection.

While UK psychologist and sceptic Richard Wiseman has criticized the parapsychological community for

widespread errors in research methods, astrophysicist Carl Sagan (1934–1996) suggested that there are three claims in the field of parapsychology that have at least some experimental support, deserving serious study as they "might be true". One of them is the phenomenon of young children reporting details of previous lives that turn out to be accurate when they could not have known about those details in any way other than through reincarnation.

Although the majority of scientists in the UK regard parapsychology as a pseudoscience, parapsychologists in Europe and the United States, such as Gary Schwartz, are in the process of conducting new research. UK physicist Brian David Josephson and some other proponents of parapsychology have spoken of "irrational attacks on parapsychology" which stem from the difficulties of "putting these phenomena into our present system of the universe".

Botanist and scientist J B Rhine (1895–1980) was considered one of the fathers of parapsychology who was committed to finding scientific evidence for the spiritual existence of humans. He became famous for his work on extrasensory perception and other psychic phenomena in the 1940s and 1950s. Since then, many other scientists and psychologists who have researched the afterlife include doctor and psychologist Raymond Moody, psychologist and parapsychologist Charles Tart, neuroscientist Michael Persinger, and cardiologist and scientist Pim van Lommel. In 1974, even Persinger proposed that electromagnetic waves carry clairvoyant information.

Left: Certain Parapsychologists are now working with scientists and other researchers to establish what is the truth behind psychic phenomena.

FORENSIC PSYCHIC EVIDENCE

There is a huge area of forensic evidence for psychic phenomena that has been amassed by psychics working with the police on investigations into missing persons and murder victims. Can it be that psychics are really communicating with the spirits of the dead?

Little research has been done in this area, but there is a stream of reports on record from the police to verify that this work is inexplicably accurate. Perhaps science is in need of a shake-up and wake-up?

Psychics are reluctant to discuss their work for several reasons:

• They often experience the same pain or fear of the victim, and do not want to pass these feelings on to others.

• Communication with the spirit of the victim can go on for some time while solving a case. Psychics don't want the information to get into the wrong hands.

• Accuracy isn't always possible. Information can be disjointed, and they have to interpret symbols and words, and can find such tasks confusing, making them unwilling to share their imprecise findings.

• In a few cases they are accused of committing the crime themselves, or can be threatened by criminals.

There are many cases on record in which gifted psychics and mediums have given police officers information about crimes. In many such cases, it is claimed that the information was transmitted either by clairvoyance, telepathy, remote viewing, or precognition. But in most cases, the information has come, apparently, directly from the deceased spirit of the victim. It is this astonishing contact with the afterlife that has baffled the police and mystified and astounded the scientific community.

Overleaf are true-life case studies from some of the most well-known forensic psychics currently working in the US. Their names have been changed to protect their identities. When considering these cases, it's difficult to imagine what can be at work here other than true interaction and contact with the spiritual world.

Right: Forensic psychics and mediums are often used by the police to detect criminals and provide valuable information about the crime scene.

Doreen is a well-known forensic psychic in the States. A case back in 1987 involved two teenage females who had been raped and murdered. Doreen provided evidence by accurately describing how the victims were murdered, including describing the letter R worn by the murderer on a piece of clothing, and how the police would catch a man with a moustache when he was 32 years old. All information was confirmed to be 100 per cent accurate by the Philadelphia police department.

Another case involved a missing female athlete. An American psychic medium, Vanessa, was recommended to the FBI. She quickly entered into the feelings of the missing victim and stated how she felt enormous fear. She also talked about darkness, tree-growth, missing shoes and jacket. She mentioned how the victim was buried in a shallow grave, near a religious statue or fountain. There was trauma to her head and the attacker knew the victim. Through Vanessa's trance state, the victim asked her own mother, "where did you put me?" Very soon afterwards, the mother confessed she shot her daughter in the head, was found guilty of murder, and sent to prison. Again, the police received confirmation of the psychic's revelations.

Psychic medium Eleanor astounded police with her accuracy regarding a missing person's case. Her evidence was channelled from the spirit of the dead man, Darrell, who said he'd been shot several times. He said there was a rope around his neck and he was lying in a swamp, face up. Eleanor said that the spirit kept repeating the word "fickle" over and over again. Captain Smith, who was working on the case, commented afterwards that he couldn't explain how she had come up with such accurate evidence. The details were exactly as Eleanor had described and the body was exactly where she had said it would be – at the South end of a specific lake in Ohio. For Captain Smith, the most chilling moment was when they arrested a suspect and discovered his surname was a variant spelling of the word "fickle".

In Pennsylvania, a psychic and psychotherapist, Elizabeth Bell, told the local police detective that he would soon be working on an old, unsolved crime. Six months later Detective Banner was given the file on an unnamed woman who had been strangled, then tied up in a blanket, and dumped over an embankment in a small community.

Right: A psychic's revelation often comes from direct contact with the spirit of the murdered victim, and can include the fear or pain that the victim felt.

Chapter 2
BELIEF

What is belief? Why is it important? This chapter looks at a wide range of afterlife beliefs that have given shape to civilizations. Whether orthodox religion, philosophy, or mystery traditions, all have been at the root of cults and cultures that look upon the afterlife as another world, or a place where one's soul could rest eternally in peace. As well as belief in one God and Pagan belief in many gods, we look at the ideas of the spirit world of various indigenous peoples, shamanic practice, and contemporary thought, such as that within Spiritism and Wicca.

CULTURAL BELIEF IN AN AFTERLIFE

Belief matters to every culture and civilization. It is what holds society together. The belief in something spiritual, a purpose for life and death, was one of the most important tenets on which great civilizations were shaped and developed.

Above: Inuit peoples of North America believed that the shaman's soul could fly from his body and contact the spirit world.

Many ancient peoples, such as the Northern American Inuits, believed that the shamans in their culture travelled between this world and the spiritual one to help cure or free us from our suffering. Others, like the Bantu peoples of Africa, believed that if we contact and honour our ancestors, we will be healed and blessed in this life, ready for the next.

Throughout history, belief in "another" realm of existence, has been the glue which has kept such communities together. If a society has a collective belief in a heavenly afterlife, or that their soul will live on in the spiritual otherworld, it becomes some kind of consolation for living in this life.

Animism

Many ancient cultures and most contemporary neopagan groups are founded on animism, or the belief that everything is imbued with spirit.

Everything, from a rock, tree, or deer to a human being, is animated with divine power. All those who pass on go to the spirit world or reunite with the Divine. In these belief systems, the spiritual world is just another part of life and each individual must discover the truth for themselves. Animism was suppressed by patriarchal religions but resurfaced in the 20th century and

Above: Animism is the belief that everything is imbued with divine energy, whether animal or tree.

is now embraced by New Age Pagan groups such as Great Goddess followers, Wiccans, Druids, and by shamanism. Neopagan beliefs in the spirit world are not founded on orthodox faith, but on individual belief and one's personal quest for spiritual truth.

Who looks outside, dreams. Who looks inside, awakens.

Carl Jung

POLYTHEISM TO MONOTHEISM

From the ancient belief in a world of spirits followed by a host of different gods, it wasn't long until one God took over.

Multiple gods

As civilizations arose out of tribal living, polytheism, or the worship of many gods, became common. For example, the Celtic belief in a pantheon of gods is rooted in early Indo-European tribal cultures that spread across Europe. Celtic warriors were fearless because they believed the spirit or soul was immortal and would be reborn again. The otherworld existed alongside the apparent one. This was considered a place of eternal happiness and immortality, to which mortals could cross at certain times of the year, through special portals found at hilltops, caves, waterfalls, and other sacred places.

The otherworld in myth

Storytellers would orally transmit ideas about what happens after we die. Most

Left: This red figure vase shows the underworld. Hades and Persephone, in the centre, hold court.

Right: Zoroaster was the first prophet to promote the belief in one beneficial God and his battle against evil.

envisioned a god of the underworld as a shadowy, illusory figure who ruled over the souls of the dead. Some traditions believed this realm was either below us or above us, or that it was filled with the souls of dead people waiting to return to the "real" world.

In Vedic mythology, the underworld was simply a mirror of the world we believe to be real. Both are nothing more than an illusion. And in Hindu belief, Brahma dreams the universe into being while he sleeps. So everything and everyone is just an illusion, and when Brahma wakes up, the universe will disappear.

In Greek mythology, death itself was something to which the gods were immune. They were all-knowing and immortal, and although they allowed us access to their wisdom and taught us skills to survive, they denied mortals the gift of eternal life. Death became a human sufferance and the gods took little interest in us.

To the Maoris of New Zealand, death is a return to the womb of the Great Mother; to the Buddhists, the eternal now; and to the Egyptians, death is the final judgement.

It was the single deity and his powerful rule of the skies and Earth who was to

take over from the earlier pantheons, such as the Mesopotamian god Marduk, and later the Middle Eastern prophet Zoroaster's solo God and his band of angels. But it was the Christians and Muslims who went on to battle to the death to prove their God was the only One.

REINCARNATION AND KARMA

Reincarnation literally means "re-entering the flesh". If a culture believes in the soul and the afterlife, then it is highly likely it also believes in some form of reincarnation.

Although the afterlife is often viewed as a specific place, as we shall see in Chapter 4, there are also wide-ranging beliefs that the soul eventually re-enters another living entity. The wandering soul needs to go somewhere. Alternatively, perhaps we believe that there is a new soul for every new life, which then vanishes into the air and is reabsorbed into the cosmos.

Reincarnation is an ancient concept. No one really knows how it began. It is at the core of many Eastern traditions, although, believe it or not, not at the heart of Buddhist or ancient Egyptian belief. Although the ancient Egyptians believed in the afterlife, they rarely believed that anyone was coming back from it. They were more interested in the transmigration of the soul, in other words, the soul's spiritual evolution in the otherworld.

If we believe that something has a "soul", what that commonly means is that we believe there is something embodied within us, an essence of the Divine that is eternal and universal. And if we also believe that we have lived a life before the present one, then we also must believe we have had some kind of in-between life after our previous incarnation. This means that after our current incarnation, we will be born again, usually after our soul or spirit has journeyed through the realms of the afterlife. The concept of reincarnation gives us not only hope, but a sense of unbelievable possibilities of what we have been and what we may become.

Soul evolution

Both religious and philosophical beliefs about reincarnation hinge on the idea that the soul survives after the death of the body. The soul then begins a new life in a new body. If you also believe in the concept of karma, then that new flesh may be human, animal, or even spiritual, depending on the moral quality of the previous life's actions.

Above: Many religions, such as Hinduism, believe that karma or moral action in one life dictates how you will reincarnate in the next life.

Many belief systems believe the individual's soul takes up residence in another body, and when that body dies, the soul eventually is reborn in another body, which is why many people are convinced they can remember their past lives. Some cultures, such as certain African traditions and followers of esoteric and mystical philosophies, believe that the soul must pass through some spiritual plane to enable it to travel from one life to the next. That's why a belief in "future lives" is based on past lives; to reincarnate into another life we must have had a past life in the first place to do so.

There are various alternative ways of defining reincarnation. For the ancient Greeks, the transmigration of the soul was concerned with its evolution in the afterlife and was known as *metempsychosis*. However, a term that

Above: The cycle of death and rebirth is known as samsara or "wandering" in Buddhist and Vedic-rooted belief systems.

was akin to the concept of reincarnation was the word *palingenesis*. This was strongly favoured by the time of Homer.

In India, reincarnation was an essential element in the sacred texts called the Upanishads, c.800 BCE. Many other cultures, including Greek philosophers, Norse mythology, Inuit and other Native American traditions, Sufism, Hindu-based religions, and modern day Spiritualism, all embrace the idea that the essence of an individual incarnates into another human body. This essence can be referred to as the soul, spirit, divine essence and so on.

In Vedic and Hindu religion, although there is a cycle of death and rebirth, this is part of the entire universal process referred to as *samsara*, meaning "wandering", and governed by the law of karma. The *atman* of Hindu philosophy, for example, is the inner self, but not a self that we can call our own, it is a self of universal consciousness. The impersonal atman incarnates into another living being, who's life is dictated by the karmic inheritance of the last incarnation.

Karma

Karma (action) is defined as the tally and consequent spiritual result of the morally right or wrong actions taken in life, which determine a person's destiny after death. However, a belief in reincarnation can be karma-free.

Karma is a simple concept. According to the doctrine of karma, how we act in one life will have an effect on the next life. In this respect, if in your past life you did "bad" things or thought evil thoughts, then in the next life you will pay the consequences. So in this life, if you are having a run of bad luck, no jobs, painful relationships, then it's due to the karmic load of your soul or, in other words, the experiences or actions of the person you were in your previous life. According to most healers, psychotherapists, and other spiritual advisors, now is our chance to make up for it.

Gods may also reincarnate and incarnate on Earth as avatars, such as Vishnu and his ten incarnations, known as the Dashavatars. Many Christian groups regard Jesus as a divine incarnation who will return again.

Buddhist reincarnation

The Buddhist belief in reincarnation is quite different to that in many other religions. In Buddhism, there is no one enduring entity that incarnates. Buddhist thinking aspires to the "no-self" rather than an entity, and it is the flow of energy, or a collection of karmic elements that moves on from embodiment to embodiment that is labelled a rebirth. This notion implies there is only a "stream of consciousness" that links life with life.

Left: Buddhism teaches that liberation from the cycle of life and death is possible if one aspires to what is known as "no-self".

Right: In ancient Egypt, after the body was mummified, protective symbols helped the soul on its way to the Kingdom of the Dead.

ANCIENT EGYPTIAN BELIEF

The Egyptians were the first to make a very big, beautiful theatre out of the journey from life to the afterlife, which became a key theme for every culture that followed.

The Egyptians mummified their dead and covered the coffin with signs, symbols, and images to protect the body on its journey. They placed figurines, possessions, and mummified pets in the tomb to ensure the person would have his favourite delights in the afterlife, too.

The Egyptians had a complex concept of the soul, which was made up of either five or six parts, depending on the period of Egyptian history. To represent the transit of the dead to the afterlife, the part of the soul known as the *ba*, often depicted as a person's head attached to

the body of a bird, winged its way to *Duat*, the Kingdom of the Dead. To get to *Aaru*, a more heavenly abode, required greater dedication, a sin-free heart, and the ability to recite spells and incantations. Only if the corpse had been properly embalmed and dressed would he be able to live in *Aaru*, the fields of reeds, where he would accompany the sun on its daily ride.

Passing through the Hall of Two Truths, the deceased's heart was weighed against the feather of truth taken from the headdress of the goddess of justice, Ma'at. If the heart was the same weight as the feather, the person could pass on, but if it were too light or too heavy, the heart would be devoured by the demon Ammit and the soul cast into the darkness. If the scales were balanced, the deceased had passed the test and was taken before Osiris, who welcomed the deceased into the

afterlife. For those who feared the test, they could recite Spell 30B of the Book of the Dead, inscribed on their heart scarab amulet to prevent their heart from "betraying" them.

Aaru, the fields of reeds

Aaru was in the East near the rising sun, and was described as a series of islands covered with reeds or rushes. It was an ideal hunting and fishing ground where, after judgement, the deceased were allowed to live for eternity.

Before reaching *Aaru*, the deceased had to pass through a series of gates, some say 15, others, 21. All were guarded by fierce demons. The deceased would have to face the ordeal of passing these guards without looking into their eyes.

Once they reached the fields of reeds, life was an ideal reflection of the real world, with blue skies, rivers, and boats. This was a perfect afterlife, with gods and goddesses to worship, and crops that needed to be harvested. In fact, the afterlife was almost a mirror image of the life the deceased had once lived. The wealthier the deceased had been, the better the situation he or she had in the afterlife. Most merchants and royalty were buried with an accompanying statue of a servant employed to do their work in the afterlife.

Social class was maintained in the afterlife, especially by the pharaohs. So when a pharaoh was succeeded by his rival, the latter often attempted to deface the tomb of his predecessor, in an attempt to stop him reaching *Aaru*.

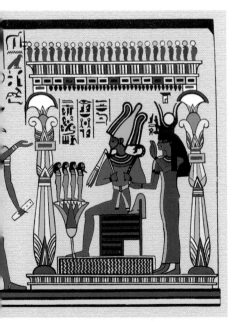

Left: The goddess Ma'at weighs the soul of the dead against the feather of truth taken from her headdress.

The Book of the Dead

The practice of including a Book of the Dead within a deceased person's tomb dates from around 1550 BCE. It developed out of exclusive funerary texts inscribed on walls and tombs of Old Kingdom pharaohs a thousand years earlier. The pharaohs believed that these texts would help them to reunite with the gods and, in particular, the creator god, Ra. Over the following dynastic period, these texts were not prepared exclusively for the pharaohs and were inscribed on the coffins and tombs of other royal family members, high-ranking officials, and dignitaries. The texts began to include spells and talismanic magic to assist the dead person's journey through the *Duat* (see page 74) and into the afterlife. It wasn't long until wealthy individuals commissioned their own texts to be written, choosing spells that suited their own personal requirements.

Written in hieroglyphs on a papyrus scroll, the book was also illustrated with scenes from the deceased's journey after death. The book was intended to give the deceased mystical knowledge in the afterlife, including spells and incantations to control the unknown world around him.

Below: The soul recited prayers from the Book of the Dead to help it reach the heavenly realm.

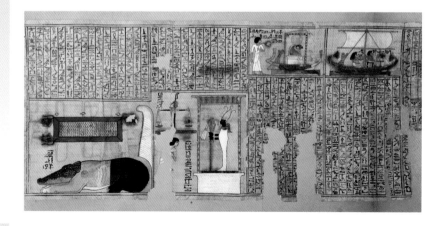

A DOOR TO THE AFTERLIFE

Thutmose III was only a baby when he became pharaoh on his father's death, so his father's wife, Hatshepsut, who was not his mother, became regent. Powerful and controlling, she ruled alone, not allowing Thutmose any authority even when he became of age. When she died, Thutmose, in revenge, had her name removed from all monuments, destroyed her statues and desecrated her tomb. It was thought that by cursing a pharaoh's tomb, the soul would not be able to reach *Aaru*, and would remain forever stuck in the dangerous territory of *Duat*. But in 2010, the Egyptian Cultural Ministry claimed to have unearthed a large red granite door in Luxor with magical inscriptions written by a powerful adviser to Queen Hatshepsut. The false door is believed to be a door to the afterlife, perhaps the one the queen closed behind her so that no pharoah could stop her from reaching *Aaru*!

Left: Queen Hatshepsut is thought to have left a secret doorway to the afterlife so she could escape being cursed by her successor.

ANCIENT GREEK BELIEF

The ancient Greek conception of the afterlife, and the ceremonies associated with burial, were an already established folk tradition by the 6th century BCE.

The popularized Greek view of the afterlife was of a dismal realm of drudgery, not much better than life on Earth, and usually so dull that there was a widespread belief that the dead longed only to return to Earth to haunt the living as ghosts. Loved ones prayed that their dead would return as favourable ghosts rather than as malevolent spirits. In theory, anyone who died of anything other than disease or old age could become a restless, bitter, and resentful ghost, such as those who died young or from a tragic accident, those who were murdered, were suicide or battle victims, or those who had neither achieved marriage nor motherhood. These were all likely to become restless, malicious wraiths. But whatever the circumstances of death, a ghost would never achieve real rest without an appropriate burial, so to ensure this extra protection, strict funerary rituals were followed by the book.

This all changed when the great epic writers Hesiod and Homer took the stage and turned this rather depressing Greek

traditional system into a stunning drama. So with literary and poetic licence, Homer and his poetic visions took the Greek world by storm. The afterlife got a makeover, albeit in both a heavenly and hellish way.

Above: Psyche, goddess of the soul, was rescued by Eros from an eternal sleep after she was tested by a jealous Aphrodite.

Left: Homer transformed the dismal view of the afterlife into a theatrical world of its own.

Homer brought the dead to life by giving them spirit, soul, body, and minds while Hesiod put character into the gods who ruled the underworld. Homer and Hesiod are usually thought by scholars to have lived about the same time in the 8–7th centuries BCE. When Homer's hero Odysseus visits *Hades*, we see the popular vision of a depressing, robot-like underworld transformed into a place

where souls have intellect and can help a hero escape his apparent fate. Hesiod's depiction of the goddess Nemesis, once the distributor of good and bad fortune, appears swooping, vulture-like, through the underworld as a goddess of divine retribution, taking what's due from the souls of men.

Psyche, meaning breath, was considered to be the soul and was thought to leave the body as a puff of wind and enter the house of *Ais*, later called *Hades*, the House of Invisibility. This underworld was imagined to be accessed by entrances on the upper world near rocks and caverns. It was filled with rivers, fire, springs, deep gorges, lakes, and gates. In *The Odyssey*, Hades and Persephone reigned over countless drifting crowds of "shades", the shadowy figures of those who had died. The epic poem did not show the underworld as a particularly happy place, apart from the Elysian Fields, but it was certainly a theatrical depiction of it, and it made people think about their future after death, rather than merely accept a miserable end.

The underworld offered punishment for the bad and pleasure for the good. The Elysian Fields was a sunlit paradise and home to those who had a led a good life.

Above: Tantalus was punished by being eternally tempted by the fruit of a tree he could never reach.

Left: The Elysian Fields were thought to be a place of permanent happiness, filled with all the beauty and goodness of the Earthly world.

Others were condemned to a recurring nightmare in the Fields of Punishment. The half-mortal and evil-minded Tantalus (most famous for cutting up his son, Pelops, and serving him at a banquet as a sacrifice to the gods) was forced to be perpetually hungry and thirsty while chained next to a fruit tree and lake that he could never reach. The deceitful king Sisyphus was forced to roll a rock up a hill, only to have it return to the bottom, where he began the task all over again – for eternity. This dismal place was one of limbo, of eternal repetition of one's sins or failings.

In Homer and Hesiod's writing, Tarturus became the darkest part of the underworld, and was described with even more horrific detail by later classical writers. Plato saw it as a dungeon of torment and suffering for the wicked. Virgil's Tartarus was filled with the writhing wraiths of the Titans and from behind the ominous iron gates was heard the clanking of chains.

Ancient Greek philosophy and mysticism

After Homer's epic poems of heroes and incest, mystical cults, such as the Orphic and Eleusinian mysteries developed, promising initiates an afterlife of happiness. The *psyche*, or soul, then became seen as separate from the body.

The earliest Greek philosophers, such as Pythagorus and, later, Plato, promoted the idea of reincarnation. These early thinkers came to the conclusion that the soul was the centre of feeling and thinking and, therefore, was very important to man. For Plato, the soul became the basis for a whole new belief system, creating a new approach to the afterlife that was to have a lasting influence throughout Western thought.

Homer's old texts of the terrors of Tarturus faded into insignificance, to become as much a mythic fantasy to the Greeks as they are now.

Left: Pythagorus claimed that he lived four previous lives that he could remember in detail, including that of a courtesan.

THE VEDIC TRADITIONS

Afterlife beliefs in the Vedic traditions that developed between 1,500 BCE to 500 CE were defined by deities ruling Heaven and Hell.

Yama was the deity who judged the souls of the recently deceased and was accompanied by his assistant Chitragupta who summed up the soul's virtues and sins. Yama sent the soul either to one of many Hells, or to Heaven, or to the abode of Pitris, the land of the ancestors. Only a virtuous person was allowed to enter Pitris.

There were two paths to get to Heaven during life on Earth – either through prayers and rituals, or piety and righteousness. Heaven was a place of beautiful celestial gardens and well-kept paths, where food and drink were plentiful. It was full of wonderful fragrances, cool breezes, delightful music, charming people. There was no fear or pain, hunger or thirst. Qualities or experiences such as old age, sweat, urine, or excretion were non-existent. However, nothing new could ever happen there. The soul was limited to repeating only the same things it had done in its previous life and, eventually, would be happy to be reincarnated yet again. The final aim of existence, according to ancient Vedic traditions, was to be reunited with one's personal choice of deity, but unlike the surrendering and dissolution of the self desired by the Buddhists, each soul sought and was believed to retain its human personality when merged with the Divine, although in a refined and purified form.

Right: The Vedic god, Yama, ruled the underworld and also judged whether the soul would be sent to Heaven or to Hell.

ZOROASTRIANISM

The initial beliefs of this ancient Persian religion were reworked, embellished, and developed by the patriarchal scribes of the Zurvan doctrine around 350 BCE. Today, Zoroastrianism is said to have up to around two million or more followers worldwide.

From the beginning, its belief system emphasized the responsibility of everyone to behave ethically in life, for their fate after death depended on it. Zoroaster lived around 1,100–1,000 BCE, although many place him around the 7th century BCE. Whatever the case, to the Greeks, Zoroaster was considered to be the founder of the Magi, the Persian astrologers and alchemists. Zoroaster believed that man had a soul which existed before birth, and would transcend the death of the body, and it was something that gave the curious Greeks a light at the end of their *Hades* tunnel.

In Zoroastrianism, which is still practised widely today, it is believed that, at death, the soul waited with the body for three days, chanting and praying for blessings. On the fourth day, a woman appears – a beautiful damsel, if the individual had been righteous; a hideous one, if they have been unrighteous. The figure represents the soul's Earthly life. She conducts the soul to the Chinvat bridge. For the pious, the bridge is wide and easy and, at the other side, they are welcomed into a Heaven of riches and comfort. The wicked, however, find the bridge as narrow as a razor, and a horrifying hag takes the soul in her arms, plunging them both, screaming, into Hell where, depending on their sins, they eat excrement and filth, are eaten by monsters, or suffer terrible punishments forever.

If the soul continues to be righteous and good while in Heaven, it will be eventually elevated to divine status, and when all the bad thoughts are eliminated from the world, the righteous dead will be resurrected to live in eternal harmony.

Right: Zoroaster developed the pantheon of ancient Persian gods into two opposing forces, Ahura Mazda, the supreme God, and the destructive principle of Ahriman.

JUDAISM

Traditional Judaism firmly believes that death is not the end of human existence. But what happens next is open to each individual's personal opinion.

It is possible for an Orthodox Jew to believe that the souls of the righteous go to a place similar to a Christian Heaven, or that they simply wait until the coming of the messiah, when they will be resurrected. To Orthodox Jews, demons torment the souls of those who committed sins in their lifetime. Alternatively, they believe that, at the moment of death, evil souls will be totally annihilated.

The afterlife or otherworld is known as *Olam Ha-Ba* and is more an exalted, perfected state of being than a place. The deceased's share in the world to come is determined by merit, by the righteousness in one's life, and the good deeds done. Interestingly, the ultimate result of such a belief is that it isn't necessary to be Jewish to attain *Olam Ha-Ba*: in fact, any person from any faith may be accepted, as long as their life was good, productive, and virtuous.

Punishment for the unrighteous takes place in *Gehinnom* (*Gehenna* or *She'ol*). Different traditions see this place

Right: In Judaism, getting to the higher realms of Olam Ha-Ba *depends on your deeds and actions in this life.*

in different ways. To some, it is a dreary, miserable, and extremely unpleasant place in which the wicked can contemplate their wrongdoing, come to realize any harm they have caused, and repent. To others it's a place of fire and torture similar to the Christian image of Hell. To yet others, it's inhabited by the demons created by each

sin and wrongful action, who then punish the person who created them.

Gehinnom can be contemplated as a place in which the soul can rest and see the actions and consequences of its life objectively, experiencing remorse for all the harm done. The penance takes no longer than 12 months, after which time, if the soul has expiated its sins, it can go on to *Gad Eden*. If it is truly wicked and refuses to repent, it either ceases to exist entirely or spends the rest of eternity suffering remorse. *Gad Eden* is viewed as a perfected spiritual state: only those who were truly righteous and pious in life go straight there after death.

CHRISTIANITY

For God so loved the world, that he gave his only Son, that whoever believes in him should not perish but have eternal life.

John 3:16

The verse above sums up the basic Christian concept of the afterlife dependent on belief in Christ. Since the earliest and most influential Christian fathers, such as Origen in the 2nd century CE or the medieval Aquinas, Christian thought has always been open to what the afterlife actually is. Nowadays, different denominations have their own perception, but all believe in some kind of spiritual otherworld.

Eternal life begins when the individual first has faith in Christ, which happens, naturally, while he is still alive. After death, some traditions profess that the soul returns to God, who gave it existence in the first place. Others believe that at the Second Coming of Christ, all souls will be judged (for a second time, in the case of those already dead, although this is now an outmoded viewpoint) and go either to eternal Heaven or to eternal Hell.

Hell was originally envisaged simply as a miserable place where unbelievers are forever separated from God's mercy and love. Later, it became a place of pain and castigation, characterized by ferocious fires and terrible tortures wielded by demons.

Heaven was even more vaguely described, apart from in the Book of Revelation. In John's vision, however, only 144,000 virgin men of the Tribes of Israel will be saved, but the Heaven in which they live will be magnificently sculpted of gold and jewels.

Generally, Heaven and Hell, for Christians, are viewed as two different physical places. One – Heaven – is for the reward of the righteous believers. The other – Hell – is for the punishment of those who scorn Christ.

Right: The souls of righteous Christian believers are rewarded with Heaven, a place of eternal bliss.

Christian asceticism
Gnosticism

Gnosticism is thought by most scholars to be a mystical offshoot of 2nd-century KA Christianity. During the 1940s a collection of ancient texts known as the "Nag Hammadi Library" was discovered in various caves in Egypt. Although most of the authors appeared to fall under the umbrella term of "Christian mysticism", it now appears that they were heavily influenced by early Greek philosophers, such as Plato. The Hammadi library collection contains Pagan, Jewish, Greek,

Above: Hell was a place of perpetual torture, demons, fire, and damnation for heretics or sinners.

and Christian writings. Yet the Gnostic notion of the afterlife was very different to the mainstream Christian or Jewish ones. *Gnosis*, meaning "knowledge" in ancient Greek (usually secret knowledge), could be achieved only by following an ascetic lifestyle. This meant denying the body's pleasures so that believers could focus on enhancing the spirit through meditation and visions that led to a direct experience of the Divine. This inner journey, undertaken in solitude, eventually led to the soul's reunion with the One. Unlike many other religions, it was not necessary for the individual to die for this to happen – it was quite possible to achieve Heaven while still alive. But even if the individual didn't manage to gain *gnosis*, they would be reincarnated until they attained their true self.

Cathars

Considered heretical by the Catholic Church, the Cathars (12th and 13th

centuries CE) believed that there were two principles or Gods controlling the world. The Good God ruled the spiritual realm, while the Bad God (often believed to be Satan) commanded the material world.

The soul yearned to return to God, but the challenges by which this could be accomplished were not for everyone. Complete vegetarianism, celibacy, refusal to kill, and a total rejection of the world required a particular kind of initiate, who was called the Perfect. To live and die in such a state of grace ensured the soul would return to the spiritual realm upon death.

Hell was existence on Earth, not a place to be punished after death. The soul was considered to be eternal and sexless, and could incarnate in a male or a female body in each lifetime. Like Pythagorus and Plato (see page 82), many Cathars believed that the stars in the night sky were souls of the Perfects returned home.

Left: The Cathars believed that the soul returned to its spiritual home after the body passed away.

BUDDHISM

Siddhārtha Gautama devised the "middle way" when he became the Buddha (the awakened or enlightened one) at the age of 35. Buddhism is more of a spiritual tradition or philosophy than a religion, and acknowledges no gods.

For Buddhists, the eternal unchanging soul does not exist. The personal, conscious entity that humans think of as "me" is, in effect, a constantly changing mental construct, an assembly of energies that "flows" from moment to moment, creating the illusion of a stable being. At death, these energies are reborn into another form, dependent on the karmic debt accrued in the previous existence.

Theravada Buddhism

The Theravada branch of Buddhism claims there are 31 levels of rebirth spread over 4 planes of existence. The lowest one is the Plane of Deprivation, which includes the eight major hells. Next is the Plane of Sensual Happiness, with the average human residing at the lowest level. Above that in ascending order are the Realm of Forms, the abode of the Devas (supernatural beings and minor deities invisible to, and more powerful than, humans), and the Formless Realms, where the beings are pure mind. Humans can ascend the levels and planes by shedding their karma throughout their lifetimes and being reborn onto a higher level. Each level is more pleasant than the one preceding it, which may, it seems, make sticking to the Buddha's "middle way" less of a challenge as the being progresses towards nirvana.

Alternatively, the being may be reborn into one of the Hells through adding karma during life, for example, by lying, sexual misconduct, or killing. Buddhist Hells are places of fire and torture, where the sufferer is burned, hacked apart, crushed, or cooked alive. However, residence here is temporary, and once the being has expiated their karma, they may be reborn on a higher level. This could also mean being reborn in a slightly less unpleasant level of Hell, if the karmic debt is very large.

Mahayana Buddhism

Success in achieving nirvana in the Theravada tradition is difficult, requiring an ascetic lifestyle and strict adherence to tenets of the way. In contrast, the Mahayana school is much easier, preaching potential enlightenment in one's lifetime. Heaven – the "pure land" – is envisaged as a place free of pain, want or sadness, decorated with jewels, lined with palm trees, and containing flowing streams of pure water.

Left: Liberation from the cycle of death and rebirth is the aim of most Buddhist teachings and, in some schools, is possible within an individual's lifetime.

NATIVE AMERICAN AND ANCIENT MESOAMERICAN BELIEFS

Most North American Native traditions (some of which still exist today) believe that all nature is imbued with the Divine and that one is reunited with one's ancestors in the afterlife. However, there is no unified vision of what happens after death.

The Mesoamerican civilizations had very different notions from their Northern neighbours. There was both a heaven for the elite and a terrifying hell filled with evil gods, demons, and perpetual torture.

Many Native Americans believe that there are two worlds – the physical Mother Earth and the spiritual world, ruled over by the Great Spirit or Great Mystery (known as Wakan Tanka to the Sioux), usually a male father figure. The spirit of the dead comprises the organic part that returns to the Earth and the numinous part that lives on after death. Beyond this, traditions vary. For the Hopi, the soul travels Westwards along a sky path, the righteous journeying with ease while the unrighteous travel with difficulty. For the Sioux, the soul goes to the Happy Hunting Ground, a spiritual realm that resembles the Great Plains but with plentiful and easily captured game. The Apache focus on survival in the physical realm and give little thought to the afterlife. For the Iroquois, the soul is judged after death by the Great Spirit, and wrongdoers are punished.

In early Native American mythology, the dead had to be sent off with the correct rites, otherwise they might come back as ghosts to haunt the living.

The Aztecs and Mayans believed in Tamoanchan – a fertile, beautiful paradise in which one could walk with the gods, feast all day and enjoy the pleasures of the flesh.

Tamoanchan had 13 hierarchial levels. But only a few were allowed access here such as royalty, advisors, scribes, and heroic warriors. Xibalba was the dark, cold, miserable Hell haunted by evil gods. It was a place of hopelessness and, unfortunately, the ultimate destination for most people.

In most traditions, where one ended up after death was heavily dependent on how one died. Victims sacrificed to Huitzilopochtli, the ancient god of war and the sun, would join the battle against

Above: Native American traditions have differing beliefs about the fate of the individual in the afterlife.

darkness in the afterlife. Some humans could be reincarnated as birds or insects, or wander the world as ghosts. Living a virtuous life didn't guarantee a place in Tamoanchan, but it certainly helped towards getting there.

The Incan afterlife was dependent on living a virtuous life, and anyone keeping to this could hope to live with the sun after death, enjoying perpetual feasting.

Those who did not suffered the dismal underworld with no food or drink. The only exception was a member of Incan royalty, who was destined to live with the sun regardless of his behaviour.

Above: Hell in Mesoamerican traditions was a place of horror and evil.

Right: Most African traditions, like the Dogon, are animists who worship the spirits of their ancestors.

AFRICAN BELIEFS

Although many African cultures had their ancient spiritual beliefs replaced by or assimilated into the orthodox religions of colonizers, such as Christianity and Islam, some continue to practise indigenous afterlife traditions such as the two examples below.

Animistic-based African traditions are orally transmitted, and share common elements, such as a belief in a supreme being, the afterlife, spirits, and gods. The two examples here stand out from others not only for their use of magic and belief in supernatural forces, but also for their

belief in a "soul" and their continued worship of their ancestors today.

Dogon people

The Dogon people of Mali in West Africa are animists whose principle deity is Ammu, the all-knowing creator god. Below him are Nommo, the water spirit, and Lebe, the nurturing earth, with a host of other good and evil spirits forever prowling the world. Primarily ancestor worshippers, the Dogon peoples' elaborate funerary rituals, masks, and regalia are well-known totems of their belief system.

At death, it is believed, the two parts of the human, the *nyama* (vital life force) and *kikinu* (the soul), are separated, and the latter joins the illustrious ancestors. Funeral rites take place immediately following death and may last for a week, while the more significant and elaborate ritual that marks the end of mourning, the *dama*, takes place some time later – possibly up to two years after the original death. The *dama* is designed to usher the spirit of the deceased to go to *Amma* (paradise). The just will then reside there, where they will live a life similar to the one they had on Earth.

Vodun

Vodun of West Africa, or Voodoo, developed out of the 18th-century slave trade, and holds that everyone has a soul that consists of two parts, the *gros bon ange* (big good angel) and the *ti bon ange* (little good angel). At death, the soul remains near the body for several days, during which time the *ti bon ange* can be captured and brought under the control of an evil sorcerer to do his bidding.

In the Ewe tradition of Togo, after death the soul travels to a dwelling place below the waters, from where it may be reincarnated as a member of its original family. In Haitian Voodoo, which is more closely allied to Catholicism, the soul will go to Heaven or Hell in accordance with the good or evil the individual did in life.

Right: Voodoo shamans contact the spirits through symbols used in elaborate rituals.

KABBALAH

In the philosophical and mystical Jewish tradition known as Kabbalah is a complex set of esoteric teachings that developed from ancient Jewish thought to explain the relationship between an unchanging, eternal, divine mystery, Ein Sof, *and the finite universe.*

The ultimate aim of the Kabbalist is to attain union with the Divine, and to do this the soul must move upwards through the seven heavens. This is a journey that can take many, many years, and even more reincarnations, as the soul grows wiser, stronger, and more perfect along the way.

There are seven figurative heavens. The first is the realm of Adam and Eve, ruled over by the angel Gabriel, and the closest in nature to the physical world; the seventh is guarded by the angel Cassiel and is the abode of God. Hell is being denied union with God, although in most traditions it is a temporary punishment. Here the soul wanders the Earth as a ghost or spectre until God can forgive whatever sin caused the abandonment in the first place.

Gilgul Neshamot is a Kabbalistic concept of reincarnation. The Hebrew word *gilgul* means "cycle" and *neshamot* means "souls". Souls are seen to "cycle" through "incarnations" as they ascend to their own level of perfection. In the tradition known as Lurianic Kabbalah there is a teaching that a cosmic catastrophe occurred at the beginning of creation, when the vessels of the *Sephirot* (emanations of *Ein Sof*, the Infinite) broke and fell down through the spiritual worlds until they became physical "Sparks of Holiness". Once all the sparks are redeemed to their spiritual source, a new Messianic Era begins. This gives cosmic significance to the life of each person as a "soul spark".

Right: The Sephirot *in the Tree of Life are the ten different ways in which God reveals his will and reflect the soul's ability to perceive God at these differing levels.*

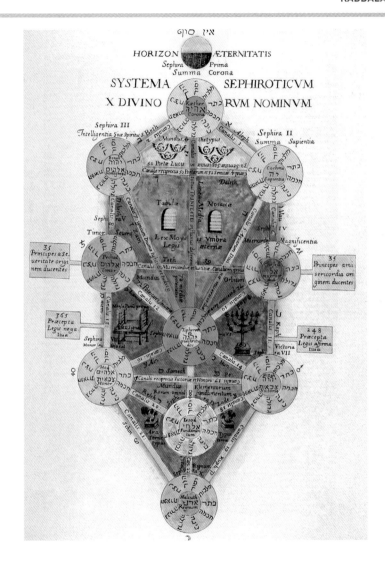

NOTABLE EUROPEAN MYSTICS

The 17th and 18th centuries in Western Europe were known more for their scientific revolution than for interest in the spiritual. Yet two notable European mystics appeared during this time.

First was a Swedish doctor, Emanuel Swedenborg, whose many writings were to influence, among others, Arthur Conan Doyle, Ralph Waldo Emerson, and Carl Jung. The second was the English artist, poet and printmaker, William Blake, who himself was influenced by Swedenborg, and who was to become an iconic figure of the Romantic Age.

Emanuel Swedenborg

The extraordinary mystic scientist Emanuel Swedenborg (1688–1772) started his career as a doctor and ended it as a messenger, it seems, for the afterlife. He believed that faith alone was not enough for a heavenly destination unless accompanied by good works. His conception of what happened after death has been likened to recently recorded near-death experiences.

At the moment of death, Swedenborg believed, the soul pulled away from the body into a spirit realm that was very close to the world it had just left,

Left: Scientist and mystic Emanuel Swedenborg developed his own theology after visions and contact with angels and spirits.

Right: Artist and poet William Blake is best known for his visionary watercolour illustrations for Milton's epic poem, Paradise Lost.

except that there could be no deception there. The soul was met by beings who Swedenborg believed were angels, after which it was greeted by the souls of friends the deceased had known in life. The soul was shown a vision of everything that had happened throughout its life – with nothing hidden – and found itself surrounded by light, which Swedenborg referred to as the Light of the Lord.

William Blake

Another mystic, William Blake (1757–1827) is best known for his highly symbolic poetry and art. His personal departure from Christianized religion might still be seen as radical, if not shocking, to traditionalists. He saw Satan not so much as an agent of evil than as a rebellious hero, bringing about change by his refusal to bow to a harsh, dictatorial God. As an advocate of the sacred quality of love and opposed to the restrictive marriages of his day, his ideals were founded on the concept of free love, and these ideals were considered to be the seeds of the free-love movement of the 1960s. He envisaged Heaven and Hell less as places to go to, and more as states of the individual self. This departure from Hell and Heaven being outside of oneself led him to believe that if both existed in the individual, one could be redeemed through forgiveness and self-sacrifice when balancing one's own inner world.

Right: William Blake was opposed to orthodox Christianity because he believed it encouraged the suppression of Earthly joys.

SPIRITUALISM

Contemporary Spiritualism is a movement made up of organized bodies, individuals, and other groups who share a belief in an afterlife. Most Spiritualists believe in contact with the afterlife through individuals known as mediums to promote healing and comfort in this life.

There are currently many different Spiritualist organizations, such as the widespread Spiritualist Church and the Spiritualist Association of Great Britain, and Spiritualist churches in Europe, Australia, and New Zealand.

The Spiritualist movement is rooted in mid-19th-century New York. At the time, a restless wave of reformers hoped to challenge not only conventional religion, but also the problems of gender and race inequality. Many of the early protagonists for Spiritualism were radical Quakers, such as Amy and Isaac Post. Amy and Isaac were friends with a family called Fox and had taken two of the three daughters into their home in 1848. These sisters had been at the centre of a scandal, having claimed that their house was haunted, and that they were in contact with the spirit of a murderer. To calm down the frightened neighbours of the Foxes, the Post family agreed to look after the girls

on the other side of New York. Amy and Isaac Post became convinced that the experiences described by the young girls were true and introduced them to their circle of Quaker friends. The Fox sisters quickly became famous for their claims to hear "rappings" – the knocks and taps of spirit messages, during their successful staged and private séances.

But in the 1880s, older sister Margaret confessed that the rappings were simply a hoax, and their reputation was ruined. Although she retracted her statement, it was too late. By then, the Spiritualist movement was besieged with fraudulent mediums, while séances, also known as group channelling, were seen as nothing more than party games.

But Spiritualism survived its defamatory critics and became a great comfort for those grieving the death of a loved one. The American Civil War of 1861–65 brought the horrors of death directly into the parlour with grim photographic imagery of battlefield casualties. As with subsequent wars, many families wanted to believe in an afterlife, or to find evidence for the continuing existence of their loved ones. One famous Spiritualist believer was Abraham Lincoln's wife, Mary Todd Lincoln. Grieving the loss in 1862 of her 11-year-old son, Willie, she organized as many as eight séances in the White House in the presence of Lincoln

Below: Spiritualism and seances became highly popular in Europe and the United States at the end of the 19th century.

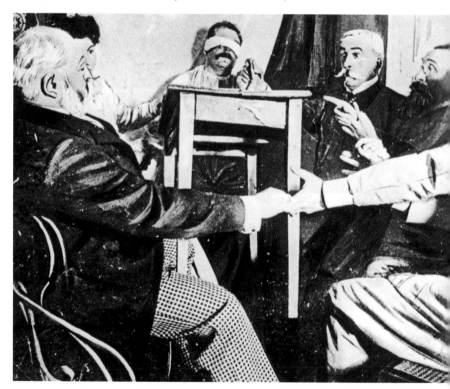

EMMA HARDINGE BRITTEN

Born in London as Emma Floyd, Emma Hardinge Britten (1823–1899) proved to have clairvoyant abilities that took her to New York, where she became a trance medium in séance work. But her real vocation was to tirelessly campaign for the Spiritualist movement. A co-founder of the Theosophical Society (see page 40), and with a long list of publications under her professional belt, she eventually married another passionate Spiritualist, William Britten, in 1870. In 1878, they embarked on a mission to promote Spiritualism throughout Australia and New Zealand.

Emma is credited with defining the Seven Principles of Spiritualism, still used by many Spiritualist bodies today. These are briefly: the existence of the human soul; personal responsibility in this life; contact with spirits and angels; the brotherhood of man; the existence of the Divine; karma; and development of the human soul.

Right: Clairvoyant Emma Hardinge Britten spent her life campaigning for the Spiritualist movement.

himself. Spiritualism also appealed to religious and radical reformers, those who rejected organized religion, and scientists of the day such as physicist William Crookes (1832–1919) and well-known author Arthur Conan Doyle (1859–1930).

Now used as an umbrella term for many different sub-movements, Spiritualism includes a wide range of beliefs and world-views. But all who follow are united in believing that the afterlife exists, and communication with spirits is possible.

Max Heindel

Born into German and Danish nobility, Max Heindel (1865–1919) was a Christian occultist, mystic, and astrologer who left Europe in 1903 to live in Los Angeles and develop his interest in astrology and the Theosophical Society. But overwork left him very ill with heart problems, and while his body suffered, his spirit apparently spent much time exploring the invisible planes and coming to an understanding of humanity and its needs.

The various Rosicrucian brotherhoods that existed in Europe and the US at the time were all based on a secret society known as the Rosicrucian Order, and were said to have been founded in late medieval Germany by legendary doctor Christian Rosenkreuz. Rosicrucianism is symbolized by the Rosy Cross, and its central tenet is the belief that ancient esoteric wisdom can provide insight into the universe and the spiritual world.

Heindel's Rosicrucian Order was described as being composed of 12 Elder Brothers, gathered around a 13th who was the invisible Head. They were known as The Compassionate Ones.

In Germany in 1907 Heindel was visited by an evolved spiritual being who claimed to be an elder brother of the original Rosicrucian Order. This adept had progressed far beyond the cycle of death and rebirth. The information he received led to *The Rosicrucian Cosmo-Conception*, a profoundly detailed and informative book about man's spiritual evolution. It also offered Heindel's views on the afterlife, including the visible and invisible worlds, the Borderland (purgatory) and the First, Second, and Third Heavens, where the soul is purified and perfected, ready for rebirth.

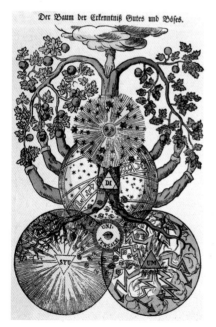

Der Baum der Erkenntniß Gutes und Böses.

Left: The Rosicrucians developed the soul's journey around the tree of knowledge of good and evil.

Right: Franz Mesmer stunned the scientific community with his theories of animal magnetism to pioneer hypnotherapy.

SPIRITISM

Inspired by mystic visionaries Swedenborg (see page 102) and later German physician Franz Mesmer, Spiritism was systemized in the 19th century by French educator Allan Kardec. Spiritism studies the existence and nature of spirits, which it defines as the immortal, God-created souls of humans.

Followers consider Spiritism to be a science and a philosophy rather than a religion. However, the main tenet of Spiritist belief states that God is the creator of all. Spiritism is particularly popular in Brazil, while organized Spiritist

Above: The founder of Spiritism, Allan Kardec, believed that individual self-improvement in this life would enhance one's future lives.

churches are prevalent throughout Latin and South America, the United States, and Europe.

Spiritist belief promotes continued self-improvement, and harmony and love between all beings. Spiritism teaches rebirth, with reincarnation explaining the moral and intellectual differences among humans who, by amending their mistakes, increase their knowledge in successive lives. The true life is the spiritual one; life in the material world is just a short-term stage, where the spirit has the opportunity to learn and develop its potentials.

Spiritism asserts that there are two realms, the physical universe and the invisible spirit world. At death, the soul joins the hierarchy of the invisible world and lives there for a time before being reincarnated as a human to continue its moral and spiritual development. While in the spirit world the soul can communicate with the living, revealing details of the spirit life, and advising and encouraging those still in the physical world.

The spirit world is made up of a large number of colonies and communities, both here and on other planets throughout the universe. As with Spiritualism (see page 105) Spiritism affirms anyone can become a medium.

WICCA

Modern-day Wicca grew out of the ancient polytheistic traditions of Pagan Europe – traditions that were suppressed or subtly assimilated by Christianity, but which still remain evident today.

These can be found in such festivities as Christmas (originally the winter solstice celebration) and Hallowe'en (originally Samhain, the night when the boundary between the visible and invisible worlds grew thin and communicating with the spirits of the dead was possible).

There are many varying traditions in Wicca, but the unifying elements are reverence for the triple goddess of the sky and stars, Cernunnos (the horned god of the natural world), the lunar cycles, and the eight sabbats – the seasonal festivals in honour of the solstices and equinoxes. Wiccan afterlife beliefs also vary, although reincarnation plays a significant role in most traditions.

The Wiccan afterlife is known as the Summerland (other neopagan belief systems also use this term to describe the afterlife), a pleasant place of repose and rest where the soul can reflect on

the life it led and evaluate its own merit. There is no Heaven or Hell in Wicca. The bad things that happen are viewed as part of the cycle of life, to be accepted, then avoided the next time around.

Right: In Wicca and other pagan religions, the horned god Cernunnos is worshipped as the spirit of the natural world.

SHAMANISM

Shamanism is the practice of communicating with the spirit world. It is common among indigenous peoples for whom the belief in animism is the core of their culture. The word "shaman" was originally a Mongolian word meaning "he or she who knows".

Having undergone initiation and transformation, shamans usually work on their own, entering into a trance-like state to invoke revelations and visions and to enter the spirit world.

Shamans act as messengers between the human, spirit, and other supernatural realms. They enter these other worlds to discover solutions to both personal and community problems and may acquire spirit guides who direct the shaman on his or her travels through the afterlife.

In many cases, these spirit guides are always present within the shaman, but in other cases, the shaman only encounters them when he or she is in a trance. The spirit guide energizes the shaman, enabling him or her to enter the spiritual dimension. Shamans may assist in soul retrieval by returning "lost" parts of the human soul from wherever they have gone. (During various incarnations, the soul might have become disconnected from the body, as well as trapped in another life, or totally lost due to physical and psychological trauma.) The shaman also cleanses excess negative energies that confuse or pollute the soul. Shamans often hunt out the essence of the soul, which can become dissociated from the body after some dramatic life-changing experience. For example, the Tucano rainforest people of South America are famous for retrieving the souls of lost animals for hunting purposes.

Traditional shamans can still be found among the Uralic people of Russia and Sibera, as well as among the small communities of Tibet, Nepal, Korea, and Taiwan, and are more widespread among the Inuit peoples of North America and Canada. Shamanism is common in South

Right: Many indigenous peoples look up to the shaman, whose role is to communicate with spirits in order to help the living.

America, particularly the Amazonian regions – for example, the *Curanderos* (shamans) of the Peruvian Amazon Basin and the well-known shamans, known as *Ayahuasqueros*, of the Uravina peoples, renowned for their hallucinogenic tea. In Australia, shamans are known as "clever men or women", or *Kadji*. In Papua New Guinea, shamans are known to exorcise *masalai* or dark spirits.

Chapter 3

THE NATURE OF THE SOUL

For thousands of years the concept of all living things having a soul has been at the root of our belief in an afterlife. The afterlife is where ancestral spirits or souls live in eternal happiness, or eternal Hell depending on one's cultural belief. But what is the soul? To most of us, the idea of the soul conjures up some mysterious essence of ourselves that we do not know but have at times glimpsed or felt we knew. Perhaps that knowing has occurred when we have been "taken out of ourselves" in moments of experiencing great art, music, love, sexual ecstasy, or meditation. It is not something we can hold onto but, by believing it is there, we have a sense of meaning. It is a symbol of our own great depths and connection to the Divine within. Looking at how different religions and great thinkers across the ages have defined the soul, and how it fits into their pictures of the afterlife, can give us insights into, and greater understanding of, this mystery.

WHAT IS THE SOUL?

Death – the last sleep?
No, it is the final awakening.

Walter Scott

In most spiritual traditions, the soul has been associated with death and the afterlife. The physical body dies, but the soul carries on eternally, whether as an individual soul (hopefully), or a World Soul (profoundly). We all ask ourselves at some point in our lives the following questions: "Where will I go when I die? Is it just lights out and nothing more? Who am I? What is the meaning of life?" Some people discover a belief to fit their soul's purpose – they find meaning in life. Even if they have to go on suffering, meaning gives them a sense of soul. But where did the idea of a soul come from? And in European traditions, how and why did these ideas unfold, change, and develop?

Eternal essence

Plato (428–347 BCE) was one of the earliest Greek philosophers to consider the soul as the eternal essence of a person. He believed that the soul is continually reborn in different bodies. Plato and his later followers believed that we already

Above: One of the greatest Greek philosophers, Plato, believed we all have our own unique soul.

have all knowledge of the universe when we come into the world because the soul is innately familiar with what he called the "eternal forms" that, according to Plato's theory, are the underlying, greatest, and fundamental truths of reality.

Plato's theory of forms

A "form" is the essence or quality that makes something what it is. For example, the essence of a cat, the essence of a table, the essence of a rock are the blueprints that make them uniquely what they are. Without this essence or "form", the thing or object would not be the kind of thing it is – there are countless cats in the world, but "catness" is the essence of all cats, for instance.

Plato believed that each individual had his own unique essence – his soul. He also postulated that the human soul carries all knowledge of the "eternal forms" (the essence and ideal form of truth, beauty, justice, and other such universal archetypes) into each physical life, but forgets this knowledge in transit. But through recognition, the soul remembers, recollects the ideas from the world of forms. This is likened to knowing the truth of something when we see it. For example, we unconsciously (at our soul

level) know the essence of a table, the essence of gold, the essence of truth, the essence of beauty – the abstract qualities of everything in existence. Our soul already knows this, but it does not come to "mind" until we recognize it. It can be as simple as suddenly having a flash of insight, remembering something we may not consciously have believed we had known before, a feeling that we know we have known something before, lived our life in a different way before. According to Plato, as we develop through our lives, our souls are, in fact, recollecting and recognizing the essence of all things they innately know, and we as individuals are not in fact learning new information at all – we are simply remembering it.

Left: According to Plato, our soul already knows the essence of the universe, and as we follow life's pathway, we gradually rediscover all that our soul knows.

WORLD SOUL

In Western philosophy, Plato's Demiurge, the non-judgemental craftsman of the universe, needed to bring his blank canvas of the universe to life.

Looking at the eternal forms, the Demiurge copied, moulded, crafted, and shaped replicas of all the perfect things he saw there and filled the universe with these copies. This means that the universe was in fact a replica of a perfect reality. The Demiurge also infused the universe with its own soul, known as *psyche tou kosmou* or the "soul of the cosmos", more commonly known as the World Soul.

It was this concept of a World Soul that was to have a profound influence on later philosophers such as Plotinus, writing in the 3rd century CE, who himself also inspired spiritual and esoteric philosophy in the West from the Renaissance right up to today.

Plotinus, intrigued by Plato's idea of the eternal forms, revived and developed Platonic philosophy. He also seized on the idea of the World Soul, developing it into a profound concept. Plotinus believed that the World Soul was a cosmic force that animated, unified, and controlled every aspect of the universe. It was not the Demiurge's creation as such – in fact, the World Soul was "everything and everywhere". To Plotinus, it flowed through everything, it was immanent.

Plotinus's writings went on to inspire 15th-century Italian philosopher and astrologer Marsilio Ficino, who translated

Right: The Renaissance magus, Giordano Bruno, was heavily influenced by the writings of Ficino and believed in the power of the soul.

not only all of Plato's works into Latin, but also Plotinus's works and many other unknown Greek texts, making them available to every academic institution in Europe and, thus, Ficino was one of the major protagonists of Renaissance and humanistic philosophy. To Ficino, the World Soul is a spiritual essence within creation, guiding life and the cosmos, while the human soul is a miniature model of the World Soul. To Ficino, the world soul contains and yet permeates each individual, so we are part of it, not separate from it. In fact, individual souls are fragments of the World Soul and so, in understanding ourselves, we understand the World Soul.

Renaissance artists saw the World Soul as the creative force behind their work. This Renaissance concept of the World Soul was to become the tenet of most esoteric beliefs in the Western world. It was already the core of Eastern beliefs, such as Taoism and Hinduism, dating back several thousand years.

TWO FRIENDLY BIRDS

The Upanishads, the sacred texts of early Hindu religion, compare the individual soul and the World Soul with two friendly birds sitting within the same tree. One of the birds (the individual soul) is eating the fruit of the tree, while the other bird (the World Soul) is simply watching his friend. The World Soul bird has no desires, no ego, no intention, while the other bird, the individual soul, is enchanted by the tree and doesn't want to fly away. The World Soul is content to wait for his friend to eat all the fruit on the tree until it is no longer hungry and is ready to fly away with the World Soul. This reveals that our hungry soul needs to feed on life, until it is ready to depart and return to the welcoming World Soul.

Above: Our individual soul is thought to be part of the World Soul.

TWO SOULS

The Homeric Greeks believed we had two souls, psyche *and* thymos. Thymos *was believed to be a physical soul, while* psyche *(see page 81) was the life force that continued to live on after death in* Hades *as one of the shades.* Thymos *was associated with consciousness by the philosopher Heraclitus (535–475* BCE*), but he also believed that the* psyche *or soul was about the fathomless deeps of ourselves.*

The Orphic mystery cults thrived a hundred years after Heraclitus and were influenced by the shamanistic cultures of the Thracians, who lived near the Black Sea. In the Orphic spiritual concept, the soul was thought to detach itself entirely from the body and exist independently after death. Cult followers had a reason to believe that death lead on to better things.

Other cultures, such as the Caribou Inuit people, believe that a person has more than one type of soul. To them, one is associated with respiration; the other, associated with personality, accompanies the body as a shadow. Traditional Chinese religion also defined two types of soul, the *hun* and the *po*, which correspond to yang and yin respectively.

Left: Known as the "weeping philosopher", Heraclitus believed that the soul carried the seeds of our character.

Right: Yin and yang are not polar opposites, but are one and the same.

Within this concept of soul dualism, every human has both an ethereal soul that leaves the body after death and a physical soul that remains consciously with the corpse.

Because the soul is unable to leave the physical world, it is often considered to become a ghost after physical death by cultures such as the Ewe and Fon peoples of West Africa.

SOUL OR SPIRIT?

Often, the words "soul" and "spirit" are used interchangeably, but there is actually a distinction between the two. It seems that while the spirit is something that can manifest in the physical world, the elusive soul is more like a butterfly – it is hard to pin down, let alone catch.

In many spiritual traditions, such as Christianity, it is generally agreed that something often known as the spirit animates the body and brings it to life. For example, the New Testament, James 2, says "the body without spirit is dead", and Psalm 104 reveals that "If you [Jehovah] take away their spirit, they expire, and back to their dust they go". Here, spirit refers to an invisible force that animates all living creatures.

In contemporary transpersonal psychology, rooted in Jungian psychology, the spirit is equated to the mind and ego. Spirit is action, it makes things happen, it does things, it loves, feeds, follows, directs life. Soul, however, recalls, remembers from other realms or past lives, it feels, profoundly knows and listens. Then, when the spirit or life-force dies, the spark of the soul returns to the World Soul. It rests for a while, its light is seen in the sky as a new star that one day falls to Earth again. In this way, the soul evolves through a hierarchy of lives through various incarnations until it attains eternal bliss.

So it can be said that the soul is the deeper essence of something eternal and enduring within us, and its source is the World Soul, whereas the term "spirit" describes our desires, instincts, conscious thoughts, and the ego. Archetypal psychologist James Hillman (1926–2011) commented that if soul is art, the supernatural, the "other" world, then spirit is fact, science, the rational, logic, so-called reality, and cause and effect. He also affirmed that "spirit" (like most scientists) rarely accepts the existence of an afterlife – it usually denies it. The spirit has a defence mechanism, triggered by the fear that all that is not this life or so-called reality does not exist.

Soul is mysterious and numinous. It lurks within. Having a sense of soul produces the feeling that you have been here before, an inner knowing, a *deja vu*. Whereas, with spirit, you might think, "OK, maybe I have been here before, so I'm going to find out when and why!"

Below: The candle flame can be likened to the human spirit, while hidden within the wax lie the depths of the soul.

Soul-making

The poet John Keats (1795–1821) beautifully summed up the purpose of life in relation to the soul in a letter to his brother and sister written in 1819. He believed that we all have sparks of some divine light within us, but this spark only becomes a true soul when it has acquired an identity. An individual life is what he called the Vale of Soul-Making. Although we may be born with a soul, we have to work at improving it, and so the "vale" is our life journey.

Yet, if we can weave both spirit and soul harmoniously into the fabric of our lives for healing both ourselves and others, freeing us from fear or pain of loss, this "Vale of Soul-Making" will make our lives happier in spirit, soul, and body.

The spirit world

If the spirit is something that activates and gives life to an individual, and the soul is the eternal aspect of each individual, phrases such as "spiritual" and "the spirit world" obviously confuse things. (Perhaps it should have been called the "soul world".) But in the context of this book, spirits, whether of ancestors, ghosts, misty shades, or horrific demons, are all considered active manifestations of individual souls.

THE ANCIENT EGYPTIAN SOUL

The ancient Egyptian concept of the soul was highly complex and, due to the many dynastic changes over the course of several thousand years, the soul was known to be made up of either two, five, or six different parts.

The *ka* and the *ba* were considered the essential components of the soul from around 2,500 BCE. It was believed that when a human was created, the *ka* was made simultaneously by the god Khnum on his potter's wheel. The *ka* was a spirit

double of the body. It followed the person around like an invisible shadow, and pharaohs believed they were being guided and protected by their *ka* throughout their lives. When someone died, the *ka* lived on in the tomb, and often the mummified body became its eternal home. Should the body be destroyed in the tomb, the *ka* would become homeless and die a second death along with the *ba* – a fate much feared by the pharaohs.

The *ba* was essentially a living person's very essence, what made them unique, their personality. To the Egyptians, one's physical head was closely identified with the whole person, while the heart was thought to be the centre of consciousness. To represent the transit of the dead to the afterlife, the *ba* was depicted as a person's head attached to the body of a

Left: The ba, *or essence, flew away from the body to the Kingdom of the Dead.*

Right: The ka, *or spirit, stayed with the mummified body in the tomb.*

bird, so that it could wing its way to *Duat*, the Kingdom of the Dead. If the *ba* was judged to be pure, it could then become a grander version of itself, known as the *akh* and could mingle with the gods.

Most bodies were placed in a stone sarcophagus or walled-up tomb. The tomb was protected by magical spells and powerful curses. If the tomb was ever robbed or the body destroyed, a statue of the deceased was placed in the tomb so the ka would remain with the statue, rather than the *ka* and *ba* both dying a second death.

THE ANCIENT GREEK SOUL

The beliefs of ancient Greece have perhaps been more influential on the religious and philosophical thinking of Western culture than any other civilization. It is from the ancient Greeks that the West derives its ideas about the nature of the soul and its journey.

Before the soul appeared as a concept in Greek thought, spirits were the intermediaries between the invisible and visible worlds. They came in a variety of guises – good nature spirits, nymphs, and personifications of abstract ideas such as forgetfulness (*lethe*), delusion (*ate*), and jealousy (*zelus*). There were also the evil spirits, known as the *keres* according to writers Hesiod (8th–7th century BCE), Homer (8th century BCE), and Virgil (70–19 BCE), not forgetting golden spirits

and watchers who observed the deeds of man and rewarded them if good and true.

Breath and shades

The human soul was first envisaged as the breath of life, the animating principle in humans and other animals. The Greek word for soul, *psyche*, originally referred to this vital breath. It left the body at death, after which it travelled to the underworld to spend eternity as an immaterial shade or pale image of the person it had once animated. Those who had been good and honoured by the gods went to the paradise of the Elysian Fields. The bad and those who had dishonoured the gods suffered in hellish *Tartarus*, while the vast majority of ordinary souls wandered the dreary Plains of Asphodel.

It was vital for the souls of the dead to drink of the waters of the river Lethe (meaning "forgetfulness" or "oblivion"), one of the five rivers that flowed through *Hades*, the underworld. This water ensured that they would forget everything about their lives and accept their fate in death. Initiates of an offshoot of early Greek religion known as Orphism, which was devoted to the

Left: The Elysian Fields were for heroes or those distinguished for their work. Even as late as the 18th century, the French philosopher Rousseau is shown arriving in this idyllic place.

literature of the mythical poet Orpheus, were taught that if they drank from the river Mnemosyne (meaning "memory") instead of Lethe, they could retain their memories and become omniscient.

However, as Greek civilization advanced, notions about the soul became more sophisticated, and a distinction was made between *pneuma* (spirit) and *psyche* (soul), not forgetting the guardian of the soul, known as the *daimon*.

Pneuma

The ancient Greek philosopher, the 6th-century BCE Anaximenes, was the first to comment on *pneuma* as "air in motion, breath, wind" and the element from which all else originated. Anaximenes observed that "just as our soul (*psyche*), being air (*aer*), holds us together, so do breath (*pneuma*) and air (*aer*) encompass the whole world".

Later, the 3rd-century BCE Stoic philosophers believed that all people are manifestations of one universal soul and should live in brotherly love and readily help one another. To the Stoics, *pneuma* was the concept of the "breath of life", a mixture of the elements air (in motion) and fire (as warmth) and was the active, generative principle that organizes both the individual and the cosmos.

With the translation of the *Septuagint*, the Greek version of the Hebrew Bible, *pneuma* became "spirit" and continued to be used as such in the New Testament. For example, at John 3:5, to be allowed into the kingdom of God, "spirit" along with "water" were said to be the essential components that a human needed.

Psyche, goddess of the soul

The concept of the breath of life as *psyche* as opposed to *pneuma* developed within ancient Greek culture to the point at which it was personified as the beautiful goddess of the soul, Psyche, who was often depicted with butterfly wings. To help understand the soul's journey as it silently flows alongside your own life journey, the ancient Greek myth of Psyche is a superb analogy.

In Greek myth, Psyche was a mortal princess who fell in love with Eros, the god of love and the son of Aphrodite. After Eros had abandoned Psyche due to a momentary lack of trust, Aphrodite sent Psyche on a series of tests to see if she was worthy of Eros's love. In the final task, Psyche was sent to the depths of the underworld to ask for some of Persephone's magic beauty potion to give

to Aphrodite. Despairing of ever being able to fulfill the task, Psyche climbed a stone tower, ready to throw herself off and commit suicide. The tower, however, suddenly spoke to her and told her how to find the entrance to the underworld. Following the tower's advice, Psyche made her way to the depths of the underworld and found Persephone, who agreed to Psyche's demand. Overcome by curiosity, Psyche couldn't resist opening the box in the hope of enhancing her own beauty. Mysterious vapours arose out of the box and sent her into a death-like sleep. Aphrodite realized that Psyche

Right: When Eros and Psyche were reunited, Psyche was made goddess of the soul.

SOUL SPARK

Pythagorus, the ancient Greek philosopher of the 6th–5th centuries BCE, believed that the soul was a solitary spark from the light of the universe. This soul spark falls into something we call life, a dark place through which the spark must find its way, lighting up the darkness as it goes, in the hope of returning to the place from which it came. The soul, animated by the spark, was accompanied in life by a guiding *daimon*, a friend, mentor, or wise soul.

Left: Pythagorus was first to believe in soul sparks.

had proved her love for Eros, so agreed to remove the fateful spell. Eros was reunited with Psyche in the land of the gods where she was honored by being made the "goddess of the soul".

This tale reveals that when the gods favour us, we can become immortal too. Yet, as Psyche's experience reflects, life is fraught with twists and turns, tests, and challenges for the individual. This offers us the chance to receive and act upon our soul's innate wisdom and knowledge (represented by the tower speaking to Psyche) as it recognizes universal truths, and thus for the soul to develop within that person's life. Through these challenges

and obstacles, the soul eventually returns to its spiritual home, a place of perfect love. The soul has evolved, enriched by its pathway though life.

Empedocles and *daimons*

Philosopher and mystic Empedocles (490–430 BCE) was the first to claim that he had, in a previous incarnation, been a *daimon* and, in fact, still was one! He believed he had once been a messenger soul, a *daimon*, that lived among the gods, who had now incarnated as a man on Earth. A *daimon* is not a demon, but a guiding wise soul who leads other souls through their Earthly existence.

Above: Empedocles was convinced that he had once lived among the gods.

A charismatic philosopher and wanderer, Empedocles claimed to have divine powers. It is recorded by the historian Plutarch that he wandered around Sicily and Greece in colourful robes, apparently worked miracles, revived the dead, and controlled the wind. His teachings were concerned with the soul's journey to achieve perfect love. In one account, known as papyrus fragment no.115, found by the University of Strasbourg in 1999, he described that when he was a messenger among the gods, he was banished from their company for eating meat. He then had to face 30,000 years of travelling every realm to nurture his soul. During his banishment he had to pay for his sin by being reincarnated into every living form in nature, to be eventually reborn as an immortal again.

Plato and the *daimon*

Plato (428–347 BCE) subscribed to Empedocles's belief that every human being was appointed a *daimon*, a guiding spirit at birth (see page 127). He called it "the *daimon* which has received us as its portionment". This invisible, semi-divine spirit guide led the individual along the right path through life and also after death, so that his soul (*psyche*) would arrive at its appointed place in the afterlife. By contrast, those who ignored their *daimon* wandered lost and bewildered both during life and in the afterlife. The wise soul followed its guide and its circumstances, but the soul who only lusted after Earthly things would flit about and, after much resistance and suffering, would be led away with difficulty by the spirit guide.

As mentioned on page 117, for Plato, the world was a defective version of his perfect world that was populated by ideal "forms", that were changeless and eternal. In that way, human beings, on the surface, were also defective replicas of each perfect soul.

Plato's allegory of the cave

To demonstrate how the eternal forms (see page 117) could be understood, and how we can be enlightened to a sense of our own soul, Plato implied that our Earthly existence is much like being a prisoner, and devised the following allegory of prisoners chained up in a cave to illustrate his idea. There is a fire behind us inside the cave, but we are unable to see it as we cannot turn our heads. We are facing a blank wall and, unknown to us, puppeteers parade objects and puppets back and forth in front of the fire, so that their shadows are cast on the blank wall

Above: Plato was one of the most important and influential philosophers in Western history.

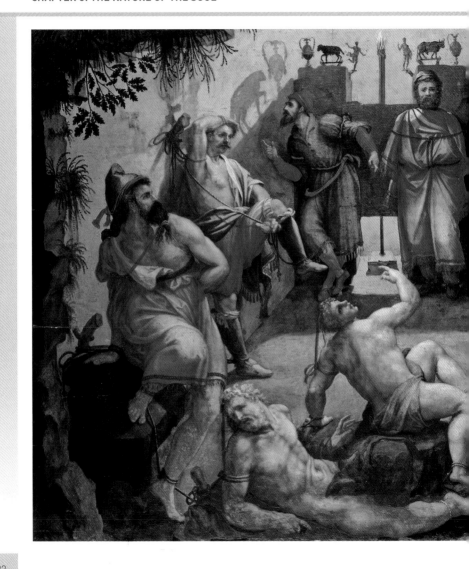

Left: Plato's allegory of the cave is also a metaphor for our understanding of the soul.

that we can see. As prisoners, we can only see the shadows on the wall, not what is casting them, and so their existence is our only reality.

Then Plato posited that, if one prisoner is freed, even as he turns around and sees the fire and the puppeteers as he leaves, he realizes that the shadows on the wall are not real. It does not take long for him to understand that there is another reality. If he then also leaves the cave, he will see that even another truth lies beyond the cave. Plato suggested that if the man then returned to try to explain to the other prisoners what he had seen, no one would believe him, because their reality was simply what they saw before them – shadows dancing on the wall.

Plato explained that the human soul can more easily perceive the world of eternal forms when not confined by the human body – the cave – but, he insisted, humans were not meant to hurry the separation of the soul and body. Their aim should be to gradually learn these things on a pathway to enlightenment. We become enlightened by changing our perception, by turning around first to see the fire, then by moving out of the cave to

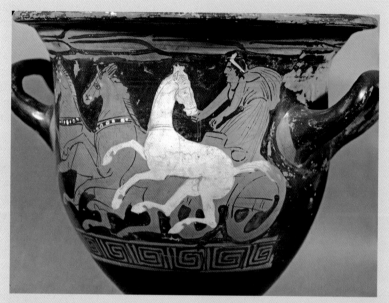

Above: Plato used the symbol of a horse-drawn chariot as an allegory for the human soul.

PLATO'S CHARIOT

In the *Phaedrus*, Plato describes how the human soul is like a chariot driven by two horses. The charioteer represents part of the soul that must guide it to truth, while one horse represents rational, moral impulses, and the other horse, irrational desires. Before birth, the chariot team encircles the outer reaches of the sky in the company of the gods, gazing at what is beyond, looking out to the eternal forms (see page 117). The chariots of the gods circle the perimeter indefinitely. Some souls have difficulty controlling the irrational horse, and so the soul plummets to the Earth. Should that happen, the soul is incarnated into one of nine kinds of person, according to how much truth it glimpsed of the eternal forms. During life, and from what the soul can recollect of the eternal forms, and with the help of other souls, it attempts to regain its knowledge to return after death to its celestial home.

see the light, and then to eventually know the place to which our soul belongs.

Aristotle

One of the greatest Greek philosophers and scholars of all time, Aristotle (384–322 BCE) had a highly complex concept of the soul. He was to have a profound influence on later Christian fathers, such as Thomas Aquinas (see page 148), and the subsequent Age of Enlightenment. Aristotle believed that everything that was alive had a soul and that it was the soul that made those things living. The soul was the form or essence of a thing.

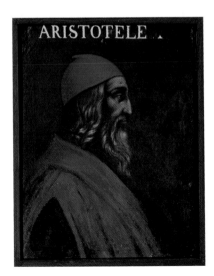

The soul was made up of three parts – physical growth, the five senses, and the intellect. The intellect or rational soul belonged to humans alone. Aristotle argued that the intellect could exist without the body and is immortal, yet was not the kind of "soul" we might imagine it to be. Rather, it was an abstract force.

Rather than being separate, the soul and the body were inextricably linked. Aristotle maintained that the soul could not exist without a body, but was not itself a body. The soul was something that belonged to the body and, therefore, only existed inside it. This, of course, implies that the soul is not eternal and that it ceases to exist at death.

Although, curiously, he maintained that the intellect was immortal, he was convinced there was no afterlife, and this latter belief became one of the major influences on modern scientific thought. Some commentators have suggested that Aristotle's use of the word "soul" is better translated as "lifeforce".

Left: The Greek philosopher Aristotle was to influence not only the Christian Church but the Age of Enlightenment and modern scientific thought.

THE INDIAN SOUL

Although Hinduism embraces a variety of different beliefs and paths, the atman *is the soul, the essential self, the true, eternal essence, and is believed to be a generic soul of all living things.*

The Hindu *atman*

Since the 3rd millenium BCE, Hinduism has considered the body to be merely the container for the *atman*, rather than the *atman* being the thing that animates the body. Liberation from the cycle of death and reincarnation (*moksha*) and union with Brahman, the Divine, is the believer's ultimate goal. The *atman* is often described as the Self, while Brahman is the Divine Self. We could perhaps equate this to the Western concept of the World Soul and the individual soul.

According to Hinduism, everyone must choose their own natural path to liberation, known as their *dharma*, but how this path is defined is less rigid than in many other religions and relies on caste and gender. Of course, there is a Hindu Heaven and Hell, but these are places of temporary pleasure and punishment, where the believer is rewarded or penalized before being reincarnated either in a lower form of life, if the karmic debt is large, or a better life,

if he has led a virtuous life. It is only when we all understand that we have a spark of Brahman (the Divine that permeates everything) within us, that *atman* can be united with Brahman, thereby attaining *moksha* from the endless cycle of rebirth. Hidden within each of us is the all-knowing, blissful *atman* who some believe will return to Brahman like a drop of water to the ocean, while others believe that the *atman* will live as a separate being in the presence of Brahman.

The Jainist soul

Sharing many of the same beliefs as fundamental Hinduism, the Indian religion known as Jainism follows a path of complete non-aggression and self-control to achieve *moksha*. To Jains, every living thing has a soul and all are equal: each soul (*jiva*) is independent and responsible for its own actions. When *moksha* is attained, the *jiva* joins other liberated souls in the highest level of Heaven: the next level down is reserved for deities such as Ambika, the protector of women. If *moksha* is not attained in life, the soul is reincarnated to try again.

If the soul has gathered bad karma in life, through ill deeds or violence, it may be punished in one of the eight levels of Hell, which become progressively colder the lower they are. However, penance in Hell is temporary: once the soul has suffered enough it is reborn to work towards *moksha* once more.

Left: According to many Hindu traditions, the body is merely the container for the Atman, *the individual soul, until it can reunite with Brahman, the Divine soul.*

THE SOUL IN TAOISM

The ancient belief of the Tao, which began around the 4th century BCE, had little concern with the individual soul, apart from when Taoism merged with Chinese organized religion from the 14th century CE onwards.

About the same time as Plato was contemplating the soul's journey (see page 204), in the late 4th century BCE the legendary philosopher and emperor Laozi completed his work known as the *Tao Te Ching*, which became the core text of Taoist belief.

Tao or Dao means the "Way", "Ultimate Reality" or "All That Is". In its original form, Taoism was a philosophical doctrine in which death was seen as a release from the corpse and was followed by immortality or ascension to Heaven. For example, the Yellow Emperor was said to have ascended directly to Heaven, while the magician Ye Fashan was said to have transformed into a sword and then into a column of smoke that then rose to Heaven.

Taoists aimed to exist in perfect harmony with the universe, which embraced both life and death. So although

Left: Taoist emperor Laozi believed that all was one, and therefore there was no separate soul.

it was good to enjoy life, there was no need to fear death, it was simply another way of being, a change from one state to another in the endless manifestations of the Way and, thus, to eternity.

As Taoism merged with Confucianism, various elements developed. This included the notion of a Hell, where those who had lived bad lives were punished, but only until they had redeemed themselves, after which they were reincarnated. Balancing Hell was Heaven, where those who had lived upright and good lives according to the Tao were rewarded by becoming illustrious ancestors and spiritually aiding the living.

As different traditions emerged from Taoism, some saw the soul as separated into the *hun* and *po*, the spirit and soul, which separate at death. The spirit or *hun* could be developed onto a higher plane of being, or could simply be reintegrated into the universe. The *po*, the soul, became reintegrated with the energies of the Earth.

THE JEWISH SOUL

In Judaism, belief in the soul is riddled with twists and turns, and there are various understandings of its nature.

Above: In some older Jewish traditions, the soul's destination was irrelevant, as living a virtuous life was vital.

Originally, there were three terms referring to the soul. *Neshamah* is the breath of God and is the intellect and higher mind. *Ruah* is the emotional aspect of the soul, and separates from the body at death. Finally, there is *nefesh*, the essence of a person connected to the physical body and its material needs and desires. The latter is similar to the concept of the animating spirit, particularly in Christian thought.

By the time of the first translations into Greek of the Old Testament in the 3rd/2nd century BCE, the soul had been unified as a unique, eternal soul that leaves the body at death. In one *midrash* (the body of works that interpret and explain Biblical texts), all souls were created during the six days of creation and are called forth by God. And it is God who instructs angels to advise the soul how to develop spiritually before entry to the individual body. In another *midrash*, the soul separates from the body during sleep and returns to it just before waking.

One major tenet of Judaism is that care of the body is also care of the soul. The soul is seen as a guest in the physical body, and both must be treated with respect so that they may coexist in harmony: this is why in religious texts there are so many commandments and instructions on how to treat the body. Both body and soul are deemed responsible for their actions and state of physical and spiritual health, so following instructions for the sake of the soul is advisable.

In early Judaism the destination of the soul after death was not seen as being particularly relevant – it was this life that mattered. As time went on, however, belief in the physical resurrection of the body, when the Jewish Messiah appears at some time in the future, became the norm. The righteous are then rewarded for eternity in Gan Eden. Gan Eden is not the same Eden as in the Book of Genesis. Instead Gan Eden is a place of spiritual perfection.

Kabbalah

According to the *Zohar*, the chief text of the Kabbalah tradition, a part of the soul leaves our body at night. When the body sleeps, the restraining chains of physical existence are broken and the soul is free to ascend to a high place in the spiritual realm, where it receives nourishment and information.

The soul contains five "levels". The first three are similar to those of mainstream Jewish religion as mentioned above. But in Kabbalah there are two other levels,

Hayyah (the universal self) and yehidah (unity with God). These are the highest soul state levels, and in rabbinic literature it is thought that only the biblical Adam was capable of achieving this level in life. The ultimate aim is unification with God. There is also an aspect of man called the zelem. The zelem is the essence of individuality, or the sense of self bestowed upon every human being. It is also likened to an ethereal body or garment which serves as an intermediary between the physical body and the soul. Unlike the soul, the zelem changes as the individual physically evolves.

At death, the *shekinah* (the female essence of God) and the Angel of Death appear to the departing soul. If the individual has been righteous in life, the soul is protected by the *shekinah* and is allowed to ascend to a spiritual sanctuary. Here, they are purified in preparation for their next life. The unrighteous are led away by the Angel of Death to the Hell-like *gehenna* where they are punished. Here, the unrighteous must make reparation for their wrongdoings and work to perfect themselves.

Right: In the mystical Kabbalistic tradition, red string is tied round the wrist as a talisman to avert danger.

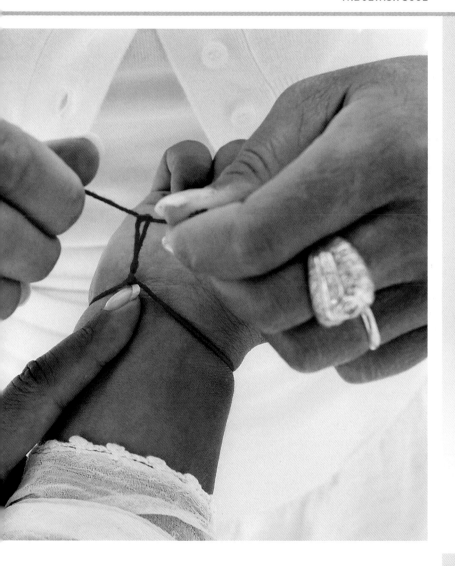

GNOSTICISM

Although hints of Gnosticism can be traced back to 300- BCE Alexandria, it did not become a codified religious and spiritual practice until 100 CE when it spread across Europe, North Africa, and the Middle East.

Gnosis is the Greek word for knowledge. In this case, it refers to a very specific form of intimate knowledge of God. It cannot be gained by study or by faith, but must be achieved by direct experience of the sacred. For the Gnostics, salvation means salvation from ignorance, not from sin.

The soul is seen as a spark of the Divine, as once perfect and capable of being so again, and its deepest desire is to return to God and its home in the *pleroma* (the realm of pure spirit). The Earth is seen as a flawed, ephemeral prison, and the human body is perceived as a cage that keeps the soul from the liberation it longs for.

There are three kinds of souls: the spirituals, destined to succeed in their quest; the psychics who succeed with the help of their fellows and by good works; and the hylics who belong to the material world and have no hope of salvation. In some traditions, help can be sought and given by spiritual beings already dwelling in the *pleroma*.

The way out of the prison is by living an ascetic life. Personal poverty is recommended (which is echoed by the Christian tenet of selling all one has and giving any money already gained to the poor). The other ways of releasing oneself from life's prison is through celibacy, near-starvation, and humility, to discipline the body and make the mind more receptive.

The soul is held to be female. Know as Sophia (which means "wisdom"), she is also a feminine aspect of God. In the 2nd century CE, and especially in Christian Gnostic sects, women were held in great regard.

Left: Some Gnostic traditions still use immersion in water, particularly in natural running water, for their ritual baptism.

THE CHRISTIAN SOUL

It may come as a surprise, but the New Testament, the original Christian text, makes very little mention of the soul. Death is referred to as "falling asleep". Christ speaks of the dead being resurrected at the Second Coming and Last Judgement.

In Revelations, the dead are defined as two groups: the righteous believers bound for paradise, and wicked unbelievers heading for Hell. But what happens in between each individual death and the Last Judgement is unclear.

Christianity grew out of Judaism, and it is logical that the Judaic notion of the soul was originally adopted into the newer faith. Over time, and especially within the Catholic church (although Christianity now includes over 40,000 different sects), a vision of the soul developed in which it seems to be imprisoned within the human body rather than an essential part of it. The emphasis shifted from care of the body (and, thus, the soul) to the pre-eminence of the soul over the body. The body is to be controlled and disciplined severely so that the soul is

Right: In Christian traditions, the souls of the dead will either go to heaven or hell.

146

worthy of ascending to Heaven, carried by angels to worship God after death.

Souls return to God, who gave them existence in the first place, to then be judged, and sent to Heaven or Hell. The Last Judgement – a time when the dead are resurrected and reunited with their soul – may seem a little superfluous, given that the souls' destinations have already been decided, but its concept serves as a caution to those living, and perhaps to ensure that followers continue to believe in their eventual salvation if they pray to God.

All Souls' Day

In the 11th century, Odilo, bishop of Cluny in France, decreed that 2 November, the day after All Saints' Day, would be celebrated as All Souls' Day – a day when the prayers of the faithful can help speed the souls in purgatory on their way to Heaven. This soon became standard practice in the Roman Catholic Church.

This date connects to the ancient Pagan festival of Samhain (see page 111), and it is likely that the celebration of All Souls' Day grew out of the widespread and very old tradition of ancestor worship. Venerating the deceased is believed to prevent their ghosts from haunting the living, but whatever the

Above: All Souls' Day is a worldwide Christian celebration to welcome the souls of the dead.

motivation, the festival demonstrates worldwide belief in the soul.

The souls of the dead are said to visit the homes of the living on the Polish Zaduszki, a version of the Catholic All Souls' Day, on 2 November. Candles are lit to welcome the soul, an extra place is set at the table, and food is offered. The Mexican Day of the Dead, also celebrated on the same day, includes festivals, carnivals, and family celebrations. It had its origin in an ancient Aztec festival honouring Mictecacihuatl (see page 196),

the Lady of the Dead, the Queen of the Underworld, but was later overlaid with Catholic influences.

In North America and the UK, Hallowe´en, meaning the Eve of All Hallows' Day, has become a cultural celebration on 31 October to celebrate the evening before All Saints' Day. Unfortunately, the spiritual element of the festival has been mostly lost to commercialization, and all that is left to link it to the past are the cartoon ghosts, spirits and children's trick-or-treating – a pale memory of the practice of placating the restless souls of ancestors.

Above: Skeletons and skulls represent dead souls on the Mexican Day of the Dead.

Thomas Aquinas

Thomas Aquinas (1225–74 CE), originally a Dominican friar and a hugely influential Christian philosopher, was canonized in 1323 CE. He believed that while the body and soul were distinct entities, with the body being born of physical matter and the soul created directly by God, one could not exist for long without the other, much as Aristotle did (see page 135).

Human beings were thus viewed as complete entities.

However, since body and soul cannot exist for long when apart, Aquinas concluded that they were reunited when the body was resurrected into the afterlife. What happened then was dependent on the life the particular individual had led. A good, pious, righteous person was granted union and unending fellowship with God in the ultimate bliss of contemplating him. Purgatory was where venial sins were punished, with a possibility of redemption, while mortal sins were eternally punished in Hell.

Left: Ghosts, spirits, and souls of the ancestors are all revered and celebrated in both China and Japan.

CELEBRATING SOULS IN THE FAR EAST

The Chinese Ghost Festival (held on the 15th day of the 7th lunar month) celebrates when Heaven, Hell, and the world of the living are all open to each other. This is when the restless, hungry ghosts of the ancestors roam the Earth and offerings of food are made to appease and persuade them to return to their rest. In Japan, the Bon Festival (held during mid-July or mid-August) centres around those ghosts who return to visit their families, and their spirits are welcomed with lanterns, dancing, and food. At the end of the day, lanterns are lit and floated along rivers to guide the spirits back to the unseen realm.

ISLAM

In Islam, the destination of the soul after death is reliant on the kind of life led.

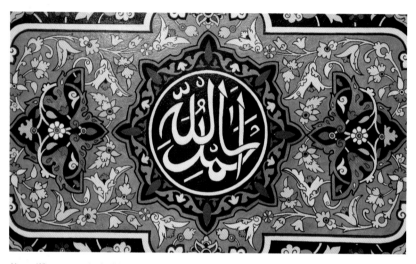

Above: Where you go in the Islamic afterlife is dependent on the judgement of souls by the angels of mercy.

The righteous are those who keep the faith, do good deeds, follow the rules, and pass on their religious knowledge to those less fortunate or wise. The unrighteous are the sinful unbelievers who defy Allah, although Allah is merciful and will pardon repentant sinners if they are sincere.

The afterlife begins in the grave. The conscious souls of the righteous are visited by angels of mercy, the souls of the unrighteous by angels of punishment. The angels question the soul about its Earthly life, its deeds, and the strength of its faith in preparation for the resurrection and final assigning to paradise or Hell.

At the Day of Judgement, everyone who has ever lived will be resurrected in their original physical body and called to account. Those who were martyrs for Islam go directly to paradise; everyone else will answer for their lives and be sent either to paradise or to Hell.

Paradise is envisaged as two gardens of transcendent beauty, where all physical desires and spiritual longings are forever satisfied and where no one can ever become bored, with the vision of Allah being the greatest treasure.

Hell is envisaged as having seven gates, all leading to an eternal torment of fiery torture for body and soul.

Avicenna Ibn Sina

The Islamic philosopher and theologian Avicenna Ibn Sina (980–1,037 CE) wrote extensively on medicine, physics, and a wide range of scientific and metaphysical subject matter. He believed that the soul was an incorporeal but very real "being" created from the Active Spirit, which came into existence when a body having the right temperament to receive it also came into existence. He believed that the soul was structured in much the same way as Aristotle had believed (see page 135), but it was there that the similarity ended. For Avicenna, the body and soul were closely linked, but the soul survived the death of the body as it was both immortal and indestructible.

However, rebirth and reincarnation did not exist in Avicenna's conception of the soul. Instead, the soul goes to paradise or to Hell depending upon its level of intellect and achievement during its life. Those who knew or cared only for things of the body would find their soul suffering once the body no longer exists, while the intellectual soul would be welcomed into a paradise shared with its equals. The potential for improvement meant it was possible to attain perfection. Those rare "souls" who achieved perfection in life would exist in a state of pure bliss.

Above: Persian polymath, Avicenna Ibn Sina.

EARLY MODERN PERIOD

With the fate of ordinary people's souls (Hell seemed more likely than Heaven) set in stone by 13th-century Thomas Aquinas, it was hardly surprising that heretics, Pagans, and sceptics searched for other spiritual clues as to whether there was something other than eternal damnation.

The dawning of the Renaissance began around 1439, when Florentine ruler Cosimo Medici became passionate about a treasure trove of ancient literature brought to his court by a Byzantine magician, Gemistos Plethon. From then on, ancient beliefs, Pagan gods, and supernatural powers animated the Renaissance world. The Neoplatonists were rediscovered, and mystery religions flourished. This was a time in which the soul was given value again.

Alchemy and the soul

Alchemy blossomed in Renaissance Europe and can be traced back to the 3rd-century CE Greek mystic and alchemist Zozimos of Panopolis, whose works were also found translated into Arabic (he was born in Egypt).

The phrases "lead into gold", "philosopher's stone", and "elixir of life" all come from the alchemical tradition, which grew and developed over the millennia until the 17th century CE, when it was overtaken by its successor, the science of chemistry. However, the new science, while owing a debt to the older art, was only about the physical qualities of elements, alchemy was much more. The elixir of life was sought to extend the life of the practitioner and immortality appeared to be the major goal of alchemy. This would, theoretically, allow the alchemist more time to refine and perfect his soul. All alchemical procedures and terms had two meanings: the physical and the spiritual. Turning base metals into gold applied to the human soul as much as to the elements, emphasizing the need for the soul to aspire to a higher, nobler state in order, eventually, to unite with the Divine and become perfect. Alchemy was very much part of the esoteric belief system of Hellenistic Egypt from around 300–30 BCE. A secret tradition, it was believed to have its roots in ancient Egypt and had many associations with the esoteric wisdom known as Hermeticism.

Above: Renaissance alchemists believed in the immortality of the soul and unity with the Divine.

Hermeticism

The legendary sage, Hermes Trismegistus, believed to predate Moses, was first mentioned in the 1st century CE by the historian and writer Plutarch (46–120 CE), and was later revered by the Neoplatonists, such as Iamblichus and Porphyry of the 3rd century CE. Although Hermetic teachings had been guarded and promoted in Harran, a centre of astrology and magic in Persia, during the dark ages, Hermeticism wasn't truly introduced to Europe until 1460. It was then that a travelling monk from the East brought the text known as the *Corpus Hermeticum*, which was subsequently translated by scholar and mystic Marsillo Ficino, to Florence. Thanks to the interest of the ruling Medici family, Ficino also rediscovered Plato (see page 116) and claimed Plato's writings along with those of the Neoplatonist Plotinus and other Hermetic texts were the key to self-knowledge. Ficino's belief that the human soul was itself divine was at the core of the Renaissance way of thinking and also at the core of Hermeticism.

Hermeticism included alchemy as one of the three elements necessary for the Great Work of reunion with God. The others were astrology and theurgy (performing miracles with supernatural

Left: Hermes Trismegistus was a legendary mystic whose followers used supernatural forces to align their souls with God.

Right: Immanuel Kant and other rationalists believe that, as God could not be proved to exist, then neither could the soul.

assistance). "As above, so below", one of the basic tenets of the Hermetic tradition, teaches that anything that happens on one plane of existence, physical, mental, or spiritual, also happens on all the others, and is often known as the law of correspondences. An example can be seen in astrology, where the positions and motions of the planets were thought to reflect the lives and characters of those living on Earth. This implies that the Divine is in everything that exists, just as the Divine is made up of everything that exists. The microcosm is man, and the macrocosm is the universe. Within each lies the other, and through understanding one, a man may understand both.

Hermetic practitioners attempt to escape from the cycle of reincarnation through a true and perfect understanding of nature, the soul, and God. In this, nature is the greatest teacher, and those who seek to be reunited with God try to live a creative life by working in tandem with the powers of both natural and supernatural forces. One's individual soul is simply a spark of the World Soul (see page 118), and so understanding of one's own soul is the key to understanding all that the World Soul is and knows.

Immanuel Kant

The Renaissance revival of ancient thought – its humanistic and passionate principles of art, magic, the Divine in nature, the influence of the stars and planets – was totally overturned by the dawning of a new age, that of "enlightenment" and the birth of

modern science. During the Age of Enlightenment, from the early 17th century through to the end of the 18th century, the "soul" became lost between the dogma of scientific, rational thought and the problems that orthodox religion now faced in the light of pragmatic thinking. A principle figure at this time and often considered the father of modern philosophy, German philosopher Immanuel Kant (1724–1804 CE), believed that reason was the source of morality. He argued that since all our experiences were filtered through our senses, we can never truly have an objective understanding of the world. It followed, logically, that all our goodness, our moral compass and, conversely, any evil we think or do, comes from within. It is not dictated from without.

Kant argued that we can never know that God exists (or that He doesn't), but in order to work towards becoming moral creatures, or people working towards the common good, we should act as though he does exist. God becomes the purpose, not the cause, and the quest for the morality granted by God gives purpose to human life. For Kant, the afterlife was "necessary" as a reward for good, even though it could not be proved to exist as could not the immortality of the soul.

THE 19TH CENTURY

For over two hundred years, reason, science and medicine, evolution, and the wonders of innovation had bypassed the spiritual world. Many secret esoteric groups, such as Hermeticists, went underground.

Yet with the growing European movement towards romanticism in art, literature, and music, by the middle of the 19th century, spiritual ideas began to creep out from the woodwork once again. Mystery schools flourished and many of them continued to promote either the soul or the spirit, or both.

Above: Blavatsky's visit to India marked the debut of the Theosophical Society.

G I GURDJIEFF

By comparison, G I Gurdjieff (1872–1949), a Russian spiritual teacher, posited that the vast mass of humans are "asleep" in a kind of hypnotic trance in which their lives are repetitious and mechanical. This is caused by the three "centres" of being (intellect, emotions, and motor functions) being out of harmony with each other. To wake up and function as a whole being, he devised exercises, physical, mental, and emotional, that his disciples had to perform.

For Gurdjieff, the sleeping human did not possess a soul. The soul was something one cultivated through great insight and spiritual teaching. He taught that the soul was not automatically immortal, but could become so through his specific methods. However, the true nature of his concept of "immortality" is unclear and today his work remains controversial.

Right: For Gurdjieff, the soul could only be cultivated through practical and disciplined work.

Theosophy

The term theosophy, meaning "divine wisdom", was in use as far back as the 3rd century BCE, and was originally interchangeable with theology. It wasn't until the Renaissance that it acquired its own definition, but became best known in connection with Helena Blavatsky (1831–91), one of the co-founders of the Theosophical Society of New York.

Universal brotherhood is a tenet of modern theosophy. The most basic principle is that all religions are just different expressions of the same source, that everything is cyclical, and that the whole point of existence is to enjoy a grand adventure. The individual soul is eternal, consisting of an inner spiritual core, holding all that is good and worth preserving, surrounded by an outer shell that is selfish and transitory. At death, the shell dissipates and the inner soul is absorbed into the World Soul , similar to Plato's World Soul (see page 118), which enjoys the pure joy and fulfillment of the Absolute. After a while, the soul feels the need to experience life again, and is reborn. It experiences countless deaths and rebirths until it has learned all that Earth can teach it. Then, it goes on to repeat the cycle on every planet in the universe.

Edgar Cayce

Edgar Cayce was an early 20th-century American psychic. His predictions and claims were to make him a celebrity, which overshadowed his more important work and his interest in the afterlife. Cayce was a crusading believer for what is known as the transmigration or spiritual evolution of the soul in the afterlife.

According to Cayce, souls live in different afterlife realms, related to the planets of our solar system. They don't actually live on the surface of planets, but on spiritual levels represented by these planets. A soul doesn't necessarily experience all these realms, and reincarnation takes place not only in the Earth realm, but also in other realms between Earth incarnations.

The soul realms

There were nine realms, equated to the nine planets of astrology. The first, symbolized by Saturn, was a level for the purification of the souls. This realm was for starting over.

The second, Mercury's realm, gives us the ability to consider problems

Above: Helena Blavatsky is one of the most influential occultists of modern spiritual traditions.

Above: American Edgar Cayce believed the soul transcends nine realms until it can become at one with the cosmos.

we begin to use our creative powers to free ourselves from the material world.

The seventh realm is symbolized by Jupiter, which strengthens the soul's ability to depict situations, to analyze people and places, things, and conditions.

The eighth afterlife realm, ruled by Uranus, develops psychic ability. This realm can develop extremes and extremism within a soul. Also, a soul can develop an interest in the occult and the mystic forces in this realm, and become open to visions, hearings, seeing, and knowing without having to have the physical contact with experiences in the mental body. This realm influences an interest in the spiritual things. Cayce believed that all psychics on Earth had a period within this afterlife realm before incarnating to the Earth.

The ninth afterlife realm is symbolized by Pluto, the astrological realm of the unconscious. The final afterlife realm is physically represented not by a planet but by the star Arcturus. This afterlife realm is a transient place where souls choose to travel to other realms and to other solar systems. But this is not "astral travel" as such, it is the soul's liberation into eternity, and is a realm which opens the doorway from our solar system into the cosmos.

as a whole. From this comes mental insight into virtue, goodness, beauty, the mysteries of the universal forces, and development to the soul.

The third of the nine soul realms is ruled by the Earth and is associated with the Earthly pleasures. The fourth realm is where we find out about love, and is ruled by Venus. The fifth realm is where we meet our limitations and is ruled by Mars. The sixth realm is ruled by Neptune, and this is where

Brahma Kumaris

A neo-Hindu group founded in the 1930s, the Brahma Kumaris' central tenet is that the soul is separate from the human body, but lives within it. For the Brahma Kumaris, the soul is a tiny point of light existing in a physical body and reincarnates 84 times. Adherents of the discipline are released from the cycle of death and rebirth after their 84th incarnation. If you are not an adherent, your soul will begin the 84 cycle again.

Brahma Kumaris believe that life only exists on Earth, that the size of the universe is much smaller than science has revealed it to be, and that time is cyclical, identically repeating itself every 5,000 years. Each cycle starts off pure, then degrades over time until, at the end, the world is destroyed (in a nuclear holocaust) in order to make way for the next cycle. Only nine hundred thousand Brahma Kumaris will survive to enjoy life in a technological paradise with thought-powered machines and extended lifetimes. Everyone else will cease to exist as all land except for India sinks under the oceans. When their time comes, they will be reborn as the cycle repeats again.

Left: Brahma Kumaris believe that the soul is separate from the body yet lives within it.

Eckankar

Eckankar is a modern religion developed in the 1960s, known as the Light and Sound of God. Eck is the Divine Spirit which appears to humans as light and sound (an audible current that can carry the soul back to God), and the ultimate aim of the Eckist is to achieve reunion with God. Each individual human soul is a spark of God and is on a personal spiritual journey to self-realization. This is accomplished by soul travel to the spiritual worlds – planes of existence that are within each Eckist rather than external realms – reachable through spiritual exercises, chanting, and meditation under the guidance of the Mahanta (the living Eck Master).

Eckankar teaches that the soul is reincarnated over and over again in order to work off negative karma, eventually becoming enlightened and able to manifest its Godlike qualities. The Eckankar afterlife is believed to be a continuation of the soul's existence in the inner worlds (the etheric or the soul planes), entered into consciously when the karmic debt is paid.

Spiritualism and soul

Mainstream Spiritualists (see page 105) postulate a series of seven "otherworlds" that are not unlike Edgar Cayce's nine realms ruled by the planets. Here, as it evolves, the soul moves higher and higher until it reaches the ultimate realm of universal oneness.

The basic "unformed" soul – filled with sin and guilt, unashamed and with no awareness of morality – moves, after death, into the first realm, which is equated with hell. This is the world where troubled souls spend a long time before they are compelled to move up to the next realm.

However, most people's souls at death move directly to the second level: a heaven thought to be an intermediate transition between the lower planes of life and hell and the higher perfect realms of the universe. This second otherworld is a place for souls to reflect and observe their lives. Resembling or mirroring its life on Earth, this plane enables the soul to work with knowledge reaped from its past life before it is able to climb the rungs of the soul ladder.

The third level is for those souls that have worked with their karmic inheritance. There is awareness, understanding, and a willingness to be redeemed. From this level the soul can begin the process of entering into a new life (if it chooses) and it is here that Spiritualists believe the most prophetic spirit messages come from.

The fourth level is that from which evolved souls teach and direct those on Earth. Many religious leaders, spiritual gurus, and evolved literary figures have ascended to this level, ready to disseminate to the world knowledge that can only be found at this high state.

At the fifth level, the soul leaves human consciousness behind. Silence, nothingness, and a still, perfect sense of being at one with the universe is what awaits this highly evolved soul. Jesus, the Buddha, and other spiritual figures are thought to have experienced this level of awareness.

Arriving on the sixth plane, the soul is finally aligned with the cosmic consciousness and has no sense of separateness or individuality.

Finally, the seventh level, the goal of each soul, is where the soul transcends its own sense of "soulfulness" and reunites with the World Soul and the universe.

Right: The realms of Heaven as portrayed in the fantasy world of 15th-century painter, Hieronymus Bosch.

Carl Jung and the soul

Carl G Jung (1875–1961) is best known for being the father of analytical psychology, one of the forerunners of contemporary transpersonal psychology. His concept of humankind's collective unconscious, archetypes, and individuation is a process by which each human being develops all the elements of his and her self to become a self-aware, whole, well-balanced, and functional being.

Jung posited a series of ancient, universal images and events that all humans share in common. According to him, these archetypes are expressions of the collective unconscious (one could say the World Soul) and play a large part in shaping human relationships and influencing human experience and feelings, and must be integrated into the *psyche* to create the wholeness of the well-balanced person.

For Jung, the soul was a special type of complex that can best be described as a "personality". It could also act as a messenger between the unconscious and the conscious mind. He asserted that the soul of a man is feminine, known as the anima, while the soul of a woman is masculine, known as the animus, and that these elements need to be in balance and integrated with the rest of the *psyche*. The anima and animus represent those aspects that are opposite to those of the persona, the outward self-image everyone presents to the external world. The anima of the cool intellectual will be sentimental and empathic, while the animus of the shy intuitive will be earthy and self-assured.

Left: The great psychologist Carl Jung believed that we needed to integrate various characteristics lacking in ourselves to make our soul whole.

Above: Jung's Red Book *is the result of the psychologist's confrontation with the unconcious.*

The characteristics of the anima are perception, intuition, forgiveness, empathy, and creativity. The characteristics of the animus are assertiveness, decisiveness, strength, courage, and ambition.

If the anima or animus is ignored or repressed, the person cannot be whole. When a man represses his feminine side (which is a strong likelihood in a patriarchal culture), this makes him less than a whole person: he may easily become brittle and unable to cope with the emotional demands of modern life. Similarly, when women ignore their "courageous" side, this puts their soul at risk, too. What Jung proposed was that we try to integrate both and thus make our "soulness" whole.

James Hillman

James Hillman (1926–2011), who trained in Jungian psychology, took a radically different view from Jung. He focused on dreams, which he saw as phenomena holding personal significance for the dreamer. Rather than looking for archetypes, the true meaning of the dream can only be found by understanding the dreamer's own associations to the images and events in the dream.

In Hillman's belief system, the World Soul or *anima mundi* is the core of ourselves. The World Soul (see page 118) shapes the fantasies and the myths of the psychology of the individual, with the ego being simply one fantasy among many others.

Hillman, using Keats' own phrase, "Soul-Making" (see page 123) argued the soul was a deliberately ambiguous concept. He viewed the soul as comprised of different beings and personalities, symbolized by the gods and goddesses of ages past. Dreams, images, and the human imagination were the language of the soul, pregnant with meaning for the individual experiencing them. In Hillman's view, all the soul wanted was to experience beauty. Continually deepening one's sense of beauty is the purest expression of soul-making. The personality traits that humans are born with are an intimate part of their soul, and should be nurtured instead of transformed or disciplined.

In his well-known book, *The Soul's Code*, he put forward the theory that just as the majestic oak is embedded in the acorn, so a person carries inside them an active kernel of truth waiting to be lived. This is similar to the Greek *daimon* describing the invisible guiding force in our lives.

Twin souls

The concept of twin souls originally came from a story, or possibly the retelling of a myth, told in Plato's *Symposium*. The story goes like this: in the beginning humans had four arms, four legs, two faces, and three sexes, male, female, and androgyne, with androgynes being the most numerous. Humans were happy, contented, and powerful – so powerful or happy that the gods felt threatened. The gods split each human into two and scattered them throughout time and space, condemning them to search the world for the other half of themselves. Without the other half of their soul, each twin felt lonely and incomplete. Naturally, those who had been male searched for the male "twin" who completed them, the females sought their female twin, while the androgynes yearned for their opposite gender twin who would make them whole again.

This ancient tale found great favour with the New Age movement. The all-embracing, tolerant, and questing nature of this movement found the idea of everyone having a twin soul vastly appealing. The concept was finally loosely codified into the belief that finding one's twin soul created a bond so strong it would last forever, the reunion – mental, spiritual, physical, and sexual – creating a transfiguring energy and profound love that could connect twin souls to their Higher Selves, or be used to help heal the planet. Each soul would be reincarnated over and over again, learning, growing, and becoming wiser with each lifetime, until reunited with their twin.

Although the terms "twin souls" and "twin flames" are often used interchangeably, there is a school of thought that considers twin flames to be a harsher concept. Twin flames may be envisioned as two mirrors, reflecting all the faults and flaws of the other in order to work together to develop and perfect one other.

Below: If you find your twin soul, you will, according to New Ageists, become whole.

NEUROLOGY AND THE SOUL

Although the scientific study of the nervous system has antecedents going back to at least 1,700 BCE, when ancient Egyptians used trepanning (drilling a hole in the skull) to cure headaches, this branch of science is a relatively new speciality.

Above: The ancient art of trepanning.

As the discipline develops, neuroscience is challenging the traditional view of the soul and body being separate entities. Recent research has shown a repeatable pattern in brain activity associated with states of religious ecstasy or transcendence such as Buddhist meditation, Sufi whirling dervishes, and the public prayers of charismatic Christians. This research is beginning to account for the differences between conscious and unconscious cognition.

Memory is a vitally important part of life for humankind. According to neurologists, human experiences, the things in human lives that make us who we are, are stored in our memory, not our soul. The brain is an amazing organ, and capable of almost anything, certainly on a mental and imaginative level. Even the universal images seen in so called near-death experiences are considered to be the product of brain activity.

According to best-selling British-American author and neurologist Oliver Sacks, humans have always had the desire to live forever and the belief in the soul that survives after death satisfies this desire.

Scientists acknowledge this desire to have a soul, but consider it to be nothing more than simply a desire.

However, with advances in neuroscience, experts like Sacks increasingly believe that there simply is no such thing as soul, and that everything human is contained in the physical body. However, this existentialist viewpoint is now being reviewed by modern physicists, particularly those researching in the field of quantum mechanics.

Above: Whirling dervishes enter a trance-like state which neurologists believe is activated by the brain.

NEW THEORY

A remarkable theory put forward by two eminent scientists states that when quantum substances that form the soul leave the nervous system and enter the universe, this is the moment of a near-death experience.

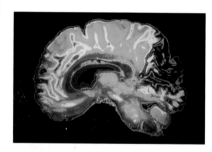

Above: The essence of the soul may be contained within microtubules inside the brain.

In this theory, consciousness is considered to be a program for a quantum computer in the brain that can persist in the universe after death. Dr Stuart Hameroff, Professor Emeritus at the Departments of Anesthesiology and Psychology and the Director of the Centre of Consciousness Studies at the University of Arizona, has advanced this quasi-religious theory. Based on a quantum theory of consciousness, he and British physicist, Sir Roger Penrose, have proposed the essence of the soul is contained inside structures, "microtubules", within brain cells. They have argued that our experience of consciousness is the result of quantum gravity effects in these microtubules, a theory that they dubbed Orchestrated Objective Reduction (Orch-OR).

In fact, Dr Hameroff holds that the soul is more than the interaction of neurons in the brain. It is constructed from the very fabric of the universe and may have existed since the beginning of time. In a NDE, the microtubules lose their quantum state, and the information is not destroyed; it or the soul merely returns to the cosmos. The concept is similar to the Buddhist and Hindu belief that consciousness is an integral part of the universe and indeed that it is really all there may be, a position similar to Western philosophical idealism. However, the Orch-OR theory is highly controversial among the scientific community. Nevertheless, Dr Hameroff believes that research into quantum physics is beginning to validate not only his own Orch-Or model, but the huge question of what the soul actually is.

TIMOTHY LEARY

Psychologist Timothy Leary proposed the Eight-circuit Model of Consciousness in the 1970s. He believed the human mind consisted of originally seven neurological circuits, which, when activated, created different levels of consciousness, which he later expanded to include an eighth level. Leary believed most people experienced the first three some time in their lives, but the last four levels would be triggered as human consciousness evolves. He also believed some people shift to these levels by using techniques such as yoga, meditation, visualization, or drugs. These four "stellar" circuits deal with psychic and mystical states of mind. It is in these altered states of consciousness, during which we move out of the conscious world of "self" and into the stream of the universe, that our psychic perception comes into play.

Below: According to psychologist Timothy Leary, altered states of consciousness can lead us to discover the world of the soul.

Chapter 4
AFTERLIFE PLACES AND BEINGS

The notion of some form of place – an underworld, Heaven, or "otherworld" – has been used to explain two of the key questions humans have about existence: "where do we go when we die?" and "what happens to our consciousness when we die?" Most belief systems developed the idea that another world was waiting for the souls of the dead, along with beings who reigned over the dark or light realms, and those who led us from life through death and on to the next world. This chapter is concerned with the most well-known places and beings associated with the afterlife, which are also valuable symbols for your own spiritual journey. Whether you've already reached a conclusion about what the afterlife means to you, are still sceptical, or are looking for an answer, the following myths and tales not only bring the afterlife to life, but are wonderful metaphors for your own spiritual search as you journey through this life.

HEAVEN OR HELL?

Now is the time to unite the soul and the world.
Now is the time to see the sunlight dancing as one with the shadows.

Rumi

Depending on the civilization or culture in question, the various versions of the afterlife are or have each been considered good, bad, or a mixture of both. In these worlds, evil spirits, angels, and demons are fearful spirits or loved guardians, ghastly attendants or beneficial gods of these realms.

There have been many tales of gods and heroes whose quests were to rescue someone or something from the underworld, such as Dionysus, who descended to the underworld to rescue Semele. In Vedic mythology, Ushas, the goddess of the dawn, was liberated from a terrifying stone cave, Vala, by Indra, god

Left: In some cultures, angels beckon from the higher realms to encourage believers to live a virtuous life.

Left: European fairy tales were often moral warnings to children not to sin. If they did, they would be at the mercy of evil spirits.

of the heavens, and in Finnish mythology, Lemminkainen, a well-known hero, is rescued from Hell by his mother. Equally, there are many tales of hellish creatures or demons who want to take over the upper world, as in the epic Hindu texts of the *Ramayana*.

The afterlife is not always a grim underworld, but can also be a resting place for fallen heroes, as the Roman Elysian Fields or the glorious Valhalla (see page 190), where Norse warriors are celebrated after death.

Some civilizations have been very concerned with carrying out the correct funeral rites in order to determine the soul's right passage onwards, such as the ancient Egyptians, who had many gods presiding over funerary rites and rituals.

Many of the underworld gods exist in shadows, are dark, menacing, and usually invisible, as was Hades in Greek myth.

In fact, in most of the earliest mythologies, the afterlife is not a particularly friendly place and provides little comfort to the living. The idea of a good afterlife, which we equate with the Christian Heaven, was scarce, except for in a few civilizations which were less concerned with the pantheons of gods and more with the animistic view of life – that is, in cultures in which there was a belief that all is one and imbued with the World Soul (see page 118).

THE EGYPTIAN AFTERLIFE

To the Egyptians, the afterlife, known as Duat, *was thought to be in the sky and was the home of gods and other supernatural beings. The sun god Ra travelled from West to East across* Duat *during the course of each night. Burial chambers formed liminal portals between the mundane world and* Duat, *and spirits could use tombs to travel back and forth.*

The Book of the Dead (see page 76) and the *Coffin Texts* were used to guide the recently deceased through the dangerous landscape of *Duat* towards their resting place as an *akh* (see page 125) among the gods. The dead had to

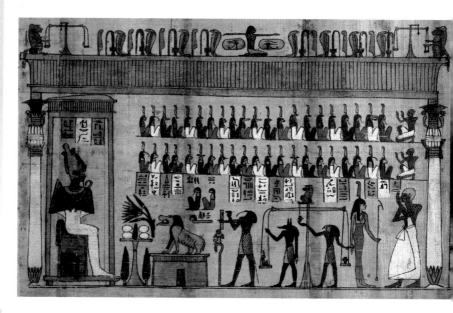

Above: Anubis, the jackal-headed god of the dead, was also the patron of embalmers.

Left: Before the dead could continue on to the afterlife their hearts were weighed and judged to see if they had still to pass some dangerous tests.

pass a series of gates that were guarded by dangerous spirits and demons. Cliffs and caverns were also inhabited by gods or supernatural animals who threatened the spirits of the dead. The purpose of the texts was not so much to guide the soul, as per a geographical road-map, but to describe a succession of rites of passage that the dead would have to pass to reach the afterlife.

If the deceased passed these tests, Anubis and Ma'at, two advisors to the god Osiris, were responsible for weighing each dead soul to determine its fate in the afterlife. Anubis was the canine god of the dead, often depicted as a jackal-headed man. As the patron of embalmers, he was also the guardian of the necropolis, a large burial area that was sometimes as large as a city. In the necropolis, priests would wear jackal masks when bodies were being embalmed to show that Anubis was present.

Ma'at, the goddess of justice, used her feather to balance the newly deceased soul. The feather represented the "perfect" balance. If your soul was equal in balance to the feather, you would be allowed to travel on to the paradise known as *Aaru*. Any hearts that were heavier or lighter in weight than her feather were rejected and eaten by the demon known as the Devourer of Souls. *Aaru*, meaning the Field of Reeds, was a highly desirable resting place where the soul would take pleasure forever in all those things he had loved during in his lifetime.

Osiris, ruler of *Duat*

The god Osiris was considered to be the first king of Egypt by pharaohs of the New Kingdom. The New Kingdom royalty and their scribes also believed Osiris taught the Egyptians about cultivation.

The myth below comes from very fragmented sources and is therefore incomplete in some details, but it is a superb analogy for our own despair at the disappearance or loss of a loved one, and how we would do anything to see them live again. Yet, it also reveals how, if we accept there is an afterlife, we can overcome our sense of loss and know that our loved one's soul lives on.

When Osiris was away on a journey, he left his sister Isis to rule in his place. Their brother Seth became jealous of Isis's elevation of status to regent and, feeling belittled, he determined to take the throne for himself. When Osiris returned, Seth set about to plot the king's death. Secretly acquiring the measurements of Osiris, Seth had an exquisitely decorated box built exactly to that size. Seth then organized a great feast to which he invited Osiris and the conspirators. Osiris suspected nothing, and when the feasting was done, Seth had the box brought out. He offered it as a gift to anyone who fitted the box exactly. One at a time the conspirators tried to fit into the box, but none did. And then it was Osiris's turn. As he lay in the box, the conspirators slammed the lid, nailed it shut, and poured molten lead in the seam to seal his fate. The deadly coffin was thrown into the Nile where it drifted to Byblos.

Isis consulted her sorcerers who told her where to find Osiris. After an arduous journey and with many adventures on the way, she eventually found the coffin and took it back to Egypt to give the king his proper funeral rites. But Seth found the coffin and, in his anger, cut the corpse into 14 pieces, which he scattered around Egypt. Again, Isis called on her sorcerers to divine where the parts had been hidden. When she had found all 14 of them, Anubis helped her to reassemble and mummify Osiris. Horus, the son of Isis, eventually defeated Seth, and when he become king, he resurrected Osiris as ruler of *Duat*.

THE CULT OF OSIRIS

The mummification of Osiris is the first to be recorded in Egyptian history. The art of mummification was perfected in about the fourth dynasty of the Egyptian pharaohs (c.2,600 BCE). It usually took as long as 70 days to complete the process and became part of Osiris's mystery religion. This was a secret following of elite priests who performed rituals and worship specifically aimed at Osiris. The secret religion promoted the belief that there would be eternal life in paradise for all who worshipped Osiris, a belief that was later assimilated into the formal religion of the New Kingdom Dynasties. The Mysteries of Osiris, a festival, was held annually at Abydos, the place where Isis was said to have found Osiris's head. This eventually became an important location for wealthy Egyptians to be buried. In the final 600 years BCE, the Osiris cult outshone all others in Egypt, and the mystery religion spread throughout the Mediterranean.

Left: Renowned for her involvement in the magic arts, Isis often consulted her team of sorcerers.

THE MESOPOTAMIAN UNDERWORLD

Sumerian myth from about 2,000 BCE, tells of how the goddess of the ocean, Nammu, gave birth to the cosmic mountain, An-Ki, Heaven and Earth. An and Ki were at first one, but they were separated so that other gods, plants, animals, and humans could be created.

With the union of Ki, Earth, and Air, Enlil, came all the other gods. Ki, Nammu's daughter, later became known as Ninhursag and was considered not only as the mother of the Earth, but her womb was thought to be the underworld or dwelling of the dead and she was known as "she who gives life to the dead". In later Sumerian myth she was replaced by Erishkigal, whose story is told on page 210.

The Mesopotamians not only revered their gods but also the souls of those who had gone on to the netherworld, albeit a terrifying place full of demons and dread. By about 1,000 BCE, a paradise, known as *Dilmun* to the Sumerians, was a land exclusively for the immortal gods, but *Irkalla*, the place for the souls of departed humans, was a dark and dreary place from which no one ever returned. In the story of the hero Gilgamesh, his companion, the mortal Enkidu, goes down to the underworld to retrieve a ball and stick, part of a hockey-like game played on Earth and, to Gilgamesh's horror, apparently is lost forever. Enkidu finds an eternally dark, quiet place, where dust covers everything. There is no joy, no eating or drinking, no companionship. It is a gloomy location, but he does recover the game implements and thankfully returns to Earth to continue playing the game. In late Sumerian and Babylonian myth, death is seen as final and absolute. Life is associated with good and light, while death is linked to bad and dark. Demons roam the underworld, and all the evil doings of mankind are projected there. It is hardly surprising that the legacy of this fear eventually evolved into the Hebrew and Christian images of Hell.

Left: The epic story of Gilgamesh included a visit to the desolate underworld for mortal souls.

Below: Gilgamesh wanted to be like the immortal gods so that he could go to paradise.

OFFENDED SPIRITS

In Sumerian belief, if a spirit had not been honoured properly in burial, it would find a way to inflict misery on the living. However, some spirits, such as those who had died violent deaths, had been criminals in life, suicide victims, or stillborn babies, were often thought to return to the living to take revenge. Most of the dead were buried under or near the home, and each house had a small shrine to the dead where daily sacrifices of food and drink were made to the spirits of the departed. People believe that by appeasing all the good family spirits they might prevent the return of any vengeful ones. But if that also failed, a necromancer was called in to exorcise the evil entity.

THE GREEK UNDERWORLD

The ancient Greeks believed that the realm of the afterlife lay somewhere to the West beyond the setting sun.

But later, with the rise of the great storytellers such as Homer and Hesiod, they began to see this netherword as literally under the earth, a place accessible from various "portals" on Earth known only to the gods and heroes. This became a powerful image in European thought and, like the Sumerian idea of eternal Hell, was to have a knock-on effect on later religions such as Christianity.

According to Greek myth, Hades ruled the underworld from the shadows, and his invisibility made him a reclusive character. He only came to the upper world when searching for a consort and, overcome by lust, he abducted Persephone who eventually became his queen for six months a year. She was allowed to return to the Earth to maintain the cycle of fertility and the seasons.

Above: When Hades abducted Persephone and took her to the underworld, all fertility on Earth ended.

Right: The Cumean Sybil's cave in Cuma, Italy, is allegedly where Aeneas found out about how to get to the underworld.

There were various entrances to the underworld. Trojan hero Aeneas descended via the Cumean Sybil's cave in Italy, passing an ancient elm tree onto which, according to Homer, false dreams clung to the bottom of every leaf. This myth implied that if your dream of returning from the underworld was destined not to come true, the dream would be left behind on Earth and you would never escape the underworld. Odysseus was directed by the witch Circe to Persephone's grove, which led to the river Styx. The only way to cross was to pay Charon the ferryman to carry your soul on his boat. Relatives of the buried dead would leave a coin under the corpse's tongue simply for that purpose. The unburied dead would wait eternally to cross the river, forever plagued by memories of the past. On the far bank lived the 50-headed dog Cerberus, who guarded the shore of the underworld and devoured any mortal who tried to enter it without paying the ferryman, or any soul who tried to leave.

There were several regions of the underworld. The worst one was Tartarus, a deep abyss and a Hell-like inferno in which sinners were eternally punished. Erebus was the deepest, most inaccessible region. Hecate, the goddess of black magic, lived here, accompanied by the Furies or Erinyes, wild, demonic female spirits who decided the torment for wicked souls. Hecate would dance across the fields with a pack of ghosts howling behind her to haunt and create fear in all those who had sinned.

Nemesis, the goddess of divine retribution, was no stranger to the underworld either. She would hunt down guilty souls who were sent to the Plain of Judgement to ensure their punishment fitted the soul's crime. The Asphodel Fields were where ordinary souls would twitter forever like birds and bats.

In Homer's epic poem *The Odyssey* (see page 81), the hero, Odysseus, sails to the very edge of the Earth where he sees a grove of trees at the junction of two rivers and arrives at the meadow of Asphodel. Here, the dead approach him in swarms, unable to speak unless animated by the blood of dead animals. Only the ghost of the semi-divine Tiresias, the blind prophet, is allowed to think and speak so he can give valuable information to Odysseus about his future, while the other ghosts must remain as shadows. Here, Odysseus meets the spirit of the hunter Orion before he is placed among the stars as a constellation, while the spirits of women who had failed to find a husband arrive in their thousands to embrace Odysseus, squeaking like bats in a cave. At the edge of the Earth is also the Pool of Lethe, where souls could drink to wipe out all memory of their lives, and the Vale of Mourning, for souls who had died unhappily in love. For those who had been virtuous, a joyous afterlife in the Elysium Fields awaited.

One strange exit route from the underworld was mentioned in the myth of Aeneas in Homer's epic work, *The Iliad*. It was known as the Gate of Ivory, through which souls sent false dreams to the upper world to deceive men. This was the gate through which Sybil and Aeneas found their way back to the Upper World, rather than the Gate of Horn, through which all that passes is made good and true.

Right: Encouraged by the water spirits, forgetting your past life was easy if you drank from the Pool of Lethe.

THE AFTERLIFE AS SUFFERING

Gehenna

The name Gehenna can be traced to a deep, narrow ravine, South of Jerusalem, where the pre-Judaic Ammonite people sacrificed their children to their god, Molech. This valley later served as the city dump and became a graphic symbol of the place of punishment for the wicked. It was called the Valley of Hinnom and, subsequently in Greek translation became Gehenna, a commonly used expression for Hell during the time of the New Testament. Gehenna, or the Lake of Fire, is referred to as the future, or final, Hell because it is where the wicked from all ages, including Satan and the fallen angels, will reside in torment forever.

Sheol

Sheol appears in both the Hebrew Old and New Testaments as a place akin to the Greek underworld. Translated, the word means both "pit" and the "home of the dead". Whatever the karma or moral choices made in life, all the dead, whether good or bad, must go to this miserable, gloomy place. But the most fearful concept for any believer is that here you are no longer favoured by or in touch with God. The characterless inhabitants of Sheol

were known as the *rephaim* or "shades". Some of the more important shades were contacted by seers such as the Witch of Endor who channelled Samuel on behalf of King Saul to obtain portents for the future. When the Hebrew texts were translated into Greek around 200 BCE, *Hades* replaced *Sheol* as the destination for the dead.

Above: In Jewish traditions, Gehenna was the eternal Hell for the wicked, while Sheol was the abode for both good and bad.

Purgatory

Purgatory is a place where merciful souls who have not been baptized or received communion will be blessed by God for eternity. A concept of the Catholic Church, the realm of purgatory must be entered by these Christian souls so that they can be purified before entering Heaven and can be sure of receiving salvation. In purgatory they will be given all the necessary rites to be admitted into the holy embrace of God.

Dis

Dis is the complex city of Hell, described in 15th-century writer Dante's epic work the *Inferno*. Dis encompasses the sixth to

Above: Dante's hellish city of Dis encapsulated the terrors of eternal damnation for all who were heretics or sinners.

the ninth circles of Hell. The most serious sins are punished in these regions of lower Hell. Dis is extremely hot and contains areas more closely resembling the common modern conception of Hell than the upper levels. The modern Christian concept of Hell derives from the teaching of the New Testament, where Hell is typically described using the Greek words *Hades* or the Hebrew word *Gehenna*. Those who find themselves in Hell are surrounded by fire, demons, and eternal suffering. The walls of Dis are guarded by the fallen angels and the Furies (the evil female spirits responsible for driving men insane). Punished to the confines of Dis are those whose lives were marked by active sins such as heretics, murderers, suicides, blasphemers, seducers, flatterers, sorcerers, hypocrites, thieves, falsifiers, and traitors.

ANCIENT PERSIAN MYTHOLOGY

In pre-Zoroastrian Persian mythology, Hell was described as a deep, terrifying well. Dark, stinking, and extremely narrow, it was filled with horrific demons, as big as mountains, who devoured the souls of the damned.

Known as the land of the Daevas, or demons, the pit of despair was ruled by the sinister god Angra Mainyu. For any lesser demons who defied the chaotic mind of Angra Mainyu, eternal torture was all that could be expected, which is why many escaped to Earth to wreak havoc among mankind. Even the weather in Duzakh was impossible to predict, with snow, hail, rain, blasting sand, and ash storms, followed by volcanic eruptions and burning larva. This desolated rocky place was arid, too hot or too cold, and nothing could survive. Throughout parts of Duzakh were slave pits called Drujdemana, where the chief demon, Vizaresh, dropped souls he had stolen who had been en route to Heaven. If the slaves refused to work in Duzakh they would be eaten by Angra Mainyu. Why the slaves were digging the well of Duzakh wider and wider, not even the other gods knew or dared to wonder.

Above: The land of demons was a stinking hole where souls became slaves to the evil gods.

AN AFTERLIFE FOR HEROES

In Norse mythology, Valhalla (hall of the slain) was the god Odin's great feasting hall for the Einherjar, the souls of the heroic Viking warriors who had been slain on the battlefield.

The roof and walls of the enormous palace of Valhalla were constructed of shields and spears. Its 500 or more doors were said to be wide enough to allow 800 men to enter marching abreast. The door, known as the Valgrind, was specially constructed out of wood. It was here that fallen heroes entered after being tested for their worth.

Once inside, the great heroes were cured of their wounds and lived an endless life of hedonism and fighting. Each morning they would don their armour, go to the practice ground and fight each other. If killed, they'd be brought back to life to endure all the agonies they had previously suffered. But each evening they would return to Valhalla to feast on the meat of a huge boar, reincarnated every day as a live boar, killed, and then eaten again.

Because the Vikings believed such an existence as to be expected at Valhalla to be perfect, older warriors who were not slain on the battlefield during their youth or active years would fall on their spears to be welcomed into Valhalla.

Left: Valhalla was a turreted palace in Norse mythology fit only for warrior heroes, many of whom had battled against the Midgard Serpent.

POLYNESIAN AFTERLIFE

Throughout Polynesia were many variations of an otherworld. The most well-known of them was the underworld of Po, in which the soul would not want to linger long after death as it was fearsome, dark, and full of evil spirits.

However, there were two other realms, known as Polotu in western Polynesia and Hawaiki in the East. Confusingly, the ancestral spirit world in the West was also called Hawaiki. This was a realm that the living could never find, but to which spirits could return. Depending on where you lived in Polynesia, this realm was thought to be in the sky, below ground, or far away across the ocean. The underground version of Hawaiki was sometimes confused with the underworld Po.

Po was divided into different regions. The most ominous part of Po was ruled over by Miru, the goddess of death, who waited with a huge net in which she caught the souls of stupid people, those who had done something wrong, and those who had had been killed by sorcery. As these souls leapt out of the real world into the otherworld, she scooped them up with her net and threw them into her huge ovens where they were annihilated.

Those who had been respected tribal elders, leaders, heroes, or just virtuous throughout life were usually given access to join their ancestors in the spirit world, which mirrored the real world. But those who died as babies or in childbirth were not so lucky and would be trapped between this world and the netherworld and dwelt in a twilight zone, only able at times to return to haunt the living and take revenge.

Above: To indigenous island peoples such as the Polynesians, the afterlife could be far away to the West, a distant land, or below the earth.

CELTIC MYTH

In Celtic myth, the otherworld, ruled by two gods, was known as Annwn and sometimes Anfwn or Anghar. A mirror-image of the physical world, this otherworld was, however, formless and timeless. The gods, Havgan and Arawn, were rivals and many legends grew around their battle to take control over the other.

Above: Glastonbury Tor is said to be one of the possible entrances to the Celtic otherworld.

Annwn is said to be accessible at the mouth of the Severn river, near Lundy Island, as well as from the top of Glastonbury Tor. Annwn, which was Christianized as the land of souls in medieval times, was filled with spirits, demons and fairies who travelled to the mortal world to trick, delude or amuse the humans that they encountered.

In the medieval Welsh collection of prose stories known as the *Mabbinogion*, Arawn persuaded the shape-changer, Pwyll, king of Dyfed, to change places with him for a year. Arawn wanted to destroy his rival Havgan and become sole ruler of the otherworld. He knew he wasn't strong enough to win but Pwyll was. One day, while out hunting, Pwyll's own pack of hounds chased off another pack that was killing a stag. The owner of the first pack was Arawn, and as recompense he persuaded Pwyll to rule the underworld for a year while he, Arawn, ruled Dyfed. Pwyll easily killed Havgan, and a year later they returned to their own kingdoms and Arawn became the sole ruler of Annwn.

In the 14th-century Welsh manuscript known as the *Book of Taliesin*, King Arthur and his knights travel through Annwn in search of the Cauldron of Plenty, the eternal source of the otherworld's delights and immortality. It has been suggested that this is the precursor to the later Grail myths. The text dates back to the 10th century CE, but scholars believe most Welsh myth was transmitted orally and thus it could date back as far as the 6th century CE. In one myth, a divine ploughman called Amaethon stole a deer from Arawn and the rather soft ruler of the underworld had to fight an enormous army that the magician Gwydion had magically transformed from trees for his good friend the ploughman. Arawn lost his deer and his reputation. He forever after became known as the gentle but rather weedy ruler of Annwn.

Above: King Arthur and his knights once travelled through Annwn in search of immortality.

BANTU AFTERLIFE

For the Bantu people of Africa, the ghost country was the afterlife and was accessed through holes and caves in the ground, but variations in the myth obviously occurred, depending on the immediate geographical landscape.

Above: For the Bantu peoples, the afterlife was a land filled with the ghosts of their ancestors.

The huge distances and changing landscape in Africa meant there was a distinct variety of local ways in which to find the land of ghosts, but also the kind of ghosts that inhabited the area. On Mount Kilimanjaro, for example, the ghost land was reached by throwing oneself into a deep pool, if you dared; for the peoples of the Transvaal, the gateway to Mosima (the abyss) was via a great ravine.

Few of these ghost lands were above ground, but in East Africa, small outcrops of trees were considered to be places of worship and mounds of earth, often called spirit hills, were all considered liable to be visited by ghosts. The trees growing in any of these sacred places were never cut down and always protected from bush fires because it was believed their roots may be inhabited by the ancestral spirits.

The Bantu have different classes of ghosts. Family ghosts – *kungu* – are honoured and propitiated throughout the generations of a family until they lose their personality and merge into a host of spirits known as *vinyamkela* or *majini*.

The *vinyamkela* are more friendly than the *majini*, but both are more powerful than the *kungu* ghosts. These ghosts are usually invisible but have moments when they appear with half a body and nothing on the other side, particularly when they return to haunt wicked family members.

BOLIVIAN AFTERLIFE

For the Guarayu people of Bolivia, the great Spirit, Tamoi, ruled the Land of the Grandfather, but before the soul was allowed to stay there it must survive a long journey of tests and trials.

There it would join its ancestors to enjoy eternal youth and the kind of paradise longed for on Earth.

Once the burial of the body was complete, the long journey began. The soul had to chose between two paths, one wide and easy, the other narrow and dark. If it chose the easy way it spent the afterlife in eternal darkness. However, the soul did not know which path was which when it first made its choice, because they looked identical.

The lucky soul who chose the narrow path first crossed a wide and dangerous river. Unless the soul took with it a bamboo pipe that would be buried with the body in the grave, the ferryman would refuse to help the soul to cross. Across the distant shore the soul now faced endless tests to ensure it was fit to reside in the Land of the Grandfather. There were dangerous rocks, terrible tortures from monkeys and birds, trees that spoke, and other exotic birds who tested the soul's ability to remain fixed in its intentions. The soul also had to pick a million feathers from a thousand hummingbirds and offer the feathers to the great Spirit. Finally, the soul had to reflect upon the things it wanted most in its life then be offered them and refuse to be tempted. When and if it managed to get past all these tests it would be honoured and allowed to bathe in the pool of eternal youth and live life as it wanted.

Left: For the Guarayu people of Bolivia, choosing a pathway led you to eternal darkness or light.

AZTEC MYTHOLOGY

In Aztec mythology, Mictlan *was the underworld where most people went after death. It consisted of nine levels. The journey from the first level to the ninth was difficult and took four years.*

The dead were accompanied by Xolotl, the god of fire and lightning. Xolotl would charge down to Earth to claim the dead, his lightning bolts causing the earth to open up so they could descend to the first level. The dead had to face terrifying challenges to move through each level, such as crossing the River of Blood, which was inhabited by vicious jaguars. Once in *Mictlan*, the dead would serve the lord of the underworld, Mictlantecuhtli, who lived with his wife in a palace with no windows. Depicted with ghastly skull, jaws open and a necklace of eyeballs, Mictlantecuhtli was eternally hungry and gobbled up any stars that fell to Earth during the day.

But there were other netherworlds that were available to the dead, depending on their behaviour in life and their means of death. Warriors who died in battle, and those who died as a sacrifice, went East and accompanied the sun during the morning, where they rose in the sky every day to show they were

Right: The Aztec rain god, Tlaloc, carried a rattle to make thunder and wore foam sandals to soak up puddles of rain into the sky.

Left: The worship of the Lord of Mictlan involved the ritual eating of human flesh and the scattering of the bones.

reborn like the sun, so that none would forget their important role on Earth.

Women who died in childbirth went to the West. Here, they would greet the sun when it set in the evening to bring a little light to their darkest day, as to die in childbirth was considered shameful. People who died of drowning, or from other causes that were seen as linked to the rain god Tlaloc, or from being hit by lightning, went to a paradise called Tlalocan.

Rain was precious to the Aztecs for the growing of crops, and any death that was connected to water was a sacrifice to the great rain god, and merited eternal heaven.

THE ASTRAL PLANE

A mysterious realm beyond the one we know, the astral plane has also been known as the "world of illusion" or "world of thoughts" because it is to here that the mind journeys to experience a different plane of existence without being hampered by the body.

The astral plane was thought to be a realm between Heaven and Earth where the heavenly bodies dwelt. Renaissance philosophers, such as Cornelius Agrippa, believed that the human soul could escape to the astral plane and discover prophetic knowledge. These astral spheres were held to be populated by angels, demons, and spirits. These bodies and their planes of being are depicted as concentric circles or nested spheres with a human body, moving freely through it.

For the 3rd-century CE Greek Neoplatonic philosopher Plotinus, the individual is a microcosm of the universe, while the material world is a dull image of the non-physical world, with various other realms in between, and the human astral body can move freely between all these realms.

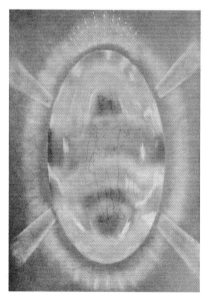

Left: The astral plane was thought to be a realm through which the soul travelled between lives.

Right: Concentric waves of light allow the soul body to move freely into other spheres.

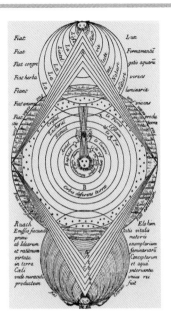

Astral projection is very similar to an experience known as "soul travel" in which, apparently, the soul leaves the body at will to visit the various planes of Heaven. The Sant Mat gurus of 13th-century India recounted soul-travel experiences, which are still practised today by the Sant Mat spiritual traditions. Originating in India, these spiritual movements use various meditation and mantra techniques to attain the eight spiritual levels described above the physical plane. Names and subdivisions within these levels will vary to some extent by movement and Master.

To the Neoplatonists, the "astral body", a link between the physical body and the soul, was able to travel to the astral plane to be at one with the stars. This form of "astral projection" has since been replaced by the idea that altered states of consciousness enable the mind or soul to travel to a non-physical or spiritual plane. On this basis, the mind is able to journey to realms that are believed to mirror the known material world, or to unknown dimensions where we can encounter other astral beings.

Some occultists of the 20th century, including Aleister Crowley, believed the astral plane stood on the threshold of timeless and spaceless spiritual planes, while the physical planes stood within time and space. It is this astral plane that can be accessed by occultists, mediums, and psychics to harness knowledge from the universe and bring it to the physical realm.

THE SUMMERLAND

The Summerland is believed to be a place of rest for souls in between Earthly incarnations. Adopted by 19th-century American Spiritualist Andrew Jackson Davis and British theosophist CW Leadbeater, Summerland is well known as the afterlife for many neopagan movements, including Wicca (see page 111).

Many neopagans also chose to believe that once one has experienced life through many incarnations and the soul has sufficiently evolved, the Summerland can also be a place of eternal afterlife. During Earthly incarnation, the soul has little, if any, recollection of the Summerland, and it is only glimpsed and recollected through near-death experiences (see page 21) or in life-between-lives regression therapy (see page 48).

Like paradise, the Summerland is a place of beauty and peace, where everything an individual soul loves is preserved in its fullest beauty. It is envisioned as containing fields of rolling green hills, lush grass, eternal sunlight, and butterflies.

It is not a place of judgement, but of spiritual self-evaluation, where the soul is able to review its life and gain

Above: American Spiritualist A J Davis wrote an influential book on the Summerland in 1868.

an understanding of the total impact its actions have had on the world. Some believe every future life is chosen and planned out by the soul itself while in the

Summerland, whereas others believe that such lessons are planned by a spirit guide or deity.

Theosophy and the Summerland

In theosophy, the Summerland is also referred to as the Astral Plane Heaven. It is depicted as a permanent place for souls who had been good in a previous life. Those who have been bad go to a Hell, another plane situated below the Earth that is composed of the densest astral matter. It is believed by theosophists that most people go to a specific Summerland created for each religious belief. Christians therefore go to a Christian Summerland, Jews go to a Jewish Summerland, and so on.

Above: According to many neopagan traditions, the Summerland is likened to an Earthly paradise.

MYTHICAL JOURNEYS TO THE AFTERLIFE

Many have tried to make their way to the underworld, either to retrieve a loved one, such as Orpheus (see page 12), to retrieve their own soul, such as Psyche (see page 128-9), or simply to fight the demons or embark on a divine or mortal quest, such as Heracles.

Below, I recount just a few of these journeys. These myths, legends, and literary tales are all powerful metaphors for your own quest to discover what the afterlife is about, just as you are doing now by reading this book. They also awaken your imagination, the very quality needed to begin the practical work to be found in Chapter 6. But most

Above: Innana's return from the underworld brought fertility back to the land.

of all, they are superb analogies for our soul's journey through this life, as it faces the real tests and trials of the Hell or underworld that life is.

Innana and Ereshkigal

Innana was the Sumerian goddess of light, fertility, and sex and was responsible for the growth of the land. Dumuzi was her consort, the shepherd king for whom she built the city of Uruk. Her twin sister Ereshkigal was the goddess of darkness who ruled the underworld.

Innana began to miss her sister and decided to visit her. Dressed in her finest gold jewellery and flowing white gowns, she arrived at the first Gate of Invisibility. There were seven altogether and, at each gate, she was ordered to remove part of her clothing or jewels. After the seventh gate, now completely naked, she finally faced her sister, Ereshkigal. But the gods who judged the dead believed she

Above: Uruk was an ancient city of Sumer, situated East of the Euphrates river in 4000 BCE.

had come to usurp her sister's throne, so dragged her off and hung her on a meat hook to rot.

While Innana was in the underworld, there was no light or fertility on Earth and the gods realized they must get her back. Enki, the trickster god, sent three immortals to descend to the underworld, who took Innana off the hook and with a magic potion revived her. Ereshkigal agreed that Innana could return to the upper world as long as she sent a replacement. On her return to Uruk, she discovered that Dumuzi had neither mourned nor cared that she'd gone. Not only had he usurped her throne, but had slept with her sisters. His betrayal was enough for Innana to banish him to the underworld as her replacement and satisfy Ereshkigal's conditions. After some time Innana regretted her decision and allowed Dumuzi to return to Earth every year for six months as a god of vegetation.

The myth of Er

The Myth of Er is a legend from Plato's *Republic* and an account of the cosmos and the afterlife that greatly influenced religious, philosophical, and scientific thought for many centuries. The word myth in this context means "account", and was used by Socrates when he explained that, because Er did not drink the waters of Lethe when on his underworld visit, the *mythos* or account was preserved for us.

When the bodies of those who died in battle were collected, ten days after his death, Er's body still remained undecomposed. Two days later he revived on his funeral pyre and told others of his journey through the afterlife.

At the start of the journey, with many other souls as his companions, Er found a place with four openings – two leading into and out of the sky, and two leading into and out of the Earth. Judges sat between these openings and told each soul which path to follow: the good were guided onto the path in the sky, while the immoral were directed below. But when Er approached the judges, he was told to remain, listening and observing the comings and goings in order to report his experience to mankind. Some souls floated down from the light-filled

Above: Er managed to cross the river Lethe without drinking any of the water, but was still under the watchful eye of Hades.

path above; others rose from below, attempting to rise from the underground.

After seven days in the underworld meadow, the souls and Er were required to travel to a place where they could see a rainbow of light. This was where souls were assigned a guardian spirit to help them continue through their next life. They passed under the throne of Lady Necessity, or goddess of Fate, then traveled to the Plane of Oblivion, where the River of Forgetfulness (river Lethe) flowed. Each soul was required to drink some of the water, in varying quantities, apart from Er. As they drank, each soul forgot everything of their past life. As they lay down at night to sleep, each soul was lifted up into the night sky, ready for their rebirth, thus completing their afterlife experience. Er remembered nothing of the actual journey back to his body. But when he opened his eyes to find himself lying on the funeral pyre, he was able to recall his visit to the afterlife, knowing he was meant to tell the world of his adventure.

Right: The journey to the underworld often began in a deep cave, where the cries of tormented souls rose through the fiery air.

Dante's descent to Hell

The epic poem the *Divine Comedy* tells the story of Dante's journey through the three realms of the dead, lasting from the night before Good Friday to the Wednesday after Easter in the spring of 1,300 CE. Dante is first guided through Hell and purgatory by the Roman poet Virgil, then through Heaven by his ideal woman, Beatrice.

The poem begins when Dante is 35 years old and lost in a dark wood, where beasts, guilt, and self-loathing all haunt

him. He is also spiritually lost and has not found the "right way" to salvation. Conscious that he is ruining himself, Dante is at last rescued by Virgil, and together the two of them begin their journey to the underworld. Dante passes through the gate of Hell, with its famous inscription, "Abandon all hope, ye who enter here".

Each sin's punishment in Inferno, the first part of the poem, is a symbolic instance of poetic justice or divine vengeance. For example, fortune tellers have to walk with their heads on

Above: Satan flapped his wings making a cold wind that froze the water and the sinners in the Ninth Circle.

backwards, unable to see what is ahead, because they had tried to predict too much in life. Virgil then guides Dante through the nine circles of Hell. The circles are concentric, representing a gradual increase in wickedness, and culminating at the centre of the Earth, where Satan is held in bondage. Each circle's sinners are punished by God in a fashion fitting their crimes: each sinner is afflicted for all of eternity by the chief sin he committed.

In the very centre of Hell, condemned for committing the ultimate sin of personal treachery against God, is Satan. Depicted as a terrifying beast with three faces, Satan is waist deep in ice, weeping tears from his six eyes and beating his six wings as if trying to escape.

The two poets escape Hell by climbing down Satan's ragged body. They pass through the centre of the Earth, then emerge in the Southern hemisphere just before dawn on Easter Sunday beneath a sky studded with stars. On the Mountain of Purgatory on the far side of the world (an island created by a huge geological shift of rock when Satan fell from the heavens and created Hell), there are seven terraces, corresponding to the seven deadly sins, or to seven roots of sinfulness. It is from here that Dante then embarks on his next epic journey to Heaven.

Journey to Zibalba

This myth was established around 500 Kᴀ. The sacred Mayan book, known as the *Popol Vuh*, recounts the legend of the twins Hun-Apu and Xbalanque and their exploits in the underworld. Later known as "hero gods", they journeyed into the underworld to avenge the murder of their relatives by the lords of hell. Xibalba, the Mayan underworld, was a dark, stench-filled place where demons and evil gods roamed. Any humans who entered there never came back to earth, which is why the twins became legendary heros in later Mayan mythology. The Mayan death gods were also known by other names such as Death God D or Death God L, and it was these two gods who murdered the twins father and uncle long before the twins made their visit.

The hero gods' relatives, their father Hun Hunahpu and their uncle Vukub, had played a game of *tlachtli*, a kind of hockey that was popular throughout ancient Mexico. Unfortunately, they lost the ball down a tunnel which lead to the dreadful realm of Xibalba. The lords of Xibalba challenged the gods at a game. But the gods were fooled by the treacherous lords, then murdered, sacrificed, and buried in the House of Gloom, a miserable realm of Xibalba that held thousands and thousands of corpses.

Many years later, the twin hero gods met a rat who told them the story about their relatives' death. The rat explained about the game of *tlachtli* and where it had been played. So the twins set off to try out the ball game, determined to meet the challenge of the demons and avenge their father's death. The twins found the tunnel, and followed the path that led down to the River of Blood and the entrance to Xibalba.

Each night the twins were tested by the lords of Xibalba. But finally the twins won by boasting they could bring the dead back to life and prove they were immortal. The lords of Xibalba demanded they kill and resurrect the Hound of Death, the guardian of the gateway to Xibalba, and cut a man to pieces and bring him to life again. The heroes did this and the underworld lords and demons asked if they could be resurrected, too. The twins reminded them they were merely dark shadows and phantoms, so the lords' powers soon waned and they were forbidden to play *tlachtli* ever again.

The ancestor's souls, Hun Hunahpu and Vukub, were sent up to the heavens as the sun and moon by the gods, and the heroes returned to the world to remind people of the immortality of the gods and their triumph over the land of the dead.

Above: In Mayan mythology, ball-game depictions were associated with the land of the dead.

Right: A battle between rival Hindu kings ended in the gods' test to see who should go to Heaven and Hell.

Yudhisthira's journey

In the epic Hindu story known as the *Mahabharata*, Yudhisthira was the king of Indraprastha and had recently fought a battle against his rival, Duryodhana. The gods Indra and Krishna wanted to test Yudhisthira to see if he was worthy of his kingship, so they sent him on a mission to find his brothers who had been killed by Duryodhana. The two gods told Yudhisthira that his brothers were in Hell atoning for their sins, while his rival

Duryodhana was in Heaven after dying at Kurukshetra where the battle between good and evil gods had taken place.

Yudhisthira didn't believe the gods, sure that his brothers were virtuous, and ordered his chariot to go to Heaven to prove that his family were there. Instead he saw his rival Duryodhana and all his demon allies. Unbeknown to Yudhisthira, the sight of his rival in Heaven was simply an illusion that Indra had placed in Yudhisthira's mind.

Yudhisthira loyally then went to Hell to find his brothers, but the sight of gore and blood horrified him. Although at first he was tempted to flee, after hearing the voices of his beloved brothers asking him to stay with them in their misery, he remained. This was an illusion, another trick to test his loyalty. Although Yudhisthira could not see his brothers, he believed them to be there. So the virtuous Yudhisthira ordered his charioteer to return to Earth alone, preferring to live in Hell with good people than in Heaven with his enemies.

Not long afterwards, Indra and Krishna appeared before him in Hell and told him that his brothers were really in Heaven, while his enemies would suffer from Hell's torment for their Earthly sins. Thus, Yudhisthira passed the test and became king, and, when he died, he was allowed to join his brothers in Heaven.

BRIEF GUIDE TO WHO'S WHO IN THE AFTERLIFE

There are hundreds of myths, tales, and people associated with the underworld and afterlife. Here is just a selection, listed in chronological order, of the most important or memorable beings, from ancient gods such as Hades, to more recent additions such as Baron Samedi, as well as brief descriptions of the difference between psychopomps, spirits, and elementals.

Ra (Egypt)
The sun god Ra crossed the daytime sky in a boat, the Mandjet, meaning Morning Boat and he used another boat, called

Meseket, the night-time boat, to cross the underworld at night. The night-time boat was controlled by a dedicated ferryman, who became known as Aken. When Aken's "ferryman" cult developed on the banks of the Nile, he became known as ruler of the underworld.

Erishkigal (Mesopotamian)
In Sumerian mythology, Ereshkigal was the goddess of the underworld and was also known as Irkalla, the name for the underworld itself. Ereshkigal was the only one who could pass judgement and give laws in her kingdom. The main temple dedicated to her was located in ancient Kutha, 25 miles or so from Babylon.

Left: All forms of life were created by Ra, who called each of them into existence by speaking their secret names.

Belet-Seri (Babylonian)

Belet-Seri was known in Babylonian and Akkadian mythology as the Scribe of the Earth who kept a list of names of all those who arrived in the underworld. She advised the queen of the dead, Ereshkigal, on the dead's final judgement. Married to Amurru, the God of Travellers, she became identified as Queen of the Desert.

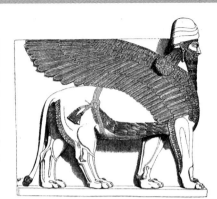

Nergal

Nergal governed the dead in some later patriarchal Akkadian myths, alongside his consort Allatu. Allatu was thought to have originally been the lone ruler of the underworld. In some texts the god Ninazu is the son of Nergal and Allatu.

Hades (Greek)

The son of the gods Cronus and Rhea, Hades, along with his brothers Zeus and Poseidon, overthrew the Titans to begin the Olympian rule of the cosmos. However, when drawing lots to see who ruled which territory, Hades was given the gloomy underworld. Hades was not very pleased with his kingdom, because he was excluded from

Above right: Nergal represented the sun at noon and the summer solstice.

Right: Gloomy Hades is depicted here with his three-headed dog, Cerberus.

Olympia and lived in perpetual darkness. Hades rarely left the underworld except on a few occasions to abduct a nymph, including his consort, Persephone, the daughter of Earth goddess Demeter.

Hecate (Greek)

Hecate was an ancient goddess associated with crossroads, fire, light, the moon, magic, witchcraft, necromancy, and sorcery. She had rulership over earth, sea and sky, as well as the cosmic World Soul (see page 118). Hecate was associated with ghosts, infernal spirits, and the dead. Shrines to Hecate were placed at doorways and entrances to cities with the belief that they would protect from restless dead and other spirits. At crossroads, food offerings were left at the new moon in honour of Hecate as protection from spirits and other evil beings.

Charon (Greek)

Charon was the ferryman who took souls across the river Styx when they arrived from the upper world with their guide, Hermes. Charon required the payment of a fee, usually in the form of a coin placed under the tongue of the deceased, before ferrying the soul across the river to Hades's domain. Anyone who couldn't afford the payment was doomed to wander the banks of the river.

The Valkyries (Norse)

The Valkyries – the beautiful yet deadly maidens of the god Odin – bore resemblance to ancient Norse goddesses of destruction who wove tapestries from the severed limbs and

Left: The ferryman Charon threw off passengers who couldn't pay their way across the river.

Left: Valkyries understand the speech of birds, have sparkling eyes, and have no scruples about seducing men.

entrails of fallen warriors. They roamed across battlefields selecting heroes for Valhalla (see page 190) then enchanted the ones that they most lusted after. Seductive yet sadistic, the Valkyries would have sex with their chosen heroes by night in Valhalla, then would awaken the following morning as virgins. They had flowing long golden hair, were depicted in white robes usually riding hot-headed wild stallions.

Also sidekicks to Tyr, the god of war, the Valkyries were sometimes shown riding wolves as they swept across the skies to seize sailors from ships, seduce them into their arms, then drop them in the ocean below to drown. They were responsible for scattering the earth with frost or morning dew that was said to be the tears that they had gathered from their victims.

Veles (Slav)

Veles was a major god of the supernatural world in Slavic mythology. Apart from the underworld, he was also associated with dragons, magic, wealth, and trickery. Often thought to be part serpent, part bull, and part human, sporting a long beard, he was constantly at war with the thunder god, Perun, as part of an ongoing epic story.

Dis Pater (Roman)

The Roman god Dis Pater took over from the original Hades and later became known as Pluto, when the Romans wiped out most of the earlier pantheons of gods in their conquest of Europe. Originally a god of the riches of the earth, he eventually became the underworld deity.

Dis Pater was commonly shortened to simply Dis. This name has since become an alternative name for the underworld or a part of the underworld, as in Dante's *Divine Comedy* (see page 205).

Orcus (Etruscan)

Orcus was the punisher of broken oaths in early Etruscan mythology (the Etruscans were a pre-Roman civilization of Northern Italy) and lived in the underworld. He was later associated with the Roman god Dis Pater and, in his later guise, as Pluto. Eventually, because of his horrific cruelty towards sinners, Orcus became associated with evil and his name was considered demonic. By the medieval period his cult developed in rural Europe where he was associated with the wildman of the woods, the Green Man, and horned gods such as Cernunnos.

Manes (Roman)

Souls of the dead who visited the living, the Manes were as popular in Roman religion as the spirits known as the Genii. The *genius*

Left: The Roman god Dis Pater was once thought to be the ancestor of the Gauls.

Right: In the Middle Ages, Orcus developed into a demonic folk figure and a monster who fed on human flesh.

was the pure spirit or essence of a place, object, person, or even abstract quality. However, the Manes were thought to be protective ancestral spirits, not unlike the Lares or hero-ancestors who were invoked as guardians in the home and family.

Akka (Scandinavian)

In Northern Scandinavia, among the shamanic Sámi peoples, the Akka were underworld female spirits. The Sámi called upon the Akka to help them in their daily life, curing disease, ridding them of evil, and promoting good hunting.

Jabme-Akka (Scandinavian)

The Samis considered the underworld to be a mirror-image of the world above. Its ruler, the goddess Jabme-Akka, was both heartless and kind: to souls of dead babies she would sing a lullaby, yet she enveloped all the other spirits in a deathly cold silence, their only comfort being the personal possessions with which they were buried.

Supay (Incan)

In Incan mythology, Supay was both the god of death and ruler of the Incan

Above: The Incan god Supay ruled a race of demons, and his festival is still celebrated in Peru.

underworld, known as Ukhu Pacha. In many South American countries, the name Supay is roughly translated as "diablo" or devil.

Miru (Polynesian)
In the Cook Islands, Miru is the goddess of the underworld who lives in Avaiki. She intoxicates the souls of dead people with kava, a deadly sedative, and burns them eternally in her oven.

Hine-nui-te-pō (Polynesian)
The much-feared goddess of Maori mythology was Hine-nui-te-pō, who ruled the night, darkness, and death. Unknowingly married to her father, the god Tāne, Hine-nui-te-pō fled in horror to the depths of the underworld on discovering her incest. As she escaped, sweeping angrily across the Western horizon, the sunset turned red.

Erlik (Turkic)
Ulgen, the god of Heaven in Turkic mythology (the Turkic peoples were indigenous to central Asia and Eastern Europe) created the first man, Erlik. But Erlik wanted to be equal to the great creator god and, to punish him for his jealousy, Ulgen sent Erlik to the underworld deep within the Earth.

Above: A spiteful Hine-nui-te-pō waits for the neverending parade of mortals to enter her world.

However, Erlik would not be beaten and, in revenge, spawned a host of evil spirits to help him conquer the heavens. With his band of demons and his nine sons and daughters he brought misfortune to the world and death to mankind. He was also known for his ability to trick shamans on their missions to take good souls to Ulgen's heaven; the souls would instead find themselves in hell.

Kali (Hindu)
Blood-thirsty and destructive, the Hindu goddess of death is usually depicted wearing a necklace of skulls. Anyone who saw her terrifying apparition, with its ghastly tongue and black flesh,

Above: Blood-loving Kali was not only the Hindu goddess of death, but also a killer of demons.

believed they were about to die. Kali's dark associations were reiterated when she became the centre of worship by the Thugee sect, a secret society feared by ordinary people. The Thugee would sacrifice humans to Kali, grabbing and strangling strangers in the street or running a knife through the victim's heart on Kali's altar. Originally, in Hindu myth, Kali was known to help the other gods in their fight against demons such as Raktabija. Raktabija had the power to come to life again from any drop of his spilt blood. Shiva sent the goddess Durga to fight him and, in Durga's frustrated anger, Kali exploded from Durga's head and lapped up all the demon's blood before it could transform into Raktabija. Kali has more recently became identified as mother goddess and protector rather than destroyer.

Di Zang (Buddhist)

According to Buddhist folklore, a monk known as Di Zang was a benevolent underworld ruler. When he first died, he went to the underworld with body and soul (unlike most inmates, who were simply souls) and then stormed around the place demanding the release of his mother who had been sent there for eating meat. With a gang of monkeys, they made such a noise that eventually his mother was sent back to the upper world and Di Zang became ruler of the dead. Once given immortality, he became a generous ruler and would sit listening to lost souls and teach them his Buddhist beliefs. Generally compassionate to all, Di Zang's underworld was very much a parallel world to the goodness and compassion of Buddhist teachings on Earth.

Emma-O (Japanese)

In Japanese myth, Emma-O was the great ruler-judge of the underworld, Yomi or Yomitsukumi (gloom-land). Yomi also meant the darkest part of night, and was originally a mirror-image world with no light, no beings, just nothingness. Izanami was originally a creator goddess, but with her untimely death giving birth to a child, she was sent to Yomi. Her husband Izanagi tried to get her back, but when he realized she was already one of the dead, he fled from Yomi. Izanami wanted him to stay there with her forever, but when he escaped back to the upper world and sealed the entrance, she vowed to torment all those souls who had just died.

Subsequently, Yomi became a place of torture and ordeal rather than just a netherworld of formless concept.

Mictlantecuhtli (Aztec)

The Aztec underworld was ruled by Mictlantecuhtli and his consort Mictecacihuatl. As the god of the dead, he was usually portrayed as a skeleton splattered with blood, with horrible protruding eyes, a collar of eyeballs, and disgusting teeth.

The worship of Mictlantecuhtli sometimes involved ritual cannibalism, with human flesh being consumed in and around the temple. He was one of only a few deities held to govern over all three types of souls identified by the Aztecs. These were souls of people who died normal deaths (of old age, disease, and so on), heroic deaths (such as in battle, sacrifice, or during childbirth), or non-heroic deaths (such as suicides or executed criminals).

Ghede (Caribbean)

In Haiti, Ghede was originally the god of love and sex. In Voodoo (see page 98), Ghede can refer to a family of spirits embodying death and fertility. These spirits known as "loas". (Voodoo has no specific pantheon or structure and relies merely on a belief in divine possession.)

From around the end of the 19th century, Ghede was amalgamated with Baron Samedi, the god of death. Devotees, when possessed by Ghede, became ecstatic, demonstrating that Ghede is also the lord of potency. The *Banda* was a group of worshippers who danced along the road under the influence of trance-inducing drugs or potions. They trailed behind one initiate dressed as Baron Samedi. Once thought to be a phallic ritual, it developed into a form of "dance macabre", leading its adepts to the edge of the underworld.

Spirit guides and psychopomps

In many traditions, lurking between the upper world and the underworld was a mysterious character, a guide who escorted the soul or the deceased to the afterlife. Known as a psychopomp (Greek for "soul's guide"), this figure never judged the soul but simply helped the dead to make their way across dangerous realms or boundaries to the otherworld. The most well-known psychopomp in Western literature is Hermes, the ancient Greek god. Below is a brief selection of psychopomps from the belief systems and myths of cultures from around the world.

Above: The ghostly souls that followed the living leader were rarely seen, but their presence was felt as a passing breeze.

Santa Compaña (Galacian)

The history of the Santa Compaña procession has been part of Spanish folk culture for hundreds of years and the legendary procession is still feared but respected by local Galacians and it is believed to be re-enacted by secret cults on All Souls' Day, 2 November.

A terrifying group of wraiths known as the Santa Compaña haunted the streets and waysides in their search for those who were soon to die. Sometimes two lines of spectres followed one living leader, who could only escape death by finding another to carry the cross he held before him. Sometimes there was one long line of lost souls who silently followed in one another's footsteps. As the procession passed by, a mist formed around the ghostly crew, but candles flickered in the gloom and the souls appeared to be dressed in hooded robes. It was believed that if you saw the procession coming, to protect yourself you must draw a magic circle on the ground and stay well inside it until the group passed by. The living leader would never remember his or her horrific experience, but would gradually grow weak and waste away unless another victim was found to replace him. The wraiths also rang bells to warn the dying that they were coming to take them away and, as the procession moved through the night, the wind stopped, dogs howled and cats fled in terror.

L'Ankou (French)

In Brittany, l'Ankou comes for the souls of those who are about to die. A true shapeshifter, this demonic spirit appears in many guises, including a tall, thin man with a long, hooded cloak, or as a skeleton with a scythe who often wears a broad-brimmed hat. He generally travels on foot, but sometimes comes in a carriage, pulled by four black horses.

Anubis (ancient Egyptian)

Anubis is the jackal-headed god of ancient Egypt who presides over the purification and mummification of the body. He is well known for his role as a psychopomp. At the time of death the *ba,* or soul of the dead, wings it way to *Duat,* the Kingdom of the Dead. Once in *Duat,* Anubis leads the soul, which still has its "heart", to the Hall of Ma'at to be judged.

The weighing of the heart ceremony was an important factor of the Egyptian mythology. In this ceremony, the heart was weighed by Anubis against Ma'at's

Above: Anubis was often depicted with a black head to symbolize the colour of rotting flesh and the fertile black soil of the Nile valley.

feather, representing truth. If the heart was heavier or lighter than the feather, the soul would be devoured by Ammit, the demon (see page 177).

Azrail (Islamic)

One of the four primary archangels of the Muslim belief system, Azrail is the "all-seeing" angel who is larger than life. One of his roles is to keep an eye on the Tree of the End, which grows in paradise. It is said that when a person is born a new leaf appears on the tree with their name on it, and when it is their time to die the leaf falls from the tree. This is Azrail's signal to come to collect their soul.

Aurora Borealis (Inuit)

For the Labrador Inuits (Eskimos) of Northeastern Canada, the Aurora Borealis is seen as flickering torch lights that are lit each night by the spirits to show the way for the deceased. When the spirits depart, the moon god, Anningan returns to chase his sister Malina the sun, across the sky.

Barnumbirr (Australian)

Barnumbirr is the Australian Morning Star who appears in the myths and legends of Northern aboriginals to show the way across the waters to the distant Island of the Dead.

Hermes (Greek)

One of the most well-known psycho-pomps, Hermes is the ancient Greek trickster god who acts as a guide and messenger between the heavens and

Above: In Buddhist traditions, Jizo (see page 224) helps dead children move from limbo to the afterlife.

Left: For many northern traditions, including the Inuits, the Aurora Borealis (Northern Lights) were thought to be spirits of the dead.

the underworld. He is also known as Mercury in Roman mythology.

Epona (Gallic/Celtic)

The horse-riding Roman-celtic goddess Epona was sacred to the ancient Gauls of France as well as the Romans. She carried the souls of the deceased on horseback to the otherworld while accompanied by three birds who were able to bring the dead back to life. She was also thought to be an ancient fertility goddess.

Jizo (Asia)

In the Buddhist tradition, Jizo is the "compassionate one" who greets people when they die. He is a popular figure in Japanese folklore and in other Asian traditions. He helps the souls of dead children who are too young to understand the Buddha's teachings and become stuck in limbo on the banks of the river Sai, unable to move on to the afterlife. To protect the children from demons, Jizo hides them under his clothes as he leads them to the salvation of the otherworld.

Types of beings

In myth and history, there are numerous accounts of spirits, ghosts, revenants, and other entities that have crossed over from the spiritual realms to appear in the so-called "real world".

Spirits and ghosts

Ghosts are thought to be the spirits or souls of the dead who are stuck in the material world, perhaps because they are attached to a place, person, event, or tragic situation. They continue to

Left: Throughout the world, ghosts are believed to haunt the living to resolve Earthly business, make amends, or take revenge.

Left: Hecate was the ancient Greek goddess of ghosts, the dead, witchcraft, and crossroads.

haunt the location associated with their attachment because they have not yet successfully crossed over to the afterlife.

Ghosts are usually harmless but are still frightening. Supernatural activity inside a home is mainly associated with tragic events that have occurred there during the building's past. The place of haunting is thought to be of extreme importance to the ghost, and so the Earthly business keeping the ghost attached to the location needs to be resolved. Mediums are often asked to visit haunted buildings to contact ghosts and help them move on to the afterlife.

Spirits should never be confused with ghosts. Spirits have crossed over successfully to the afterlife, but they can visit the material world at will or return to the spiritual one. A ghost always remains in limbo until Earthly problems are resolved.

Examples of spirits include the Empusae, sent by Hecate in Greek myth to guard roads and devour travellers. They uttered a high-pitched scream like the banshee of Celtic myth. Empusa was the beautiful daughter of the goddess Hecate and the spirit Mormo. She feasted on blood by seducing young men as they slept before drinking their blood and eating their flesh.

The Sanskrit term *preta* means "departed, deceased, a dead person", from *pra-ita*, literally "gone forth, departed". In classical Sanskrit, the term refers to the spirit of any dead person as well as a ghost or evil being. Pretas are believed to have been false, corrupted, compulsive, deceitful, jealous, or greedy people in a previous life. As a result of their karma, they are afflicted with an insatiable hunger for a particular substance or object.

In Japanese traditions such as Shinto, the soul is known as a *reikon*. However, there are two different kinds of *reikon*: one who is at peace after death, and the other who transforms into a restless wraith, stuck in limbo between the physical world and the afterlife. This distressed *reikon*, which is known as a *yūrei*, is usually a person who died an unnatural or traumatic death or who was not given the correct funeral rites. If the *yūrei* has any attachment to the physical world it will return to haunt the living in revenge for its limbo state. The *reikon* who was given the proper funeral rites, or who died a peaceful death, can leave the place of limbo and move on to the afterlife in eternal peace. It will then look down favourably on family descendants.

Elementals

Elementals, fairies, and land spirits are thought to attach themselves to a place or person but, unlike ghosts, they can be mischievous, dark, or demonic. This energy is often described by Wiccans as "sparkling" in the case of fairies, or "dense" when describing goblins.

Elementals first appeared in the alchemical works of highly respected Swiss physician and mystic Paracelsus in the 16th century. Paracelsus believed that elementals occupied a place between mankind and spirits. Traditionally, there are four types – gnomes, undines (also known as nymphs), sylphs, and salamanders. They are known as elementals because each of these groups represents one of the four elements used in astrology. Gnomes were thought to be the spirits of the earth, undines or nymphs were water spirits, sylphs were the spirits of the wind or air, and salamanders were the spirits of fire.

In contemporary esoteric practices, such as Wicca and Freemasonry, elementals are often invoked or called upon during ritual work.

Shadow people

Shadow people are thought to be dark, vague, human-shaped entities, often seen in our peripheral vision. They can also be seen in the moments between wakefulness and sleep, appearing behind our eyelids in the "in-between space" between light and dark. They are rarely thought to cause any harm.

Right: Whether hallucination or paranormal entity, shadow people are real enough to many who have reported seeing them.

PART 2

Encounter and Experience

Chapter 5

CONTACT WITH THE AFTERLIFE

We may have an understanding of what people believe about the afterlife, but do we really know what goes on there? How we respond to what we hear depends very much on our personal belief system or religion. There is a wide range of accounts of near-death experiences, encounters with angels, and out-of-body experiences. Whether from personal accounts or researchers in the psychic fields, this chapter offers information to help you bring the afterlife to life.

ENCOUNTERS

*Six weeks after his death, my father appeared to me in a dream...
It was an unforgettable experience, and it forced me for the first
time to think about life after death.*

Carl Jung

Throughout history, people have recounted their personal experiences of the spiritual world through contact with the spirits of ancestors, psychic work, and locking into the psychic energy of the universe to see the world from outside of ourselves. Taking an open-minded view of these experiences not only helps us with our own healing processes in this life, but may even contribute to those in our future lives.

Many people are wary of telling others of such experiences for fear of being laughed at or fear of experiencing some kind of spiritual reprisal. But the very secret of the contact itself can become as healing as the actual experience. For many of those who have experienced such contact, it is as if they are in collusion with the loved one in the spiritual world, in as intimate a relationship as the one they may have experienced in life. But like any dark horse, the more you bring it out into the light, the more you realize that we all perhaps share similar secrets.

There are certain types of encounters that many people have experienced, some of which are outlined here.

Below: We all reveal the odd secret, but a supernatural experience is one thing we often keep hidden forever for fear of ridicule or scorn.

AFTER-DEATH COMMUNICATION

Although near-death experiences (see page 21) are rated as one of the most popular forms of evidence for some kind of afterlife or spiritual realm of existence, it is after-death communication (see page 24) – communication with the spirit world – which leads the way to convincing most people of some form of consciousness after death.

EMDR

Dr Allan Botkin, a clinical psychologist with over 15 years of experience in the treatment of psychological trauma and grief, uses the psychological technique EMDR (Eye Movement Desensitization and Reprocessing) to induce direct spirit contact. He discovered by accident how this technique can help a client to experience an authentic spiritual contact with a deceased. The client was able to better understand their loss or grief and EMDR helped their psychological healing, often opening them to an entirely new belief system. With induced after-death communications (ADCs), most people believe their reconnection is real, but they do not have to believe in the authenticity to benefit from its profound healing effects.

Being contacted by the deceased without any kind of psychic intermediary, such as a channeller or medium, has proved to be as profoundly life-changing as the discovery of electricity.

ADC experience

Between 1988 and 1995, American writers and researchers Bill and Judy Guggenheim interviewed 2,000 people from all over the US and Canada, ranging in age from children to the elderly, who had experienced an after-death communication. The interviewees came from diverse educational, social, economic, religious, and occupational backgrounds. The Guggenheims' conservative estimate is that at least 50 million Americans have had one or more ADC experience. In their study, they collected more than 3,300 first-hand accounts of ADCs from people who

233

spontaneously and directly had such communications. No third parties, such as hypnotists, psychics, mediums, or devices of any kind, were involved.

Spirit visitation

Below is a true account of an after-death communication from a client who shared this experience with me in my work as psychic astrologer. The names, places, and personal details have all been changed for confidentiality reasons.

Anna is a 28-year-old fund-raiser based in London, England. After her mother died of cancer, she described an unexpected sighting of her just six months later. It was a Tuesday morning. Anna had just got out of bed and was still feeling half-asleep, but as she gazed into the bathroom mirror, she saw her mother standing in the hall behind her. There was a soft glow all around her mother, who smiled, waved, and blew a kiss, then faded away.

Anna rubbed her eyes, believing she was dreaming, and thought nothing more of it, until a few days later when her younger brother called her to meet for a coffee and catch-up. Anna's brother was at university studying medicine and it was rare for them to spend time together. Over coffee he said to her, almost embarrassed, that he'd seen their mother on Tuesday morning walking through the park on his way to college. He was sure it was her, because she had waved the way she always used to wave, with both hands, then blew a kiss, and was gone. Anna revealed her own experience to her brother, and both were dumbfounded by their similar experience. It seemed from that moment on they became closer, both believing they had truly seen their mother appear from the spirit world.

Another client, although ashamed to admit it, revealed how she always smelt her deceased mother's perfume when she was sitting in the garden relaxing. She first thought that it was the flowers, or that the neighbour had the same scent. But when she also caught a whiff of the same perfume just before a near-fatal accident on her bicycle, she was convinced that her mother's spirit had helped to save her somehow.

Left: The commonest forms of ADCs are through the senses. We might glimpse our loved one across a crowded a street, or smell their perfume in the midnight air.

SPIRIT SIGHTINGS OF FLIGHT 401

Perhaps the most extraordinary and well-known case of after-death communication relates to the ghosts of Flight 401.

When jetliner Flight 401 of Eastern Air Lines crashed into a Florida swamp in December 1972, 101 people were killed. Yet two of those people – the pilot, Bob Loft, and flight engineer, Don Repo – have since been the subject of numerous reported sightings. Not that they were seen alive, but it seems their ghosts haunt the airline planes that had been fitted with the wrecked 401's salvaged parts. The spirits of Loft and Repo were described in detail. They were not only reported by people who had known them personally, but were also identified after sightings from photographs by people who had not known them. However, it was not until some of the undamaged parts of the aircraft were subsequently recycled onto other planes that the mysterious incidents began to be reported.

The strange tales of the ghostly airmen of Flight 401 circulated in the airline community. An account of the paranormal happenings even appeared in a 1974 US Flight Safety Foundation's newsletter. John G Fuller, the bestselling author of the book *The Ghost of Flight 401*, carried out an exhaustive investigation into the hauntings with the aid of sceptical airline personnel.

Although Eastern Air Lines refused to discuss the matter, researchers have interviewed numerous individuals claiming to have encountered the ill-fated pair on other airplanes built by Lockheed. It seemed almost as if Loft and Repo had devoted their afterlives to watching over the passengers and crew of Lockheed-built passenger planes.

Right: The spirits of airline pilots killed in a crash communicated with crew on other planes to help them avoid similar danger.

REINCARNATION, PAST LIVES, AND IN-BETWEEN LIVES

Dr Michael Newton, best-selling author of Journey of Souls *and* Destiny of Souls *is a hypnotherapist who began regressing his clients to access memories of their former lives.*

He believes it is possible to perceive the spirit world through subjects who are hypnotized or in a state of heightened consciousness. Clients in this altered state are also able to tell him what their soul was doing between lives on Earth. His books represent ten years of his research and insights and help people understand the purpose behind their life choices and how and why our soul, and the souls of those we love, live eternally.

Michael Newton's hypnotherapy is designed to reconnect the client with their soul self. He believes that each person is so much more than the physical aspect that they believe themselves to be. He suggests that we are a combination of the energies, experiences, and learnings of countless previous lives. Each life is a set of contrasting experiences that embody the variety of lessons our inner, eternal self seeks to learn in its quest for development and perfection. The core eternal self, always searching for growth and new levels of understanding, is our soul self.

He believes almost three-quarters of all souls who inhabit human bodies on Earth today are still in the early stages of development. Souls end their incarnation on Earth when they reach full maturity. An advanced soul is one who is patient, calm, and has exceptional insights and they often work in the helping professions. The advanced soul radiates composure, kindness, and understanding toward others, such as Mother Theresa. Not being motivated by self-interest, they may disregard their own physical needs and live in reduced circumstances.

Case studies

The late Dr Ian Stevenson served as chairman of the Department of Psychiatry at the University of Virginia School of Medicine. For 40 years, he

Above: Much research is being carried out today regarding where our soul goes between lives.

investigated children who spontaneously remember past lives (see page 239). Most were in countries in which reincarnation is an accepted part of their culture, but several of his cases involved people in Europe, where the idea is not considered part of religion and, therefore, are more curious for their apparent claims.

Gladys Deacon

One case was that of Gladys Deacon who wrote an account of her past life in the *Sunday Express* in 1935. Dr Stevenson interviewed her in 1963. One of the most interesting observations from those who work with past-life therapies is that phobias in this life are usually connected to the manner of the past-life individual's death, and this was certainly the case with Gladys.

Gladys was born in 1900 to Roman Catholic parents in a small town in England. She recalled how, as a child, she always loved the name Margaret, and later found out that her parents had nearly called her that. As a young girl, she went on a trip with her brother to Dorset, a place she'd never been to before, by train and remarked on how familiar everything seemed to her. She recounts how she told her brother she'd lived here once before, and remembered running down a hill too fast with two grown-ups holding her hands and how they all fell down and she hurt her leg. She remembered she was called Margaret at the time, and was wearing a white frock down to her ankles with little green leaves on it. The source of

Left: Childhood memories can sometimes be from a past life.

Gladys's memories of an apparent past life remained a mystery for the next 17 years.

During another trip to Dorset in 1928, the 28-year-old Gladys unexpectedly received confirmation of her past-life memories. She had been travelling with her employer in a car that needed a tyre change not far from Poole. While they waited, they were invited to have tea in a nearby cottage. It was then that Gladys saw herself in an old portrait, exactly as she had described herself to her brother many years previously, even down to the patterned dress she had seen in her vision.

At the time, no one believed her, but she eventually discovered that the child, Margaret, had died from a terrible leg injury sustained from running down a hill with two dairymaids who had tripped and fallen on top of her. Margaret never recovered and died two months later. On the back of the portrait was written, "Margaret Kempthorne, born January 25, 1830, died October 11, 1835". Gladys was born on 11 October 65 years after Margaret had died. This was enough to convince her of the validation of her past-life memory.

Right: After a plane crash in the Toros Mountains, one reincarnated soul remembered how he really died.

Erkan Kilic

Erkan Kilic was born in Adana, Turkey, on 13 March 1962, just a few days after the fateful airplane crash that killed a 35-year-old nightclub owner called Ahmet Delibalta. Erkan was one of fifteen children in his family and before Erkan could even speak, he demonstrated a great fear of airplanes. This could be triggered by seeing or

hearing an airplane in the sky and lasted until he was about three years of age.

When Erkan was only three years old, he reported details of his death in a past lifetime. He told his mother, Latife, that in his previous life he had gone to Istanbul to find a singer for his nightclub. On the way back from Istanbul, their plane crashed in the Toros Mountains. Erkan also recounted that when he was Ahmet, he didn't die in the crash, but died later from freezing to death in the mountains. Dr Stevenson was particularly impressed by this statement, as everyone associated with this reincarnation case thought that all the victims had died on impact. Only those very familiar with the investigation of the crash knew that some passengers, including Ahmet Delibalta, did survive the crash and later froze to death.

OUT-OF-BODY EXPERIENCES

Dr Charles Tart is a transpersonal psychologist who is particularly interested in altered states of consciousness and is well known for his research in parapsychology.

One of his case studies involved a young woman who had frequent out-of-body experiences (OBEs – see pages 30–4) while in his sleep laboratory for four nights. It appeared that her out-of-body experiences occurred in conjunction with a non-dreaming, non-awake brain state, characterized by predominant sloweddown alpha activity.

The case of Miss 2

Miss 2 came from a broken home and had been hospitalized for several weeks for psychiatric treatment about a year before the sleep study. The experiment was aimed solely at understanding OBE

Right: OBE reports help researchers to understand the spiritual world.

phenomena, and Miss 2's psychological problems were not being studied.

Miss 2 woke once or twice during a night's sleep. Each time she said she had found herself floating near the ceiling, but otherwise was apparently wide awake. This condition would last from a few seconds to half a minute. She frequently observed her physical body lying on the bed, then would fall asleep again. As far as she could recall, these experiences had been occurring several times weekly throughout all of her life.

As a child, she hadn't realized there was anything unusual about them. She assumed that everyone had OBEs and never thought to mention them to anyone. Dr Tart set up an experiment to see what was actually going on. He recounts how he went into his office down the hall and, on his desk, opened a table of random numbers, turning to a page also at random. He then threw a coin onto the desk to land on the page, again at random, and copied the first five digits immediately above where the coin landed. He wrote the digits about five centimetres high onto a piece of paper in black ink. This five-digit random number series was slipped into an opaque folder while entering Miss 2's sleeping room. He then slipped the paper out of the folder and onto a high shelf without at any time exposing the paper to her. This would only be clearly visible to anyone whose eyes were located approximately six and a half feet off the floor or higher, but was otherwise not visible to Miss 2. Throughout the night Miss 2's brainwaves were recorded, and early in the morning, at around 6am, Miss 2 awoke, and without knowing that Dr Tart had planted the paper there, she immediately called out that the number series 25132. This was the numbers Dr Tart had randomly chosen. In terms of probability, this was a 1 in 100,000 chance.

Dr Tart believes that the OBE is a valid psychic experience and he also believes that the evidence of the paranormal is at last bringing science and the spiritual world together.

Left: Altered states of consciousness are the main triggers for OBEs and soul travel.

NEAR-DEATH EXPERIENCES

Life is continuous, and is Infinite.

Edgar Cayce

There are numerous books now available filled with NDE case studies and accounts (see page 21). One of the original researchers of the near-death phenomenon, Dr P M H Atwater, began her work in 1978 and her books, such as *Beyond the Light*, have become NDE classics and are well worth reading.

Edgar Cayce

One man who had more induced near-death experiences than anyone else was the great American psychic and mystic Edgar Cayce (1877–1945). Cayce's experiences reveal aspects about the nature of the "tunnel" so often described in near-death experiences (see page 21). According to Cayce, while in a self-induced trance state he made thousands of visits to the otherworld. During many of his apparent journeys, he came across the so-called Hall of Records where all knowledge is stored. This place has been described by many people who recount near-death experiences. Cayce revealed that his unconscious mind, which he

identified as the soul, would leave his body and explore the dimension where all unconscious minds are connected – a dimension similar to Jung's concept of collective unconscious. It is in this the realm of thought, imagination, dreams, after-death, and near-death states where all things are possible. Edgar Cayce described in four different publications his journeys.

Cayce describes one visit in which he enters the tunnel of light as if moving up through a very large column, and as he ascended the column, beings on either side of him would call out to him for help or to attempt to attract his attention. Cayce believed that any deviation from the column and the beam of light would mean he would not be able to return to his body. As Cayce passed on, there was more light, movement, sounds, music, laughter, and birdsong,

Right: The psychic and occultist Edgar Cayce allegedly experienced thousands of NDEs using trance-hypnosis.

until there was only light, colour, and a perfect luminosity. He recalls that quite suddenly he came upon the Hall of Records. It was a hall without walls or ceiling. He was conscious of being handed a large book and inside was the knowledge that he knew he had always wanted: the secrets of the universe. This near-death experience left Cayce with a profound belief that it was possible for all of us to reach the great storehouse of all knowledge through spiritual work in this life, and he went on to write about spiritual practices, such as channelling and mediumship work, in an attempt to prove this was possible.

Carl Jung

The psychotherapist Carl Jung (1875–1961) was fascinated by dreams and the unconscious, but he, too, experienced what could almost be described as an NDE. In his famous account, Jung found himself suspended far above the Earth. Then, from the direction of what appeared to be the outline of Europe, an image of his doctor (Dr H) floated up to him. He was framed by a golden chain

Left: Jung famously experienced an NDE following a heart attack. His vivid experience was curtailed by his doctor, who asked Jung to return to Earth.

or a golden laurel wreath. Jung knew at once it was his doctor appearing to him in a god-like form as an "avatar". (An avatar is a manifestation or incarnation of a god on Earth, such as the Hindu god Vishnu.) There was then a silent exchange of thoughts between the men. According to Jung, his doctor had been ordered by the Earth itself to deliver a message. This was a protest against Jung going away and that he no right to leave the Earth and must return. The moment Jung heard this, his NDE ceased.

After this experience, Jung felt a violent resistance to his doctor because the doctor had brought him back to life. Also, the fact that the doctor had appeared in this form indicated to Jung that the doctor was soon to die. And not long afterwards, the doctor did indeed die.

Ernest Hemingway

The American writer Ernest Hemingway (1899–1961) had a near-death experience that was a close encounter with death itself, and this experience transformed his whole outlook on life. He recounted what happened during World War I after he was wounded by shrapnel while fighting on the banks of the river Piave, near Fossalta, in Italy. From the convalescent home in Milan he wrote a letter to his family, making this

Above: Ernest Hemingway's NDE gave him inspiration for one of his characters in A Farewell to Arms.

cryptic statement: "Dying is a very simple thing. I've looked at death and really I know". Years later, Hemingway explained to a friend what had occurred on that fateful night in 1918. He remembered how an Austrian mortar bomb exploded in the darkness. "I died then. I felt my soul or something coming right out of my body, like you'd pull a silk handkerchief out of a pocket by one corner. It flew around and then came back and went in again and I wasn't dead anymore".

Deeply affected by this near-death experience throughout his life, he admitted to never being as arrogant or careless as he once had been. In his book *A Farewell to Arms*, his character Frederic Henry undergoes a similar confrontation with death. "There was a flash, as when a blast-furnace door is swung open, and a roar that started white and went red and on and on in a rushing wind. I tried to breathe but my breath would not come and I felt myself rush bodily out of myself and out and out and out and all the time bodily in the wind. I went out swiftly, all of myself, and I knew I was dead and that it had all been a mistake to think you just died. Then I floated, and instead of going on I felt myself slide back. I breathed and I was back".

Arthur Yensen

Back in 1932, Arthur E Yensen, a newspaper cartoonist, decided to take some time off to research his weekly cartoon strip. Since his main character was a hobo, Yensen decided to become one for a while. He bummed rides throughout the States until, one day, a young man in a convertible car picked him up on the way to Winnipeg. Driving too fast, the car hit a three feet-high ridge of gravel, flipped, and somersaulted across the road. Both men were thrown through the soft top of the car before it crashed into a ditch. The driver escaped unharmed, but Yensen was injured, losing consciousness just as two female witnesses rushed to his aid. He recalled how the landscape gradually faded away and instead came a bright new beautiful world. For almost a minute he could see both worlds at once. Finally, when the Earth was gone, he found himself in what he thought must be Heaven. In the distance were snow-capped mountains and a shimmering lake containing clear, golden water. Beyond some trees, he saw a group of people playing and singing, some of whom came to greet him and inform him he was in the land of the dead. It seemed as if he had been there before, and remembered what was on the other side of the mountains. This was his real home, and now it seemed that on Earth he had been merely a visitor. Not wanting to leave, he was told that he must return to continue his work, and when his work was done on Earth he could come back to stay forever.

Arthur Yensen later became active in politics, an authority on organic gardening and nutrition, and was singled out as one of Idaho's "most distinguished citizens". He broke the college rules where he taught by sharing his near-death experience in class to prove that life has purpose. Ironically, Yensen was still questioning whether or not he had fulfilled his life's work when he finally returned "home" in 1992, having been a quiet benefactor of thousands.

Alice Morrison-Mays

A housewife called Alice Morrison-Mays nearly died after giving birth to her third son. Two weeks after his birth she fell into a coma and was rushed to hospital. She recalls how, from somewhere above her near the ceiling, she watched as they began to wrap up her arms and legs and tilted her body so that her legs were up in the air. She remembers vividly being angry, until the scene changed and she was no longer in the room. She found herself in a timeless, beautiful place with changing colours and "rainbows of sound". Floating on thin air, she became aware of other loving, caring beings hovering near her. They appeared "formless", and clouds and delicate shifting colours moved through and around them all. They said they were her guides and helpers. She became aware of an "immense presence" coming towards her, a "light being" that permeated everything. It was "explained" that she could remain there if she wanted; it was a choice she could make. She became aware again that she needed to make a choice and knew she must go back for the sake of her child. Almost instantly she re-entered her body through a silver cord at the top of her head and heard someone near her say, "Oh, we've got her back". She was told she had "two pieces of placenta as large as grapefruits" removed.

Morrison-Mays told no one except her husband about the monumental experience she had just had. After a hip replacement operation 12 years later, Morrison-Mays entered an altered state of consciousness that she continued to slip in and out of for six months. Throughout this lengthy visionary experience, she received lessons from "the other side". Her life has been profoundly affected ever since and she has become well known for her spiritual healing and experiences.

Dianne Morrissey

Renowned for her research into the paranormal, when the late Dr Dianne Morrissey (1949–2009) was 28 years old

Right: Visiting the afterlife, whether induced or by accident, leaves most people with feelings of joy or a sense of enlightenment.

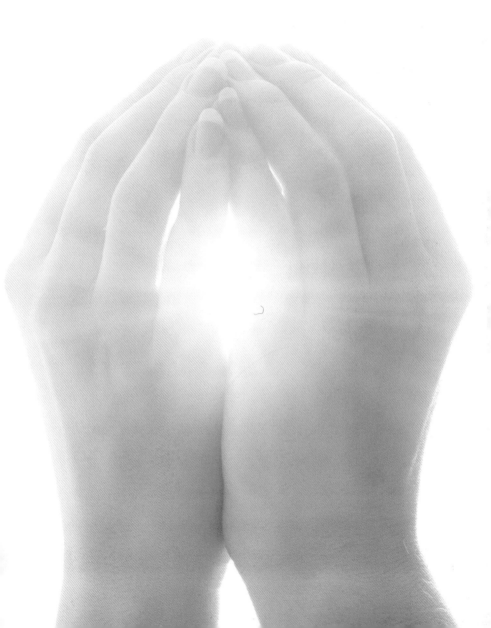

she was electrocuted and experienced a profound NDE. Her experience transformed her entire life.

During Morrissey's NDE she had observed her physical, soul, and spirit bodies simultaneously. While immediately outside of her physical body, she noticed how her soul body was attached to her physical body by a "silver cord". Later, she encountered her spirit body lying on a kind of "Heavenly bed" far above the Earth. She described herself as being at one with "the light" and suddenly knowing every grain of sand on every planet, in every galaxy, in every universe. This light held within it the knowledge of every book in every language, from the beginning of creation to the end of time. As she returned to her physical body, she knew that something within her could never die, and that she could never die. Then, with a jolt, she landed fully back in her body.

Later, she admitted that the one reason she was sent back was to help people feel better about dying, and to help them learn that death is not an end, but a new beginning.

Left: Many subjects return to Earth knowing they can help others come to terms with death.

Durga Jatav

In 1986, researchers Dr Ian Stevenson and Dr Satwant Pasricha documented 16 cases of Indian near-death experiences. Below is one of them.

When Durga was about 20, he had been ill for several weeks, suffering from what had been diagnosed as typhoid. When his body "became cold" for a couple of hours, his family thought he had died. He revived, however, and on the third day after revival he told his family that, at the time during which they experienced his body as going cold, he had been taken away by ten people. He attempted to escape, but the people cut off his legs at the knees to stop him. He was then taken to a place and sat before a crowd of people who looked at his papers, but told him they didn't want him there. The guides were told to take him back. But Durga replied that he couldn't go back without any feet. He was then shown several pairs of legs. One pair he recognized as his own, and recalls that, magically, they were reattached. He was then sent back with the instructions not to bend his knees so they could mend.

A few days after Durga revived, his sister and a neighbour noticed marks on Durga's knees which had not been there before. These deep fissures that appeared on his skin in front of his knees were still visible scars in 1979 when Dr Stevenson interviewed him, nearly 30

Right: NDEs are often described as having blurred visuals, bright lights, figures, and a sense of peace.

years later. Durga's older sister, who was also interviewed, corroborated his account of his apparent death and revival.

There had been no bleeding or pain in his knees other than discomfort following the "instructions" to keep his knees in a fixed position. X-ray photographs taken in 1981 showed that there was no abnormality below the surface of the skin.

CONTACT WITH ANGELS

The spiritual world is filled not only with the souls or spirits of the dead, but realms within realms of other guides, watchers, and angels. The artist Michelangelo (1475–1564) once commented that he saw an angel in the marble and carved until he set him free.

From the earliest angels, such as the winged goddesses of ancient Egypt to the rococo *putti* of 18th-century art, the symbol of the angel and its message changed considerably over the years. Originally, the angel's message was from the Pagan gods. "Angel" meant "messenger", and an angel was simply an intermediary between two worlds. Later, Christianity adopted the messenger as its own, and angels became associated with the Heavenly henchmen of God.

Influential angel believers include Irish mystic Lorna Byrne, whose first memoir, *Angels in My Hair*, has sold over half a million books in 50 countries, and British-born Diana Cooper, whose spirit guide Kumeka revealed to her the truth about orbs (see page 29), Atlantis, angels, and ascension. American author Doreen Virtue is the founder of Angel Therapy, based on the idea that communicating with angels is the key to healing.

Above: In many religions, angels are believed to come to Earth as messengers of God. These messengers are depicted as putti in Baroque art.

Left: Guardian angels watch over us, and it is said we all have an angel who walks beside us all our life.

There are many claims of visitations or angel sightings. Below are just a few.

Saint Cecilia

The musically talented virgin Cecilia (3rd century CE) was the daughter of a Roman senator. As was the custom, an arranged marriage was agreed to a dashing young man, Valerianus, who still believed in the pantheon of Roman gods. Cecilia had already converted to Christianity. On their wedding night, Valerianus wanted to consummate the marriage, but Cecilia told him she was secretly betrothed to an angel who guarded her virginity. Valerianus, desperate to see the angel and desperate to bed his beloved, agreed to visit the Christian bishop and be baptized. His conversion to Christianity would ensure him a sighting of both the angel and the bed chamber. On his return home, the angel crowned the couple with roses, then left for Heaven. But other family and friends of Valerianus wanted to see the angel too and so agreed

Left: The Christian patron saint of music, Cecilia, sang with the angels when she died a martyr.

Right: Jeanne d'Arc's signature. Her visions of angels and archangels were believed to have led to the end of the Hundred Years War.

to be baptized. As the conversions to Christianity mounted, Cecilia was arrested by the still-Pagan Roman senate and was sentenced to death by suffocation in the bath. For unknown reasons she escaped her terrible fate, but was hacked to death by an executioner instead, and took several days to die from her wounds. As she died, she is said to have sung with the angels, and was later to become the patron saint of music.

Jeanne d'Arc

Honoured as a political heroine in France since the time of Napoleon, Jeanne d'Arc (1412–31) has remained a symbol of feminine courage and wrongful execution. But what was most important about the religious crusade she undertook at the end of the Hundred Years War was that she utterly believed that God was sending her messages through the angels. Her visions of angels, including archangels Michael and Gabriel, and many other hosts, have also led to speculation that maybe angels and the spiritual world can help those who want to change the course of history for the better.

Teresa d'Ávila

Carmelite reformer Teresa d'Ávila (1513–1582) did much to revive the cult of mystical spirituality in the Catholic Church. She ran away from her home near Madrid hoping to martyr herself upon the daggers of the Arab invaders. But she was found in time and sent to a nunnery. Like many mystics, she began to suffer from a variety of nutritional diseases, but her dedication to the study of medieval manuscripts gave her time to recount all her "mystical experiences" or ecstasies. One was her encounter with an angel who awakened her soul to reunite with God. She described how she saw an angel close beside her. He wasn't tall, but he was very beautiful and carried a long golden spear, the tip of which was on fire. The angel thrust the spear into her heart and, as he drew out the fiery point, it felt as if he was removing all of her insides, but leaving her on fire and with love for God.

Emanuel Swedenborg

Swedenborg (1688–1772), a Swedish-born 18th-century scientist turned mystic, claimed to have written most of his books while guided by angels. One of his works, *The Delights of Wisdom Pertaining to Conjugal Love*, is filled with lengthy dialogues with angels about the wisdom of love, including hidden allusions to mystical transcendence through sexual union. Swedenborg recounted how the angels approved of certain forms of sex, but only if it was the most mind-blowing. He also wrote extensively on life after death, drawing on what he believed were his own real experiences in the world of angels, claiming that this world was in many ways quite similar to the natural world. His work also reveals how angels in Heaven do not have an ethereal or ephemeral existence but enjoy an active life of service to others. They sleep and wake, love, breathe, eat, talk, read, work, play, and worship. They live a genuine life in a real spiritual body and world. According to Swedenborg, we in the natural world can only see angels here when our spiritual eyes are opened.

Left: Teresa d'Ávila is renowned for her, some say, orgasmic experience with an angel.

Below: With his spiritual eyes open, the mystic Swedenborg wrote most of his works accompanied by angels.

William Blake

"Guarded by an Angel mild", William Blake (1757–1827), poet, painter, and mystic, was already discussing his visions and communications with Heavenly beings at an early age.

He saw angels both in his head and in the fields. He recounted to his father as a child of seeing a "tree filled with angels, bright angelic wings bespangling every bough like stars". His parents beat him for his imaginings, but he was given courage and support by the archangels to create his art and writing – the angels enjoyed his works.

Many thought Blake to be mad, including the poet William Wordsworth. But Blake's paintings unveiled him in a new light when Satan was depicted as the Angel of Revelation. Blake's depictions of angels are numinous but edgy. The angels are not only spiritual beings, but filled with human failings, too.

Rudolf Steiner

Austrian mystic and writer Rudolf Steiner (1861–1925) began his spiritual career in the Theosophical Society and eventually developed his own belief system known as anthroposophy (see page 46). Steiner believed in all spiritual entities and described many visions or experiences of their presence. He believed that angels are our invisible guides and lifelong companions. He described how angels interact with other spiritual hierarchies and believed that, through our dreams, we plot our future with our angel guide. He believed angels came to us so we could learn complete religious freedom.

Billy Graham

The evangelical spiritual advisor to many a US president, Graham became one of the few 20th-century media stars of religion. His work has converted many of little faith to accept Jesus Christ as their saviour. His work, *Angels, God's Secret Agents* led the way towards the

Left: William Blake was inspired by the archangels for his numinous art.

Right: Belief in angels is at the core of Rudolf Steiner's successful mystical philosophy.

emergence of a new belief that angels can help us in all we do, and even fight for us. Sharing his angelic crusades with over two hundred million people worldwide, he believes that angels are there to defend us with "drawn swords". His revived Christian angels have since become a source of reassurance and protection in times of dread. This recent passion for angel revival has come leaping back into the collective consciousness as a powerful healing and spiritual aid, as well as for comfort and guidance.

Vassula Ryden

Best known for her compilation of thousands of messages from God in 1985, Vassula believes in her own guardian angel. While writing a grocery list when living in Bangladesh with her family, she felt a tingling sensation in her fingers and an invisible presence guided her hand to write in a totally different hand-writing style and content from her own. The words read, "I am your guardian angel and my name is Daniel". She recounted how the angel returned for the next few days, and how they spent many hours

communicating. Believing she had been called by God to promote Christian unity, she is now involved in organizing world events in an attempt to reconcile all Christian denominations.

Elisabeth Kubler Ross

Angels are often reported by individuals who have near-death experiences. This was researched extensively by Elisabeth Kubler Ross in the late 1960s resulting in her book, *On Death and Dying*.

By the 1990s, Ross became interested in how young children are aware of

Left: Angels were apparently responsible for Billy Graham's evangelical crusade worldwide.

Above: Contacted by her guardian angel, Vassula Ryden now promotes Christian unity.

angels as they approach death. Whether "playmates" or guardian angels, she believes from the moment we come into this world to the moment we end this physical existence, we are in the presence of these guides who wait for us and help us in the transition from life to life. This is very much in line with Plato, Pythagoras, and many of the most ancient mystics and philosophers who believed in the *daimon* or guiding spirit (see pages 129 and 131).

Stigmatics and angels

Stigmatics also recount vivid visions of angels and other spiritual entities, the earliest recorded being that of Saint Francis of Assisi in the 13th century. While praying during a fast, a seraph appeared to him. Humbled by the sight of the six-winged angel on a cross, the angel transformed into a vision of the crucified Jesus. After the angel had departed, Saint Francis discovered a deep wound in his side, marks of iron nails, and wounds bleeding in his feet and hands. A fellow priest, who had been praying with Francis at the time, was the first to recount the phenomenon of stigmata, when he commented that the angel gave him the gift of the five wounds of Christ.

Padre Pio

The charismatic Padre Pio (1870–1968) lived like a New Testament apostle in San Giovanni Rotondo, Foggia, Italy, and was known for his miracle-working and mystical experiences. He cast out the Devil from possessed individuals, was beaten by demons in his cell, and conversed with angels who visited him to translate his foreign language "fan-mail" and guide him when attending to the sick. Many sceptics tried to prove he was a fraudster, but as his cult built, so did his delusions, and most of the psychological and scientific communities dismissed him as psychotic. Then in 1918, he received his first visible stigmata which strangely stayed with him for the next 50 years of his life and no one could ever prove he faked it.

Garbandal

The mountainous region of Cantabria in Northern Spain is not the best known area of Europe, nor is it much visited, except for one small village known as Garbandal that has remained unchanged for over 50 years, where an extraordinary angel sighting took place.

Right: One of the first recorded stigmatics, Saint Francis believed that his wounds were given to him by a seraph.

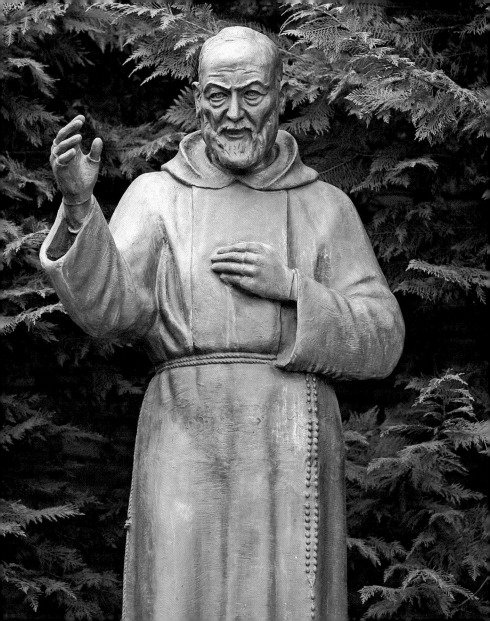

One summer's night in the 1960s, along a dirt track road on the outskirts of the small village, four 12-year-old girls heard a sudden clap of thunder above them. They looked up to the sky and gasped in fear and awe when they saw a golden angel appearing from the clouds. It was 18 June 1961, and for the next eight days Conchita, Maria, Jacinta, and Maria-Cruz reported repeated visions of the archangel Michael, who had come with a message that they were soon to be visited by the blessed Virgin Mary. The girls soon became famous for their visions, not just among Catholic believers, but throughout the world.

Soon after the archangel's visit, the Virgin Mary appeared as Our Lady of Carmel, patroness of the Carmelite Order. The girls fell into trance-like states and their ecstatic walks around the village began. They wandered throughout the village streets, sometimes running fast down the steep mountainside, sometimes even backwards up it. As their astonishing feats became known, more and more spectators arrived to see their strange ecstasies, and to ask the girls to offer up personal objects to the Virgin

Right: Archangel Michael's visitation to four young girls turned the small village of Garabandal into a thriving centre for pilgrims.

Mary to be blessed. They repeated divine messages to the world about miracles, warnings, and punishments, and how people must look into their souls for spiritual truth. In their trances, the girls were insensitive to pain, bright lights, and other external stimuli, and however many sceptics tried to prove them fakes, they seemed truly enraptured by their supernatural visitations.

Above the village is a steep hill on which stands a group of nine pine trees. It was here that an angel with a golden chalice told the girls he would give them Holy Communion and that they must let the world know, so that all could witness the miracle. On 18 July 1962, the town was crowded with visitors all waiting to see the event. At midnight Conchita went into a trance and fell down on her knees in the midst of the crowd. Lamps and torches focused on her. Cameras clicked. Reproduced in many magazines, books, and websites is a shot taken from an old video film of a wafer appearing in Conchita's open mouth, supposedly being placed there by an angel. One witness, a Spanish farmer, wrote, "I was standing at less than an arm's length from the girl...

Left: A controversial miracle occurred in 1962 among the pine trees above the village of Garabandal.

Her face was angelic. I can certify that she was there motionless, moving neither hands nor tongue. In this motionless position she received the Sacred Host... I was an unbeliever until that day".

Along with the massive press coverage, public curiosity, and the later accusations of fraud, the controversy turned Garabandal into a circus act. But the apparitions ended, and the controversy calmed down. Saint Pio of Pietrelcina and Saint Teresa of Calcutta believed and supported these apparitions, and although the Catholic Church has never refuted them, it has never fully approved them either.

Garabandal is today a centre for pilgrims, attracting thousands of people from around the world. People go there to be blessed by Our Lady of Carmel, others in the hope of seeing an angel. But whatever happens here in this simple village high in the mountains, this is one of the places in the world where angels seem to bring us the comfort and protection we are all seeking.

Donna Gatti

Contemporary healer and angel aficionado Donna Gatti runs a school for spiritual enlightenment known as the Angel Academy, based in the USA. Her first mystical experience occurred when she was four years old. Contact from an angel known as Dalia changed her life and led her into contact with archangels such as Michael and Uriel. During a near-death experience that took place while in surgery, she experienced being out of her body and watching the doctors trying to save her from a distance. From her astral plane, she seemed able to fly and was surrounded by an ocean of white light. It was then she saw two angels who offered to help her go home. Since then she has seen angels as large as tower blocks, and others only the size of a pinhead.

A 2008 survey by Baylor University in Waco, Texas, polled 1,700 people and found that 55 per cent of respondents, including one in five of those who say they are not religious, believe that they have been protected by a guardian angel during their life. A 2007 poll found that 68 per cent of Americans believe that "angels and demons are active in the world", and a US Associated Press poll in 2011 revealed that 77 per cent of American adults believed in ethereal beings.

Left: Angels are currently thought not only to be guardians and healers, but guides between this world and the otherworld. Seeing an angel is thought to be a sign of psychic ability.

ARCHANGEL MICHAEL

Michael is usually depicted in the story from the Old Testament when he defeats Satan, the ancient dragon-serpent, and drives him out of Heaven along with the fallen angels. Usually shown with sword in hand, he is the ultimate spiritual warrior and God's henchman. Legendary sightings include Michael's visit to Earth at Monte Gargano in Italy in the early 6th century CE, which led to an annual feast being held in his honour. He was seen three times in the 8th century by Saint Aubert, the bishop of Avranches in France, who was instructed by Michael to build a church on a small island off the coast of Normandy, now known as Mont Saint-Michel. Several miracle healings were reported when the church was being built, and Mont Saint-Michel remains one of the greatest Catholic pilgrimage sites in the world. Michael was first an angel of healing, but later became known as protector and leader of God's army against evil forces.

Right: Christian sanctuaries dedicated to Archangel Michael first appeared in the 4th century CE.

CHANNELLING

Channelling is the ability to contact spirit guides and to act as a conduit for information, either on behalf of others, or for oneself.

However, channelling is also a term which can imply that the individual has channelled information, whether an idea, a creative inspiration, a solution, or a healing force, from their own contact with the universal storehouse of knowledge rather than directly from a spirit. The channeller can also access information from the psychic world via deities, plants, animals, and even the landscape.

Trance-channelling was performed by a shaman in many indigenous tribal cultures as a means to travel to the spirit world. Modern shamans often use drums, spinning dances, meditation, and vision quests to achieve this deeper state. Most channellers these days remain in an altered state of consciousness rather than an unconscious state. In a conscious state, the channeller is in

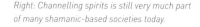

Right: Channelling spirits is still very much part of many shamanic-based societies today.

Left: The founder of theosophy, Helena Blavatsky, believed that spiritual truth could be discovered by channelling the spirits of ascended masters.

control of the communication pathway and can close the door at any time.

Spirit guides

Spirit guides are one or more entities who watch, teach, heal, and help the channeller on their journey into greater awareness. The number of spirit guides a person has varies within that person's experiences. Some channellers communicate with their Twin Soul. Teaching-spirits can go by many names and connect with more than one person at a time. Sometimes spirits come to the channeller for a specific purpose, such as creative abilities, healing issues, spiritual development, and resolving problems. Popular and well-known channellers include the late American psychic Jane Roberts (1929–1984) and her spirit guide Seth, British-born Margaret McElroy, now living in India and spirit guide Maitreya, and American, J Z Knight and Ramtha (see page 284).

Ascended masters

When the soul of an individual attains the highest possible spiritual state, or arrives at a spiritual realm where it is close to the World Soul, it is often known as an "ascended master" a term coined by the Theosophical Society during the 19th century. This apparent "ascension" to higher things allows the individual's soul or spirit – or, some say, even their consciousness – to be of service to mankind. From their spiritually elevated place in heaven, teachers or gurus such as Jesus or Mother Teresa can aid us in our own soul's journey through life. According to Theosophists, ascended masters are similar to the saints of Christianity or the bodhisattvas of Buddhism.

In the 19th century, Madame Blavatsky, the founder of theosophy (see page 157), brought attention to the existence of ascended spiritual leaders when she channelled messages from beings she called "Mahatmas". These "masters" were highly evolved beings who lived in the Himalayas. She commented, "from them we have derived all theosophical truths". Her well-known spirit guide was "Koot Hoomi" or "Kuthumi".

Blavatsky's successors in the Theosophical Society, Annie Besant and Charles W Leadbeater, developed the idea of ascended masters, and wrote many of their alleged biographies and past lives. The best known is Saint Germain, also known as "The Master Rakozi" or Master R, believed to have ascended after what was believed to be his final incarnation as Sir Francis Bacon and, according to the theosophists, son of Queen Elizabeth I and

Lord Dudley. His previous incarnations included a high priest of Atlantis, Merlin, and Christopher Columbus.

In the middle of 18th-century France, Count Saint Germain spent much time in the company of King Louis XV and Madame Pompadour. Notorious for conjuring diamonds out of his pocket, the Count apparently revealed the secret of the elixir of life to various courtiers. Thought to be an alchemist, by the 19th century his legendary status also included that of ascended master.

Celestial beings

It is believed that celestial beings have survived death on their own planets or in other universes and have come from the spirit world to enlighten those on Earth who are willing to listen.

The *Urantia Book* is a spiritual and esoteric book that originated in Chicago between 1924 and 1955. There is still much speculation as to who was/were the author/s and controversy over its claims. Urantia was the name given to the planet Earth, and the book's intention was to unite religion, science, and philosophy into a new worldwide belief system. The information within it, it was claimed, has been written by celestial beings. Two notable musicians, Stockhausen and Jimi Hendrix, both carried the *Urantia Book* with them wherever they went.

There are several offshoot Spiritualist groups who similarly work with Urantia's Divine "Father and Mother" who supposedly appeared on this planet at one time in human form.

Inspired by Urantia, the US-based Teaching Mission network claims to work with some of these celestial teachers. The Mission is for sincere seekers who want to connect to an advanced teacher, and to develop a personal relationship with God. An offshoot of the Teaching Mission, is the Center for Christ Consciousness, where followers believe that they receive love and teaching from the Divine Father, known as Christ Michael, and a Divine Mother, known as Nebadonia. (Nebadon is the name for the universe where celestial beings originated.)

There are also two other spirit beings who communicate with the Center's followers. These are Aurora, a celestial being who helps people become more cooperative, tolerant, patient and accepting of other people. Welmek is a celestial teacher who lived a human life on a planet with a very advanced civilization. Welmek offers new insight into how the universe operates. His thoughtful and considerate messages are inspirational.

THE GRID

Another current approach to accessing information from the spiritual plane is called reading the "crystalline grid".

This "grid" is a bit like a switchboard connecting everyone and everything in the universe, which vibrates to certain frequencies. This concept developed from the concept of sacred geometry, an art-science that is dedicated to the study and applications of the harmonic power of the universe via symbolic numbers and patterns.

These permeate all nature and consciousness and are considered the universal code of creation.

When a person channels, they are tapping into, or rather plugging into, the frequency of the "grid". For example, if you want to channel a specific spirit, you just plug into their frequency signature and listen to their message. Obviously you have to find this frequency first, rather like tuning into a radio station. Each "station" or vibration encompasses a specific frequency of information. These have correspondences with colours, chakras, auras, and occult symbolism.

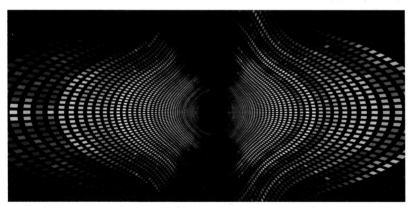

Above: Tapping into the energy of celestial harmonics is a way of accessing the spirit world.

FAMOUS CHANNELLERS

Many have claimed to be able to channel spiritual entities, the most well known being Jane Roberts and J Z Knight.

Jane Roberts

In 1963, American author and poet Jane Roberts began to receive important messages from a male personality who eventually identified himself as Seth. Soon afterwards, Roberts reported that she was hearing the messages in her head. She began to dictate the messages by entering a trance state. She said Seth at first took control of her body and spoke through her, while her husband wrote down the words she spoke. The couple referred to these experiences as "readings" or "sessions".

Roberts claims she has also channelled the world views of Rembrandt and Paul Cezanne via automatic writing on an old-fashioned typewriter.

For around 20 years, right up until her death in 1984, Roberts held regular trance sessions in which she spoke on behalf of Seth. The messages from Seth that were channelled through Roberts consisted mostly of monologues on a wide variety of spiritual, political, and religious topics.

J Z Knight

American J Z Knight has attracted such notable figures as Shirley MacLaine and Linda Evans to her teachings. She claims to bridge ancient wisdom and the power of consciousness with the latest scientific research. Criticized as being "kindergarten metaphysics" by mathematician Martin Gardner, Knight runs a school of enlightenment in Washington, USA. The "spirit guide" or ascended master, known as Ramtha allegedly appeared to her for the first time in her kitchen in 1977.

According to Knight, Ramtha was a Lemurian warrior who fought the Atlanteans over 35,000 years ago. Ramtha speaks of leading an army over two and a half million strong and conquering most of the known world (which was allegedly going through cataclysmic geological changes). According to Ramtha, he led the army for ten years until he was betrayed and almost killed. Ramtha says he spent the next seven years in isolation recovering and observing nature. He later mastered many skills, including prophecy and out-of-body states. Ramtha taught his soldiers everything he knew for 120 days, bade them farewell, rose into the air and, in a bright flash of light, ascended to Heaven. He made a promise to his army that he would come back to teach them everything he had learned.

Above: The spirit guide Ramtha first appeared to J Z Knight in her kitchen in 1977.

SHAMANS AND PSYCHIC HEALING

Shamanism is based on the premise that the visible world is pervaded by invisible forces or spirits that affect the lives of the living. There is currently a revival of shamanistic practice, called neoshamanism or core shamanism, introduced by American anthropologist, Michael Harner in the 1980s.

The shaman

Although diverse in their methods, depending on geographic and cultural needs, each shaman shares the common belief that so called "reality" is filled with invisible forces such as spirits and demons that influence the living in both positive and negative ways. These spirits play a key role in the society or culture in question. Shamans can leave their mortal body to engage in this spiritual world, and can cure illnesses and communicate with spirit guides, often animals.

Totems such as rocks or stones are commonly used by shamans. These items often have their own "spirit" and magic powers. Some shamans claim to have learned the healing powers of plants directly from the plants' spirit. In the Peruvian Amazon Basin, shamans known as *curanderos* use songs to evoke spirits, but before a spirit can be summoned it must teach the shaman its own song. Spirits can be animals, plants, or even rocks. Among the Siberian peoples known as the Selkups, the sea duck is a spirit animal and belongs to the upper and lower world. Similarly, for many Native Americans, the jaguar is a spirit animal because jaguars walk on earth, swim in water, and climb in trees. Thus jaguars belong to all three worlds, sky, earth and the underworld.

Once an initiate has transformed to a shaman and is ready to contact the spirit world, the shaman is implanted with magical talismans. To travel there, the shaman must first enter a trance-like state, usually induced by self-hypnosis, tobacco, drugs (such as psychedelic mushrooms, *Datura*, deadly nightshade, and ayahuasca), rapid drumming, sweat lodges, vision quests, and other rituals.

Contemporary work

There exist three different categories of contemporary shamans:

1. Traditional shamans who strictly follow indigenous practices according to their culture.
2. Shamans who attempt to fuse old traditional rituals with Western ideas by including new-age ceremonies and other mystical elements suited to the modern-day practitioner.
3. Those shamans who may be separated from their indigenous culture but who are called upon to serve the local community and rediscover their shamanic heritage.

Left: Trance-like states induced with drugs, drumming, music, or chanting take shamans into the spirit world.

Modern-day shamans and healers

There are many contemporary healers and shamans, but as an example here are two very different approaches to shamanism. The first is a fusion of techniques; the second is a more radical method, which is commonly known as "psychic surgery".

Robin Gress

Modern-day shaman and healer Robin Gress studied with the founder of The Foundation for Shamanic Studies, Michael Harner, for three years. A qualified psychotherapist, Robin's healing work combines clairvoyance, intelligence, and compassion. Her natural awareness and connection with non-ordinary realities enable her to easily access and traverse the shamanic realms and, with the help of her spiritual allies, provide transformational healing to her clients. Robin's healing practice blends core shamanic techniques such as soul retrieval, power animal retrieval, extraction, de-possession, and ancestral work along with her mediumship and channelling abilities.

Left: Contemporary shamans work with a wide range of techniques, from spirit ancestors to soul retrieval.

John of God

Calling himself a medium and a healer, João de Faria, also known as "John of God", is one of several psychic surgeons practising in South America. Not far from Brasilia in Brazil, John of God performs "surgical operations" that are either "invisible" or "visible". Claiming to act as a channel for God's healing power, he says he has no recollection of what happens during the operations.

Back in the 1970s, John was persuaded by spirit guides and spiritual medium Chico Xavier to move away from his small village to help more people. He was advised to move to the small town of Abadiânia. By 1978, John had set up his healing centre, which first consisted of a chair outside his home on the main road into town. People would come from miles around to be healed and it wasn't long before John's reputation reached not just countrywide, but worldwide. Since 1965, millions of people have consulted de Faria and thousands have reported being cured. Although physical healing is claimed by many, others also report that they are emotionally and spiritually healed, too.

De Faria has always said that he encourages medical and scientific investigations into his work to help mankind. He even invites doctors and surgeons into his healing sessions to monitor his work. De Faria offers two types of "surgery": the "invisible" operation is usually the most popular option. For this, the patient sits in a room alone and meditates while John of God enters the spirit world in another room. He then recommends meditation as part of the ongoing cure, and asks the patient to make frequent visits to a particular waterfall as part of the healing process. The "visible" operation is not so popular and not so well documented. For this method, De Faria apparently performs literal physical surgery and the client is given a "spiritual anaesthetic" of special mineral water and the combined spiritual power of volunteers meditating in another room. De Faria insists that, if patients continue to take all the medicines he gives them, they will be cured.

De Faria believes that he can also perform "virtual" psychic surgery when a patient is too ill to make the trip. He then performs invisible surgery on a surrogate patient, thus sending out the healing energy or "surgical procedure" via the spirit world.

John of God's work has been under much scrutiny, and he has been arrested several times for practising medicine without a licence.

Above: João de Faria encourages his patients to go on walks to a nearby waterfall as part of their treatment.

Chapter 6

EXPERIENCE AND HEALING

Personal knowledge of the otherworld only comes with belief and a respect for both yourself and others. This chapter gives you easy exercises and rituals to follow that will allow you to take the first steps on the road to experience of the afterlife. With a little time, dedication, and an open mind, you can embark on your own work with the spiritual world for healing and comfort – for yourself and your own soul, and for others in this life, too.

PSYCHIC POWER

My soul is from elsewhere, I'm sure of that, and I intend to end up there.

Rumi

Accessing your innate psychic power allows you to tap into the World Soul (see page 118), the cosmic energy field that flows through all things, connecting everything in the universe as one, including the past, the present, and the future.

Benefits

By working with your own psychic abilities, you can harness the power of the spiritual world, for self-healing, dealing with grief, contacting the spirits of loved ones, and for understanding your own soul's journey, in this life, the afterlife, and future lives, too.

This chapter includes step-by-step exercises and rituals to help you develop your innate psychic powers. You can learn the basics of psychic work, such as channelling, automatic writing, contacting and meeting your spirit guide or angel, and retrieving information from your spirit guides. The chapter includes practical guidance on past-life and in-between life regression, as well as trying an exercise in the shamanic practice of soul retrieval for yourself.

Right: A crystal ball can help you to connect to the spiritual world.

ARE YOU PSYCHIC?

Yes, you are.

Everyone is psychic because everyone has a soul and therefore an innate ability to connect to that spiritual place within ourselves. As self-help author Dr Wayne Dyer says, "We are spiritual beings having human experiences'.

The psychic world may not be very obvious because it is invisible. But the invisible will become clear to us if we start to perceive the apparent world around us in a different way.

Psychic ability is the capability to "see between things", between trees and houses, the spaces between tables and chairs, the gap between Earth and the furthest star. This "between-things place" is where there is oneness, and where and how everything is interconnected. This space between every atom, cell, or electromagnetic wave is joined by spirit or soul, and connects everything. Those who state that psychic abilities do not exist, or that claim they have no psychic ability, have yet to discover their own innate psychic perception. If you feel you haven't quite found your psychic ability yet, then now is the time to start working with it.

But first you must learn the basics. Don't be tempted to jump to the section you're most interested in. Follow the exercises in the order in this chapter, and you will then be ready to choose one of the psychic techniques to connect you to the spiritual world.

Begin by learning about the psychic world around you, and follow the pathway with rituals or exercises which increase both your own inner belief, but also will enliven your soul. Before you move on to guided psychic development work you need to learn about protection from negative energy, both in the "real" world around you and from the other realms too. Then you can get started on bringing to life your true psychic self.

USING PSYCHIC POWER TO ACCESS THE AFTERLIFE

Channellers, mediums, and psychics all draw on psychic powers to access the spiritual world or afterlife. But what is psychic power? Psychic power is the ability to tap into the supernatural world through clairvoyance, ESP, sixth sense, or other mystical means.

As with any power, whether it be political, religious, or scientific, there are always those who will abuse or corrupt that power. This is why it is very important to be 100 per cent sure that when you work with psychic power to access the afterlife you are doing so for the good of the whole, including yourself.

For hundreds of years, in the Western world at least, contacting spirits and other spiritual entities has been associated with evil and was considered particularly heretical by the Church. It is hard for some of us to disengage ourselves from this notion, so many people, when they first start their spiritual quest, feel guilty or embarrassed that they're doing something that was, and in some traditions, still is, considered "wicked". This is a mindset we must overcome if we are to work seriously with our soul, because it is through our psychic "senses"

that we can reach down into our soul and discover its connection to the universe.

Our innate psychic sense reveals information that would normally be unavailable or hidden. This paranormal ability to perceive things that are not normally recognized by the five senses brings us into contact with supernatural or spirit worlds. This is why you must also learn to protect yourself from the wearing energies of the psychic world itself and the negative invasion from those around you who may cast doubt, fear, or scorn upon your belief.

You must believe

Like any work or passion, if we don't believe in what we're doing, it's not going to happen and we won't get the results we're looking for. Belief generates thoughts, feelings, and awareness, which are followed by action and resolution.

Above: A belief in the afterlife can help you to realise your interconnection to all things.

So the first thing to think about is what kind of afterlife do you believe in? Have any of the different beliefs in this book inspired you to follow a new pathway, or have you found your own individual one? Do you want to channel spirits or ascended masters (see page 281), find your guardian angel (see page 339), or simply reach down to heal yourself and others from the depths of your soul? Or, like many neopagan groups, do you simply yearn to feel at one with the World Soul and to resonate in your interconnection to all things?

When you have clarified your belief, then you can begin to work through your soul's connection to the universe. This is the moment when, as any psychic knows, the magic happens, the light shines, and healing begins.

HOW TO BELIEVE

There are no rules about belief except that you must feel it deep inside, strongly enough to be sure in your heart and soul of that belief. This belief is that the afterlife, spiritual world, or other realities are accessible if you open yourself to perceiving the invisible spaces between things.

We all know that the Earth revolves around the sun. We all know that, without the sun, there would be no life on Earth as we know it. We know this, so we believe it, and because it has also been "confirmed" by science, it helps many more of us to trust in that knowledge. But long before Galileo was put under house arrest in the 16th century for trying to demonstrate the Earth orbited the sun, not many people believed it at all. In fact, the idea of a sun-centred system was ridiculed, scorned, and considered heretical. First proposed in the 3rd century BCE by Greek philosopher Aristarchus, it took more than a thousand years to find a scientific "reason" to confirm the belief.

If you are willing to wait a thousand years or so for evidence of the "afterlife" before you can even begin to believe it, then it's unlikely you would be reading this book. So start believing now.

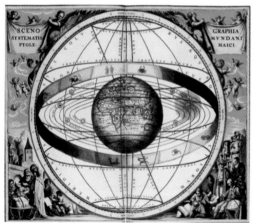

Left: Until as late as the 16th century, most people believed that the sun revolved around the earth.

Right: Shape your personal belief around those ideas that you find inspiring.

Belief exercise

You may believe everyone has a "soul", and that the spirits/souls of our loved ones are looking after us. You may believe the afterlife is a place filled with light, or that we are all stars in the sky. You may believe the afterlife is filled with spirits, or that the universe is "one" and the afterlife and this life are part of this wholeness. You may believe that your soul is connected and part of the World Soul (see page 118), and that you are a bright spark in the light of the universe. The following exercise will help you to explore your beliefs.

1. Make a list of all the things about the afterlife that you believe without thinking about it too much.

2. Gaze out of the window, or up at a cloudless sky for a few minutes when you are calm and relaxed, and wonder at the infinity of it all. If the universe is infinite, that means you are, too.

3. Now write down the things that you do not believe – this may take longer. You may need to look through this book again at ideas and concepts to help you decide what is right for you, what is wrong. You may not believe in the ancient gods or spirits, but ask yourself, why don't you believe?

4. Write down the names of loved ones, ancestors, anyone in history who's passed over who has fascinated you. If you knew them, write down what your relationship with them was, and how you feel the relationship is with them now. For example, you may have lost your mother some years ago. Do you still have deep feelings of love, hate, fear, or resentment towards her? Have you come to terms with these feelings, if negative? If not, why not? A little self-awareness helps you to be more open to the beliefs that you are beginning to "shape" for yourself.

Whatever you believe, believe it with all your heart and your soul will care for you. Lastly, you need to believe in yourself.

Seeing is believing exercise

Here's a simple exercise to help you begin to "see" in a different way.

1. First practise this technique. Hold up your finger at arm's length so that it is level with your eyes. Focus on your finger for a few seconds, then take away your finger but keep focusing on the empty spot, the "space" between you and everything in the distance. Soon, your eyes will refocus on something in the distance. With practice, you can learn to hold this gaze into the "emptiness spot" for as long as possible.

2. Next, hold up your finger again but, this time, don't move your finger away. Instead, divert your focus to an object in the distance way beyond your finger – maybe a tree, a wall, or another building outside. Your finger will go out of focus, but it is still there, it still exists even though you're not looking directly at it.

3. Now practise this with a friend. Ask your friend to stand still and, from about 1–2 metres distance, focus on their face. Then, when you are ready, ask them to move away slowly to the right or left out of your sight. Continue to hold the gaze at the spot they were in (as you did in the previous exercise with your finger). This time, the "empty

space" is much larger, so you are literally expanding your ability to see "between things". It won't be long until you can "see" with your psychic sense.

Below: Techniques such as "seeing" between objects, can help you to align with the unseen forces of the universe.

PSYCHIC PROTECTION

We are all sensitive beings, capable of picking up on the good and the bad around us. Psychic protection offers us a whole range of invaluable techniques that we can use to keep ourselves safe from a range of outside influences.

These outside influences include people who generally have negative mindsets, people who would like to manipulate you in some way, as well as negative or difficult spiritual and environmental energy. It is important that you find a form of psychic protection that suits you, and one that you can summon up whenever you feel you need it.

First, to learn how to protect yourself from everyday psychic negativity from other people *in this life*, follow the grounding and protective bubble exercises on the next pages.

Left: We must learn to protect ourselves from negative energy in this world before we can do so in any other.

Right: Grounding exercises help you to relax your mind while remaining aware of psychic energy.

Ritual to ground yourself

When doing any psychic work, it is important to still be aware or mindful of the natural world around you. This means that you are not only physically, emotionally, and mentally in tune with it, but you also know that you can return to a safe place at any time in the course of your spiritual work.

Sit cross-legged on the floor or on a comfortable chair with your feet flat on the ground. Close your eyes and relax.

1. Imagine you are literally rooted to the spot. Down from your spine grows a series of strong tree roots penetrating the depths of the earth. Now imagine yourself, the tree, with your branches filled with leaves and blossom, the spirits of nature. These spirits are your guardians and are there to protect you from any negative energy.

2. Settle your bottom further into the chair or floor and now feel the strength of your trunk, thousands of years old, your roots reaching down into the ground beneath you. You have made a strong connection to the ground and you can never be uprooted.

3. Now stand up, close your eyes, and this time imagine the roots are connecting your feet to the ground and the earth beneath you. You can imagine this even when walking, as each step you take brings you back in touch with all your roots.

4. Once you have imagined this for a few minutes you can take a deep breath, relax, and slowly open your eyes.

Above: Imagine an invisible bubble of light keeping you safe and protected.

Protective bubble

This protection ritual is to help you fend off negative energies from people around you. Our personal space is exactly that, and this is a great exercise to perform every morning before going to work, or before making any journeys, or meeting strangers, or entering social situations in which you might feel vulnerable.

1. Sit in a quiet place with your eyes closed. Focus your mind on an imaginary bright white light as if it were a motionless orb in front of you. Watch it grow brighter and brighter until it is larger than a balloon.

2. Gradually watch as the light begins to envelop you, surrounding your whole

body like a huge bright bubble, not only above, behind, and around you, but beneath you, too. Visualize the outer surface of the light becoming a protective crystal all around you.

3. Say to yourself, "This light will protect me from all negative energies. This field of light will be with me for always. No negative thoughts will be entertained in me".

4. Hold the image for a couple of minutes and then let go of it gradually. Before leaving your imagined bubble of protection, say, "My bubble is always there, even though I cannot visualize it". Now open your eyes and come back to normality.

You can at any moment throughout the day, recall the image of the bubble to reinforce its protection around you.

ACCESSING THE SPIRITUAL WORLD SAFELY

Before you begin any journey into the spiritual world for the first time, if you arm yourself with a treasury of psychic self-defence, then there is little that can harm you. It's not just the unknown factors from the spiritual realm that may slow your progress or create scepticism. It is the very mistrust and scorn engrained in the Western *psyche* (particularly) that can hold up your psychic development.

Establish right from the start of your psychic exploration the following points:

- Accept that you are responsible for your choices.
- This work is being done for the good of others as well as yourself.
- It is only you who controls your thoughts and your thoughts don't control you.
- You truly believe in yourself and in your power.

- Remember that if you are negative, you will attract negative energy to you.
- If you are positive, you will receive positive energy.
- You will always remain objective and will never get emotionally involved with spirits or clients.

DEVELOPING YOUR PSYCHIC SENSE

Often know as ESP, intuition, clairvoyance, and the sixth sense, psychic awareness and the ability to "see" through the veil of illusive reality is where our true psychic abilities lie.

Many psychics, such as clairvoyants, mediums, or channellers, often experience the spiritual world via the senses: sight, sound, touch, and hearing. These senses become conduits for their sixth sense.

Most of nature's own energies pass our senses by, so it's hardly surprising we don't notice energies from the spiritual plane. We see what we want to see, hear what we want to hear.

The exercises on the following pages will tone up three of your most important senses – touch, sight, and sound – and make you more aware of things you wouldn't normally see, touch, or hear. That means you can soon start to interact with other energy fields, whether spiritual or material.

Sound

Many psychics "hear" spiritual voices because they tune into a different "frequency" and hear sounds that most people don't. To tone up your psychic hearing, listen to all the sounds around you as you sit peacefully at home. Alternatively, find a tranquil place in nature and listen to the many sounds that come out of apparent silence. You will hear sounds however quiet you believe it is. Once you're in tune with your psychic hearing, you will begin to pick out sounds that come from the "spaces in between" the things you normally know as sounds. In nature you may hear thunder in the distance when normally you wouldn't have heard it, the rustle of leaves in the breeze, a twig falling onto soft earth. When you are more in tune with your psychic hearing, you may hear a phone ringing before your phone actually rings, whispering spirit voices in the rain, tinkling music in the trees, or the flap of birds' wings when there are no birds.

Left: Getting in tune with nature is a great way to get closer to the spirit world.

Touch

Below is a simple exercise to maximize your sense of touch.

1. Place a leaf, fruit, or crystal in the palm of your hand. All these objects have their own electromagnetic energy fields. Sit quietly, close your eyes, and concentrate on the object and what it feels like in your palm. Is it warm, soft, cold, hard? Does it make your hand feel warmer or colder, does it give you a sense of a different energy to your own?

2. Now touch the object with the fingers of your other hand. Gradually move your fingers about 5–8 centimetres away from the object and you will soon be able to feel the subtle energy, either warm, cold, or vibrational, drawn into your own energy field.

Continue to work on this exercise to increase your psychic touch. Some psychics receive messages from the spirit world by touching or holding the objects of loved ones, whether deceased or simply missing, to try to contact them or find out where they are. This is known as psychometry.

Left: White quartz crystal has a powerful electromagnetic energy field.

Above: Sometimes we only see what we want to see and not what is really there.

Sight

There is much we don't see, even in the material world. Below is an exercise to help you start to perceive things and the "spaces between things", in a different way.

Hold your finger out in front of you at arm's length and at eye level and stare at it. As you focus, be aware of everything else around it, but without focusing on anything else. Begin to note other things in the room or landscape. Gradually increase your awareness of things around you as you still concentrate on your finger. This will exercise your peripheral awareness as you mentally look from the corners of your eyes, and while your pupils are still focused straight ahead. Be aware of things going on almost behind you.

Clairvoyance

Clairvoyance is often known as having "second sight" or being able to "see clearly" with the "inner eye". Clairvoyants can retrieve information about people, work with the spirits of the deceased, and can find missing objects or reveal hidden information. "Clear awarenesses" or *sidhis* are reported in ancient Hindu texts as a kind of perfect awareness achieved through meditation. In the world of mediumship; the word "clairvoyant" usually refers to seeing or feeling the presence of spirits.

Developing your clairvoyant skill

First of all, how clairvoyant do you think you are? Try reading the six statements that follow without thinking for too long about each of them before agreeing or disagreeing.

- I often "know" when someone is about to call me on the phone.
- I often "see" what people are doing even if they are far away.
- I feel immediately if someone is kind, generous, or untrustworthy.
- If a friend has a problem and needs help, I know before they tell me.
- I can read other people's minds.
- I have dreams that come true.

If you agree with at least three of these statements, then you are probably a natural clairvoyant.

Left: A clue to your own psychic ability is when you instinctively know someone is about to call you on the phone.

Right: Imagining what you want to happen throughout the day can actually make it happen.

Exercise for developing your sixth sense

This exercise will help you to believe in your own intuition or sixth sense. Trust in your psychic perception for a day and avoid trying to make logical decisions if at all possible.

For example, as you go to work one morning, you have a choice to make – you can either take the bus or walk. If you wait for the bus you may be late. It's raining, there's a long queue, people look cross and impatient. If you walk it may take a long time and you forgot your umbrella, but you'll get to work even if you're late, you know exactly how long it will take to get there. Rather than try to work out what to do based on logic, act on intuition. What is your "soul" or inner voice saying to you?

Follow this up during the day by taking a stroll to your favourite café or shop. *Before* you get there, let your "psychic" sense inform you what you might expect to happen. Can you "see" a beautiful dress waiting to be bought, or a pair of shoes that "speak" to you as you pass by a shop? Is there someone you know chatting to a friend on a street corner, will you bump into a beautiful stranger?

Throughout the day, push yourself to follow your intuition, follow up your hunches. Work with your sixth sense until it becomes an everyday experience. You may not always be right but, with practice, the sixth sense can become your best one.

Meditation

Used by many Eastern spiritual traditions, meditation brings you to a deeper state of consciousness in which you become more aware of other realms of existence and the ability to tap into spiritual energy.

How to meditate

1. In a quiet place, sit cross-legged on the floor or in a straight-backed chair with both feet on the floor, and with hands palm down on each thigh.

2. Imagine that there is a string attached to the top of your head that is holding you up towards the sky. Close your eyes. Become aware of your feet on the floor, your hands on your thighs, and any sounds in the distance. Become aware of every part of your body. Slowly concentrate first on your toes, then work upwards from your feet, bringing your awareness to each part of your body. Notice how your body feels – are you warm, cold, fidgeting, or calm? Don't judge yourself or your feelings. Simply observe the thoughts going through your head, as if you are an observer outside of yourself. Imagine these thoughts as birds, flitting in and out of the branches of the tree of life.

3. Now turn your attention to your breathing. Each time you slowly breathe in, count one, then as you breathe out, count two, and so on. If your mind wanders, turn your attention back to your breathing and start at one again.

4. Focus on every in and out breath and number. Do this for five minutes.

5. Carry on breathing, but stop counting and observe the stillness of your mind. Observe how peaceful you are. Be aware of that mindfulness, but do not attach yourself to it mentally. You will soon discover that if you repeat this meditation every day for ten minutes, you'll begin to notice yourself being mindful of everything you do or say in daily life, too.

Instead of counting your breaths, you can also repeat a mantra in your mind to block out any rogue thoughts. This can be a simple affirmation, such as "My psychic sense is awakening" or a more spiritual mantra such as *Om mani padme ohm* (meaning "All hail the jewel in the lotus").

THE BENEFITS OF MEDITATION

- Your mind, thoughts, and emotions are calmed.

- Helps you achieve a state of passive alertness.

- Enables you to communicate in a different level of consciousness.

- Gives you better access the spiritual world.

- Makes you mindful but aware, and you are no longer attached to the material world.

- Allows you to discover new insight into the true nature of reality.

- Helps to focus psychic ability.

- Lowers brainwave frequency to the alpha level.

- Enables your subtle body energy to "merge" with universal energy.

Left: The meditative state takes us away from the noises in our mind.

Visualization

You've already experienced a few simple visualization techniques as you've been going through this chapter. Below is a deeper visualization ritual to help you amplify your higher state of consciousness and open your mind to the spiritual realms.

Sit quietly somewhere and close your eyes. Think of someone you love. Imagine them in your mind – the shape of their face, their hair, the clothes they wear, the things they do. In your mind, create a mental picture of the way they do things, a bit like a mini movie in your head. Next, imagine them speaking to you. Hear their voice, their laugh, and then imagine them touching, kissing, or just hugging you. You can practise doing this at any time of day.

The more often you practise, the more you'll prepare yourself for the time when you are ready to open your imagination to the spirit world. In fact, our imagination is the part of our mind, originating from the right side of the brain, that creates these visual images. The imagination, according to Jung, is the connection between the conscious and unconscious mind. As such, it is the channel through

which all that we do not yet know (the unconscious otherworld) comes through to us, but also through which we connect to it. Visualization techniques stimulate your imagination and open this, the most mysterious communication channel of all. If you find it hard to visualize, keep practising. It won't take long until you can.

Colour visualization

The following visualization exercise will open you up to the power of the imagination by using specifically the colour yellow, a powerful symbol of communication itself.

Make sure you give yourself at least ten minutes to perform this exercise.

1. Sit quietly. Create a mental picture in your mind of a huge bubble above your head filled with the colour yellow, like the sun. In your mind, you reach up and pierce the bubble with your finger until your finger is inside the bubble. Now imagine the colour slowly flowing through your finger into your hand. Imagine the colour yellow flowing gently and silently through your arm and up into your shoulder. Now it flows across your chest, down your other arm, up into

Above: Yellow is symbolic of solar energy and the power of the life-force.

your head, and then through your body, down through your legs, until it flows throughout you and you are filled with the colour yellow.

2. Now imagine you feel full, wise, concentrated, centred, and filled with light as the sun. Stay with this image for a few minutes. Gradually let the

colour yellow wash slowly back up through your body towards your fingertip so the yellow flows back into the bubble.

As yellow is symbolic of the sun, don't forget that every time the sun shines, you are being washed with vibrant solar and universal energy too.

Spiritual protection rituals

Before you attempt to contact the spirit world, it's important to be nurtured and in tune with the psychic energy of the World Soul (see page 118). It is your own soul's connection to the World Soul, or universal energy, that gives you psychic strength and power. Performing these protection rituals in the following order will always ensure you are prepared.

Protection ritual one puts you both in touch with the World Soul and its golden light of protection so that whenever you contact the spiritual world, you will be blessed and safe.

Once you have perfected spiritual protection ritual one, begin to practise spiritual protection rituals two and three. You must perform all three rituals consciously each time you are about to embark upon any contact with the spirit world. They don't take long and, like the earlier psychic protection exercises (see pages 302–5), they form part of the practice of psychic work.

Working on these rituals regularly is a bit like being a sportsperson – you need to prepare yourself as a beginner,

or even as a long-term practitioner. Tennis players don't just run out onto the tennis court to play a match without getting themselves in shape first. Before they play, they stretch their bodies, tone up their muscles, and get themselves prepared psychologically. Similarly, once you have created your psychic light bubble around you as per spiritual protection ritual one, the next thing you must do is set aside a few minutes to practise spiritual protection rituals two and three.

Right: Gentle exercises, such as creating a psychic light bubble around you, will help you to invoke your own psychic power.

Spiritual protection ritual one: Reviving your soul energy

This is a technique based on the simple colour visualization mentioned previously (see page 314), and is an important psychic protective ritual when working in the spiritual realm. Again, take as long as you like, but about five minutes is enough to revive your soul energy.

1. Sit quietly and close your eyes. Imagine a bubble of golden light hovering just above your head. Imagine that it floats a little lower down, just in front of you, at about an arm's length away from you. Imagine that you pierce the bubble of golden light, which is filled with peace, calm, and harmony. From your finger, it flows through your hand, up your arm, and across your shoulder to the top of your head. It then slowly permeates your entire body, filling every pore, emanating throughout all your chakras, your aura, and subtle body energies, until you are surrounded and infused by a golden light of protection.

Right: Imagining a bubble of golden light brings peace, protection, and spiritual contact.

2. Now imagine the World Soul (see page 118) in the bubble. It is light, breathtaking, illuminated by magic, the universe, and the essence of yourself. Imagine you want to connect to this World Soul because it is all that is good, perfect, and true.

3. Stay with this image for a few minutes.

4. To disengage from the World Soul bubble, simply imagine the colour yellow now flowing out of you. Gradually, it flows through your body towards your arm as you reach out towards the bubble surrounding you. Imagine all the colour yellow returning to the bubble. Now put your hand back to your side and imagine the bubble fading away into air around you. As you open your eyes, recall your interconnection to this unknown realm.

5. Thank the World Soul or universe for its help and protection.

You can repeat this visualization technique any time you feel a "disconnection" to the universe. Practise it at least once a day for four weeks as a beginner to tone up your soul connection, and then perform it once a month, around the full moon, to boost your psychic awareness.

Left: Beyond the moon, the universe awaits your reconnection to it.

Right: Candles are used in rituals as they invoke the power of spiritual forces.

- I am filled with confidence and good intention.
- I can transform any problem into opportunity.
- I feel good about my unique self.
- Changing my beliefs changes my life.

3. Now you must affirm belief in your soul's connection and love from the spiritual world. Say aloud seven times each of the following statements:

- I know and believe in my soul and its journey.
- I know and believe in all those spirits and souls upon whom I call.
- I know and believe this to be work for healing and comfort.
- I know and believe in the soul of the universe.
- I know and believe in the interconnectedness of all things.
- I know all that I have already said to be true.

Spiritual protection ritual two: Affirming belief

To ensure your intention is positive and your spirit and soul strong, these affirmations are a vehicle for good contact with other realms.

1. First, sit quietly in a room. Light a candle or incense if you feel like creating a more spiritual atmosphere. If you prefer to do this in daylight, sit near an open window and let the natural light shine upon you, or sit out in the garden or in a natural setting. Close your eyes.

2. First you must affirm your self-belief. Say aloud seven times each of the following statements:

4. Now put your hands together, as in prayer, and give thanks to the divine source, deity, or imagined spiritual being you prefer. If there is none, then just give thanks to the cosmos or the universe.

Spiritual protection ritual three:
Sacred space

1. First, you need to set up a dedicated "altar" or a sacred space or place to honour your ancestors or loved ones in the afterlife. Those loved ones who have passed over will always give you wisdom, protection, and guidance through their love for you. However, not all spirits want to be contacted, and some prefer solitude while others may not be available at the moment we choose. Of course, they still want you to receive healing and comfort from the spiritual world and most

want you to carry on "relating" to them from your physical plane of existence. Even if you had a "bad" relationship with your father, his soul is no longer hampered by inhibitions and human complexes and will always be there for you even if you have negative memories of him. By honouring and respecting him, you will begin to lose those negative thoughts and feelings about him and gradually heal your own inner self. Even if outwardly you may still feel or show signs of anger towards him, or can never consciously forgive him for something, the inner workings of your soul will slowly heal you and your relationship with him.

2. This sacred space can be simply a shelf or even a wall. Place photos of any deceased people who were "family" to you, whether you were blood related or not. Only place photos of the deceased in this space, not living people.

3. Go there each time you want to perform any spiritual work. Make a small offering, perhaps a flower or even some sentimental object that connects you to your loved ones, or anything you feel is right. It may be a written message or a favourite quote, but it should be something that is important to you and them.

4. Then, simply *talk* to your ancestors aloud, or in whispers. Thank them for everything you have, and ask them to guide your soul and protect you.

5. Then sit and listen in stillness for any messages that come to you. You may feel a presence, or just an intuitive feeling. You may feel or sense nothing, but over the next few days you may notice signs of communication, such as synchronicity (those moments where something happens and means something to you in relation to your loved one). They may be trying to contact you in a symbolic way.

If you do this every day for a few minutes, you'll start to notice real progress in your ability to become aware of loved ones' spirits as well as in opening up your psychic perception and ability.

Left: Set up a sacred space devoted to your ancestral spirits to invite their help.

LEARNING SELF-HYPNOSIS

Hypnosis comes from the Greek word hypnos *meaning "sleep".*
Hypnosis is very similar to the trance-inducing techniques of meditation.

However, hypnosis can take us into a deeper level of awareness, unlocking the door to the world of the unconscious, where memories, past lives, and even recollections of future lives are stored in the universal storehouse of knowledge.

In 1843, the Scottish neurosurgeon James Braid (1795–1860) coined the term "neuro-hypnotism" (sleep of the nervous system). Braid's work subsequently influenced a French country doctor, Ambroise-Auguste Liebeault (1823–1904), who was later acknowledged as the founder of hypnotherapy. Hypnosis has become part of mainstream psychotherapy, and in 2005 the American Psychological Association published the following: "When using hypnosis, one person (the subject) is guided by another (the hypnotist) to respond to suggestions for changes in subjective experience, alterations in perception, sensation, emotion, thought or behaviour. Persons can also learn self-hypnosis, which is the act of administering hypnotic procedures on one's own".

Self-hypnosis: stairway to your soul

Currently, self-hypnosis is used to help reduce stress and make lifestyle changes, and is often used to get in touch with your higher self or spirit guides or for accessing recollections of past lives.

Self-hypnosis technique

Before you begin, ask for protection and guidance from a higher source, and then perform spiritual protection rituals one and two for preparation for psychic work (see pages 317–319).

1. Now light your favourite candle or place sacred objects in a special space, light incense, or make prayers that will help establish your feeling of being supported, safe and guided.

2. Next, find a comfortable place and, most importantly, make it clear to yourself what your intentions are before you begin. For example, you could say to yourself that you have a specific objective of finding a past life that will be of use to you to give you

Left: An altered state of consciousness, such as hypnosis, can lead you to discover your soul's home.

knowledge of why you have certain issues in this life.

3. When you are calm and relaxed, it is time to release yourself from the concerns of the body. Imagine the golden light surrounding you, just like the protective bubble you used in protection ritual one. This time, you will be using it as a healing source for emotional wounds.

4. Visualize your bubble of golden light all around you and imagine and feel the light moving gradually throughout your body. As it permeates your fingers, hand, arms, and then your body, moving down towards your toes, it is relaxing and healing you. As this golden light moves through you, say to yourself (either aloud or in your head), "This golden light is working through, every second, every inch, every cell of my body to heal and nurture me".

5. Next, close your eyes and slowly count down from the number 20. Do this with one out-breath and in-breathe for each count. Imagine, as you count, that you are descending a beautiful golden staircase into the psychic basement of yourself.

Above: Down an imaginary staircase, you will find the centre of yourself.

6. Your mind is deepening as you descend the staircase. If you can't remember which number step you are on, it doesn't matter, just let your mind "find" a number, and keep going down until you reach the bottom step and number one in the count. Be aware of your intention to find your psychic basement at every step as you descend. If you don't feel you've "arrived" deep enough, then start from the beginning again.

7. When you arrive at the bottom of the staircase, you will intuitively know you are there. Now let your imagination lead you into a garden of healing, peace, and love. This represents the centre of who you are, this is where your soul lives, and it is the place where you are now supported by the divine power of the universe, or the World Soul.

8. As you enter, ask the World Soul to guide and protect you, then go into the healing garden and relax. Stay there for a while, at peace, feeling nurtured and safe.

9. When you are ready to leave the garden, begin the slow count back up to 20. Take it as slowly as you did when you descended the golden staircase. But as you reach the final three steps, say aloud, "I will now come out of this state on the count of three, feeling refreshed and relaxed. One – I am coming out of the state refreshed and revitalized. Two – I am now opening my eyes, fully energized. Three – I am now in my normal conscious state, aware of my journey".

Follow this ritual for a few weeks before you progress to any regression work. Little by little, as it becomes easier and more natural, you may begin to move beyond the attainment of this hypnotic state to the actual use of the state, which you will learn about in the next few pages.

Above: Using self-hypnosis you can access your centre – a garden of healing, peace, and love.

EXPLORING PAST LIVES

Have you ever thought you were a famous person in a previous life? Do you sometimes have flashes of memories that seem to be nothing to do with your current life? Are you open to the idea of reincarnation – that you have lived other lives before and that you will again?

Currently in psychological circles, therapists conclude that, if an individual believes they have experienced a previous life, it can be beneficial to explore their experience of that previous existence in order to help them to understand their purpose or role in this life.

Memories of past-life experiences

If you answer yes to most or all of the questions below, then the chances are that you are recollecting some sense of a past life.

Above: Our recollections can sometimes derive from a past life, rather than from this one.

- Do you have an overwhelming desire to visit a certain place, but don't know why?
- Are there any places you would never like to visit, but you don't know why?
- Do you ever experience déjà vu?
- Do you love reading about certain periods in history?
- Do you hate certain periods in history?
- Do you have irrational phobias?

- Do you meet new people and feel as if you have met them in another life?
- Is there any city or part of the country you really identify with?
- Do you recognize "old souls" – people who may have been on this planet before in another incarnation?

PAST-LIFE EXPERIENCE CHECK LIST

Below is a list of the most common characteristics of belief in, or experience of, a past life, or a sense of reincarnation referred to in psychological circles.

- Memory of an existence or incarnation prior to the present one.

- Recounting of information you wouldn't normally know about the past.

- A sudden ability to speak a language unknown to you.

- The existence of birth marks/scars that are unexplained and may be related to significant or fatal past-life wounds.

- Memories of a past life that have similarities to this life.

- Inexplicable knowledge of places, locations, and buildings related to a past life.

- Preference for unusual foods, tastes, fashions similar to those of a past life.

- Existence of a phobia linked to problems in a previous life, or manner of death in a previous life.

- Recognition of unknown people that were family members in a previous life.

One of the most common signs of a past life is experiencing déjà vu – the sensation that you have met a person before or have visited some place previously. Sometimes, this déjà vu feeling is a sign of a past life that involved a particular person or in a specific place.

The French phrase "déjà vu" means "already seen". The phrase was coined by Emile Boirac (1851–1917) in his book of psychic research, *L'avenir des sciences psychiques*. When we experience déjà vu, we have a feeling that we are experiencing something that has already happened to us before, perhaps in another dimension or time. You recognize something about that moment, almost as if you are witnessing yourself doing something a split second before you do it. It feels both familiar, yet strange. Déjà vu can also refer to the experience of future lives as well as past ones, because you may be experiencing something that is going to happen, not merely something that once happened in the past.

Many scientists and psychologists have tried to prove déjà vu to be merely a neurological fault between short-term and long-term memory, while parapsychologists believe it is related to past-life experiences. Other forms of "déjà vu" include *déjà vecu* (already lived), *déjà senti* (already felt), and *déjà visite* (already visited).

Symbols

If you experience vivid, detailed dreams of being in different times and places, you might find that they may contain symbols and metaphors that need to be interpreted so that their meaning and message can become clear. These symbols are just as important as apparently real experiences. Through the symbolic world, we access the spiritual one directly, which is one reason why symbols have been so important in most religions and esoteric cults, and to artists and writers. The word symbol comes from the ancient Greek, and means "thrown together". Symbols are universal archetypes thrown together,

representing the so-called "unknown" and, thus, often represent the space between the things we label on a daily basis. For example, a table and a chair are words for something we recognize, but between the table and the chair is a shape, a form, a sensation that is often unrecognizable, but can be described in a symbolic way. So dreams are often symbolic of what we once were, or will be.

Your talents, abilities, likes, dislikes, attractions, and aversions can also be clues to past lives. You might feel yourself being drawn to certain people or cultures, even if you've never had a personal experience of them. You might find you are able to learn certain subjects or foreign languages while others are more difficult. Or you may have an intense interest in particular historical times and events. These attractions and aversions all suggest some kind of previous experience of the thing in question.

Soul companions

It is quite common to travel through each life with the same soul companions. These can be soulmates, families, or even the people you work with. From these souls we learn spiritual lessons, and although our relationship to those people may change with each life, the souls don't. For

Above: Finding your twin soul or a "soulmate" can be a life-changing experience.

example, your husband in one life might reincarnate as your daughter in another. In this sense we never lose our loved one. Twin souls, however, find each other and lose each other over a course of many lifetimes, but there is a small ritual you can do to attempt to make that connection with your twin soul in this life.

Finding your twin soul

Twin souls are thought to be originally one soul that split into two at some point on its journey between lives. Twin souls are true mirrors of each other, and when they do meet up in life, the two people discover an incredible affinity, yet rarely recall they were once one soul. Twin flames, on the other hand, sense immediately they meet that they have known each other before. They usually fall passionately in love, then go their separate ways again, because each soul needs to evolve further before it can commit to a final reunion. Twin souls, when they do meet, tend to stay with each other for life.

If you feel you have not found your twin soul and would like to put out a message into the universe to find your twin soul, then start with this simple ritual.

1. Place an empty photo frame (it can be as beautiful or as ordinary as you prefer) on a small shelf or wall, away from any other photos. Nearby, light two candles, one to the left of the photo frame, the other, to the right.

Left: To find your twin soul requires action, imagination and, most of all, belief that you will do so.

2. Stand or sit between the lit candles and close your eyes. Allow the light of the universe to enter you, as described in spiritual protection ritual one (see page 317), and then begin to visualize faces in your mind. Who do you see? To begin with, you might not "see" anyone. But you may have a flash of intuition or a moment's symbolic awareness. For example, such as a place you must go to on your next holiday, someone's name written in lights, a job vacancy, or a new sport you must try out. This type of information can set you on a course of action that leads you to your twin soul, or allows them to find you.

3. Now send out a beautiful message to your twin soul, such as "We shall be together in this life and nothing or no one can stop us; let the light of the universe shine through us both so we will be revealed to one another".

4. Now, open your eyes and gaze into the empty photo frame, knowing that, soon, you will face the one who makes you feel complete. If you're lucky, you may even glimpse an image of your twin soul already in your mind.

A GENTLE PAST-LIFE REGRESSION EXERCISE

Since the success of the 1970s book Life After Life *by Raymond Moody, publications and the media have been overwhelmed with reports of afterlife or near-death experiences (see page 21).*

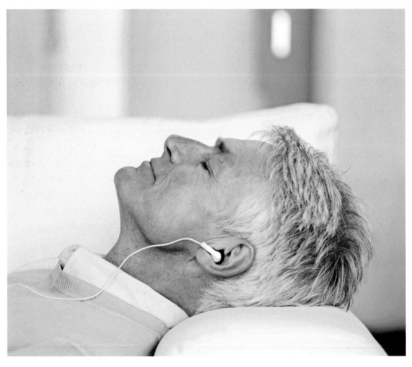

Above: A gentle and relaxing visit to the past can help self-awareness in the present.

If you are interested in trying past-life regression, the technique below is a gentle one. Please note that if you have any anxiety problems, or any sense of foreboding about what you might discover, it would be better to work with a past-life regression therapist. Treat this exercise as an adventure to discover where your soul has been, rather than looking upon it as a negative event. Whatever you see or recall from a past life will be valuable to you in this one.

But most of all, if at any time you feel uncomfortable, then simply and calmly tell your self to return to the "count" and walk back up the staircase to the material world.

Make sure you have completed spiritual protection rituals one and two (see pages 317–319). Then follow the self-hypnosis technique (see page 323), until you arrive in the garden of healing.

The following passage is your basic past-life regression script. You can either record yourself saying this, so you can listen to it while in your garden of healing, or simply remember it (it's not too difficult) and repeat it aloud or in your head as you go along.

Past-life regression script

Now that I'm in the garden of healing, I see a golden temple with many arched windows, like cloisters, around the edge of a courtyard garden. I choose a window, one that is open, or seems to "speak" to me, and that I find strangely familiar. I look through the window to see a stage play going on, or a scene being acted out from a movie.

I thank my spirit guides who are standing beside me to support and protect me. Even if they are invisible to me, I know they are there.

I can now look through the window, and I begin to see characters from history, events, people I don't know. I am watching it all an objective observer. Here I see remnants of a past life, symbols, signs, words spoken, faces, and I may even experience feelings from these moments.

I turn away from the window as I have seen enough for one session. I thank my spirit guides and the cosmos for being there, and now return to the staircase.

Use the ascension up the staircase as described in the self-hypnosis exercise (see page 323) to bring you back to a state of consciousness. Take your time to return to your conscious state. Once the count is finished, relax for a while, then write down notes about what you have seen.

If at any moment during the session you feel apprehensive, make your way back up the golden staircase.

Don't expect instant results. In order for the past-life regression to work, you must observe it and not judge anything while it is happening. Once you are "awake", analyze what happened, and determine what parts of it meant something to you, if anything. Do reflect upon the imagery for at least a week before returning again. Repeated practice can lead to emotional healing in your current life, or bring you to terms with loss, but don't push yourself. If you have any issues about regression, don't try it until you are sure you are psychologically ready, or work with a qualified therapist who can reassure you along the way.

Right: A journey to a past life is like walking through cloisters and seeing in each window a different aspect of your own soul.

ANGELS

Making contact with a personal guardian spirit, whether a Christian angel or Pagan daimon (see pages 129 and 131), confirms to us that there is always someone there to look after and comfort us.

Guardian angels and diamons

The guardian angel was known as a *daimon* in Greek mythology and in neoplatonic and later esoteric traditions. The *daimon* is our true guardian spirit who accompanies our soul and guides us from birth to know our true calling and destiny. Later on, in Judeo-Christian religion, it became known as an angel from a Greek word, meaning messenger.

Your angel has been with you throughout time, guiding your soul's journey from life to life. However, very few of us are aware of our soul's companion. By developing your psychic powers you can recognize the presence of your own personal guardian angel or

Right: According to many traditions, each of us has our own guardian angel who will come to us when we need comfort or protection.

WELL-KNOWN ANGELS

Camael – angel of joy

Cathetel – angel of the garden

Charoum – angel of silence

Ecanus – angel of writers

Elijah – angel of innocence

Hadraniel – angel of love

Hael – angel of kindness

Isda – angel of nourishment

Liwet – angel of inventions

Nisroc – angel of freedom

Paschar – angel of vision

Pistis Sophia – angel of creation and wisdom

Perpetiel – angel of success

Raziel – angel of mysteries

Samandiriel – angel of imagination

Sofiel – angel of nature

Uriel – angel of creativity

Yofiel – angel of divine beauty

Zagzagel – angel of wisdom

daimon. However, if you prefer to call on a named angel, then the list on page 336 will help you to decide which one is right for you.

If any of these names resonates with you, the angel in question, and the quality it represents may be of importance to you. But very often it is the fantasy or imaginary friend we had as a child who is our true guardian angel. If you can remember their name, they may be the one you need to get to know again.

Left: Imagination is the key to reaching out to your guardian angel.

Right: Rainbows were thought to be bridges to the divine realm of the angels.

Finding your guardian angel

The following exercise will help you to find your own guardian angel or diety. Before you begin, perform spiritual protection rituals one and two (see pages 317–319) .

1. Find a quiet place to sit comfortably where you won't be disturbed. Close your eyes and relax.

2. Imagine that you are on a beach, with the azure sea lapping gently on the sandy shore. As you turn away from the beach and look inland you see a golden chariot, drawn by two white stallions. There is someone sitting in the chariot. You can't quite make out who it is but you know they are there to protect and care for you. As you walk over to the chariot, a rainbow appears, one end falling far beyond the horizon and the other ending only a few steps from where you are standing.

3. You walk towards the rainbow and stand inside the rainbow's spectrum of colours, which radiates through you. Your whole being is filled with rainbow light and you feel at one with the universe.

4. Ask for your angel or deity to appear. You want to know who they are. You can now see, hear, touch, or feel a figure next to you who is bathed in the rainbow light. In your mind or out loud, ask the angel their name, and it will come to you. The name may be in symbolic form, or you may hear it, see it, or feel as if someone is whispering their name to you. It may be a strange name, or it may feel very ordinary. The angel may be your childhood imaginary friend. After you have received their name, ask them to show you signs in the coming weeks that they are truly your guardian angel.

5. Thank the angel by name and slowly watch as the rainbow vanishes and the chariot with the white stallions pull away into the distance, carrying away your guardian angel. Now gradually come back to your normal consciousness by ascending the staircase as in the self-hypnosis exercise (see page 323) and open your eyes. Finally, write down the name of your angel, even if it was a strange name with odd letters or a code. This will have meaning for you at some stage in the days or weeks to come.

In the weeks to come, look out for signs that your angel is there. For example, you might pick up a magazine in a shop and open it randomly, and there on the page is the name of your angel, or some symbol that you can associate with that name. If it's an unusual name, be alert to symbolic meanings. For example, say the name of your angel is Traiz. You might be out for a walk through the park one day and notice how the sun is glinting through the "traiz" or trees. This kind of association is a sign that the angel is there for you.

You can call on your personal guardian angel at any moment to guide you. Most importantly, use your imagination to interpret symbols that you see during your daily life as suggested above. It's quite likely that your angel won't appear to you as a person or an image. You may hear a voice, feel a presence, or have moments in which you intuitively feel as if you are being protected. Your imagination is the link to your psychic world. It is through your imagination and the interpretation of symbols that you will be able to find your guardian angel so that they can guide you in this life, too.

Right: Angels may not appear as you expect them to, although the presence of a white feather or dove can signify that an angel is nearby.

SPIRIT GUIDES, DEITIES, AND ASCENDED MASTERS

Apart from knowing that a special angel or guardian is watching over us, we can also make contact with other spirits, gods, and goddesses who help us get through difficult times, and point us on the right pathway when we have to make choices.

When contacting spirits or deities, affirm that you are doing so for the good of everyone and everything in universe and thank the spirits for their guidance.

Deities

Some of us prefer to call on a chosen deity from many of the different cultural pantheons of gods that have been worshipped throughout history, such as the Hindu pantheon, the Greek deities, or the Norse gods.

Obviously, there are thousands of different deities, so this is very much an individual choice, depending on your belief system. For example, you might prefer to call on Cybele, the Greek Earth goddess, or Maya, the Hindu goddess of illusion, and simply add their name into the following ritual.

As with any psychic work, if you are truly looking for good guides, it is the

"good guys" who will come to you. If at any time you feel you are under any form of negative influence, do not continue with this work. Please be sure to read about psychic protection (see page 316) before undertaking any work with spirits.

Spirit guides can appear in many different guises, both as symbolic imagery in our everyday world, or as a visual, oral, or other intuitive or imaginative experience that gives us a sense of their presence in the psychic realms.

In the following ritual, you will be reaching out into the spiritual world to them, so ensure that you perform the spiritual protection rituals, one, two, and three (see pages 317–320) first, to empower you and reinforce your spirit guide's assistance.

To help you find your spirit guide or deity, perform the following simple visualization technique.

Finding your spirit guide or chosen deity

Once you have performed spiritual protection rituals, one, two, and three (see pages 317–320), close your eyes and relax. Now imagine the golden light bubble all around you, as you used in the self-hypnosis ritual (see page 323).

1. Imagine you are in a forest glade. Around you are high trees. You feel at one with nature. You are in your golden light, knowing that no one can harm you, nothing can disturb you, and that you are safe.

2. You sit upon a grassy bank and see another warm, golden light in the distance between the trees. You know this is a friend that you have met before in some other life, in some other place, and now you wait for them to come to you. Call gently in your imagination for them to come to you. As the golden light moves closer to you, ask their name, then ask them what you want to know. Once you have discovered an answer, or just felt the presence of a guide, thank them and return to normal consciousness. Do this by gradually counting down from ten, each count lasting for one in-breath and out-breath. When you reach one, open your eyes. Now finish by stamping your feet twice on the floor. This is a traditional sign to any spiritual entity that may still be lingering on that you have finished the session and that they should return to their world.

3. Next, write the spirit or deity's name on a piece of paper and keep it folded safely in your drawer or desk. The more you use a word or name things, the more powerful it becomes to you personally, and will enable you to contact your spirit guide, who is there in the invisible world to support you. At any time you can call on this guide to help you. Also, you might like to wear a talisman associated with your spirit or deity.

4. If you are ever in the countryside or on a beach, write the name of your spirit guide in the sand or spell it out with pebbles or stones. There is so much spiritual energy in every rock, flower, tree, and the essence of nature itself, that it is here that we are often most able to communicate with our guides.

Types of guides

Besides angels, deities, and spirit guides, there are a host of other guides available. Throughout many civilizations, contact with the spirits of specific animals, ascended masters, teachers, ancestors, and even with plants, rocks and trees, fairies, ghosts, and elementals has been seen as the key to healing, protection and comfort in this life. Trust your spirit guides. Any time you need to make a decision they will be there for you.

Power animals

Animal guides were used to help and protect shamans and priests during their spiritual journeys. The power of an animal guide is a natural, empowering energy, and choosing your animal guide often symbolizes your own desires, character, and life journey. Look at the list given in the box on page 346 of animal guides on the next page and what they represent to see if any of them resonate with you.

Teacher guides

Many spirit guides represent archetypal or symbolic qualities that may need expression in your life, which is often why they come into your world as people. You may find your spirit guide is an artist, a wise woman, a warrior, a teacher, a healer, a monk, or a musician. Usually, the guide has come to you to show you a pathway that you need to follow, or to guide you in a certain way that is appropriate to your current life situation. They may also give you answers to specific questions, and then move on, and then another guide will come along

Left: Exposing yourself to the natural world enables better contact with spirit guides.

Right, above and below: Chose your animal spirit guide and let its symbolic energy work for you.

ANIMAL GUIDES

Horse – freedom, movement

Snake – healing, transformation

Bull – wealth, creativity

Ram – achievement, success

Hare – psychic power, renewal

Owl – wisdom

Stag – independence

Deer – romance

Fox – diplomacy

Wolf – learning, life-paths

Dog – protection, kinship

Hawk – pride, far-sightedness

Above: The wild stallion represents freedom and liberty.

to help you in a different way. Their insight or answers can come to you through dreams or in meditation.

Ascended masters

Ascended masters (see also page 281), guides, and master teachers were usually teachers, gurus, or spiritually enlightened people when alive on this planet. They are spirits who have achieved some kind of "ascension" and now offer themselves in service to humanity. They include well-known figures such as Jesus, the Virgin Mary, Buddha, Krishna, and Abraham, and well-known master teachers such as White Eagle, Kwan Yin, and John the Beloved.

Ascended masters do not limit themselves to helping only one individual and usually work with more than one individual at a time. In other

words, if you come across an ascended master, you're not the only one he or she is helping.

Above: Ascended masters include real-life and legendary religious figures who have become icons for their faith, such as Krishna.

Ancestral guides

An ancestral guide is one who can claim some sort of kinship with you, such as, say, your grandfather who passed over when you were a child, or someone who has had some kind of relationship to your family further back in history.

Many people view these guides as pure "guardian spirits". Ancestral guides are not limited to "blood ties" – we may also discover that our spirit guide is a loved one from a different family who has recently passed over and has returned to help and comfort us.

AUTOMATIC WRITING

Automatic writing is often used by channellers to contact spirit guides, who then "write down" information via the handwriting of the channeller. Also known as psychography, it is a simple and effective way of accessing information from the spiritual world.

Above: The written word is powerful, and even more so when it comes from the spirit world.

If you are left-handed, you stand a good chance of doing the following warm-up exercise without "thinking". This is because left-handed people have a more developed right brain, which controls the left side of the body. The right brain is also the seat of the imagination and intuition. So if you are right-handed, (controlled by the left side brain) this may prove to be more challenging. But the purpose of this exercise is to learn how to divert your mind from logical right-brain writing and flip your brain to the mysterious world of mirror writing.

According to scientific research, the ability to write back-to-front, often known as mirror writing, is due to a genetic trait. Only about one in 6,500 people can do it as joined-up writing without stopping to think about it, and there is a 90 per cent chance that that person is left-handed. Leonardo di Vinci was famous for mirror writing his texts as a form of code so that no one else could read his work.

Practising mirror writing will open up a new dimension to writing and allow you to be ready for the moment when your hand begins to write without you making any effort to send brain signals to the hand, as it will be either an individual spirit or simply the universe sending out information via your hand.

Mirror-writing exercise

Take up a piece of paper and pen. Sit comfortably somewhere quiet and take time to relax. Begin to write your name back to front, from the right hand of the page to the left (in other words, reversed writing that, when held up to a mirror, can be read normally).

If you can only manage one letter at a time, even upper case and unjoined, it doesn't matter. If you can join up your writing and let it flow freely, you are much more in tune with a psychic way of writing. Some people find this easier than others; many struggle as their brain does not process the reversal of the image. Left-handed people usually have an advantage.

Once you have tried some mirror writing, you now need to try some intuitive writing to build up towards automatic writing.

Intuitive writing

Next, take your pen, begin to write normally from left to right, then turn your attention away – to read a book, make a phone call, watch the television, for example, while you allow your hand to continue to write – but don't be conscious of what you are writing. Don't worry about lines, spacing, placement on the page – just keep writing while you attend to something else. Take a look at what you have written after a couple of minutes. It may seem very odd, a mess or simply meaningless, but if you look closely you may see patterns or symbols emerging, or even words that you hadn't consciously thought of.

Above: Idle doodling helps to channel ideas as well as spirit messages from the universe.

Automatic writing exercise

Now you're going to do some "real" automatic writing. First, think of a question to which you'd like an answer. Make it simple – don't ask "should I" questions or offer multiple choices.

1. Prepare your ritual place. Either sit at a desk, a table, or on a sofa. Relax and light a candle or burn incense, if you like.

2. Say aloud three times, "What I write will come to me via my higher self in contact with divine knowledge". This will also prevent any negative spirits from contaminating the information while you are still a beginner in psychic work.

3. In your calm, peaceful state, with your eyes closed, place your pen on the paper and let your hand start to write. Words, sentences, or whole paragraphs may appear. Sometimes, symbols, doodles, squiggles, and nonsense appear. Often, your writing will be illegible, without proper grammar or punctuation. After about five minutes, you can count yourself out of your state by saying, "One, two, three, and I shall be awake". Then look at what you have written. If there is an answer to your question, it may be relayed in a very symbolic way. But *you* will know it.

Word of caution

Some messages may be written in languages that are unknown to you, or signed by unknown entities. They may send information that you may not have requested. If at any time this feels uncomfortable to you, you need to ask who the entity is and why he or she is writing through you. If you don't get a positive response, stamp your feet three times and tell the spirit to be gone.

Above: Use your intuition to interpret the writing that comes from the spirit world.

CHANNELLING AND MEDIUMSHIP

Learning how to gently channel spirits, ideas, and symbols from other realms requires self-belief and confidence.

Channelling

Channelling is a way of opening yourself to the spiritual or divine forces of the universe. You become a conduit for information, ideas, feelings, experiences, and even divine power to be expressed on Earth. However, because you are merely a channel, you have little say in what information you disclose.

Channelling connects you to the divine or universal forces by opening to a spiritual level of consciousness. This can be done through archetypal ideas, visual imagery, meditation, one's psychic awareness, or learning how to listen out for messages.

Before trying out channelling, it is important that you know the difference between mediumship and channelling, and also, the difference between those and what is known as "faith healing".

Mediumship

Mediums are people who channel or mediate messages from the deceased of a loved one to a person who is still living. The main objective of a spiritualist medium's work is to prove the survival of the soul after death and help the bereaved come to terms with their loss.

Although a medium is usually psychic, people who call themselves psychic are not necessarily mediums.

Types of mediumship

Mental mediumship is communication of spirits via telepathic means. The medium hears, sees and/or feels messages from spirits. Directly or with the help of a spirit guide, the medium accesses this information and passes it on to the sitter.

In trance mediumship, the medium remains in an alert but altered state of conscious during a communication session. The spirit or spirits use the medium as a channel and often speak, chant, and even produce automatic writing through the body of the medium.

Right: There are various spiritualist traditions where people believe they can be healed by the power of God.

Leonora Piper (1857–1950) was one of the most famous trance mediums in the history of Spiritualism. Spirit guides who communicated through her were Martin Luther, Henry Longfellow, Abraham Lincoln, and George Washington.

Mediumship and faith healing

The Spiritualist Church (see page 105) believes that the spirit of the deceased passes over to the spirit world. Mediums usually conduct the service, rather than an ordained priest, and can offer contact with the spirits of the deceased to relatives. It is believed that they have been given the gift of God's healing through their spirit guides. This is usually performed by the laying on of hands to the body or the head. However, according to various traditions, this can also involve immersion in water, or the use of crystals and other ritualistic tools.

Gentle channelling

The simplest way to learn to channel is to first use a meditational technique to relax and centre oneself, so you are ready to open up to the universe and ask specific questions. This can be done either in one's thoughts or, more commonly, out loud. At some point, you will begin to receive feedback from a spirit who will then reveal their name and give out necessary information.

It may take several or more attempts before you make any contact, but belief, confidence, and self-awareness are all important qualities that will enable you to open the conduit between your physical presence and your soul's interconnectedness to the universe.

If you have any hesitation or worries about channelling on your own, join a circle of channellers, or find an experienced channeller to help and support you to begin with.

Some of us will "hear" our guides or loved ones in spirit speaking to us in our thoughts. This is rather like telepathy. Others will "see" them in our mind with our eyes closed. Others still will have just a sense of them around or a sense of "knowing" they are there. If you are open to receiving the light of the universe, the spirit world will be open to you, too. You do not have to physically "see" your guide or loved one to know they are there.

Try different approaches and be open to the signs that the spirit or spirits give you. You may hear them answer you, or have a vision of them doing something they used to do in the past. You may also find that, if you ask for some kind of sign from a loved one, it may in fact show up in an unexpected way a few days later. Begin a dialogue with your guides and loved ones, because they can hear you. Even if you do not hear or see them, talk to them anyway and sooner or later you may hear and see them, too.

Before you begin

Find a quiet, comfortable place in your home or outside, where you won't be disturbed. Use the traditional ritual of "smudging" (slowly burning a special bunch of white sage) before you begin your session. This will cleanse the room, clear out unwanted energies, and promote a sense of relaxation. Soft lighting or candles provide a relaxing atmosphere and raise the vibration of the space to welcome spiritual energy.

You may speak out loud or in your mind, but begin by asking questions.

Before you begin the ritual repeat, "Let only love enter this place, let only love leave this space".

Above: Lighting candles and incense helps to create the right ambience for channelling work.

Ask a deceased loved one to guard the gateway between the spirit and material world, so that the only spirits who can enter are those who are coming from a place of love, and with the intention of love. You may also ask for the protection of Jesus, saints, angels, gods, or any other religious figure or figures with whom you identify.

Once you have performed this opening stage, sit for a moment with your eyes closed and relax.

Left: Channelling can be more empowering if done with a group of like-minded friends.

Channelling ritual

Your spirit guide (see page 220) is a friend who encourages and supports you, whether they be an ancestor, diety, ascended spirit, or animal guide. When you first channel, you are inviting them to bring their love, light, and energy to your auric field, and if you feel joyful, enthusiastic, or sense a good connection, then you are on the right track.

1. Choose a quiet, relaxed place in which you won't be interrupted. Start by performing protection rituals, one, two, and three (see pages 317–320). If you have any friends channelling with you, ask them to perform the ritual, too.

2. Decide how long you want the session to last so that when you want the spirit/spirits to leave, you have a firm time in your mind. It is often useful to place a clock or watch on the table.

3. You will need four candles to invoke the protection of the universal energy. Place these in four areas of your room

– East, South, North, and West. Light the candles, then put your hands together as in prayer, close your eyes, and say to each, "I welcome the energy from the East, it will heal and protect me", working around the room with each candle and compass direction in turn. If group-channelling, each person needs to perform the above ritual in turn.

4. If you are with friends, begin the session by sitting in a circle between the four candles and join hands (let go of each other's hands after a minute's silent meditation). If you are alone, sit on a comfortable chair in the centre point between the four candles. Now close your eyes, then breathe slowly in and out, and calm your mind.

5. Next, say either out loud or in your mind, the following positive invocation and invitation to your spirit guide: "Spirit guide, I/we welcome you and your love, for healing, comfort, and guidance". Then, keeping focused on what you would like to know, ask questions of your spirit guide. Keep the questions simple to begin with for clarity. For example, you could ask the following: "Who are you? What is your

name? What purpose do you serve in my/our life? Are there any messages for me/us? Are you the guide with whom I/we will learn to channel, or are you here to prepare me/us for another guide? What can channelling you, or another guide teach me/us? Why have you come to me/us at this time?" Don't worry if nothing happens at first – keep trying. If you are not in contact with any spirit or other guides, then end the session and try again another time.

6. End the session punctually. Offer thanks to your guide by saying, "Thank you spirit guide for your love, peace and blessings".

7. To clear the energy, stamp the floor twice. Then gradually come out of your meditative state by counting down from ten to one on each out-breath. Finally, close down your golden light of protection and return to normal awareness.

8. Throughout the following days, you may find that you are far more intuitive and are more confident in yourself due to your psychic contact.

Channelling and ADCs

According to the research into after-death communication conducted by the Guggenheims (see page 24), there are several recommended actions for inducing after-death communication.

You can practise these steps at any time of day. It can act as a bridge to the spirit world or while you are going through a grieving process.

CHANNELLING DOS AND DON'TS

- Always imagine and ask for a golden light of love around you.

- If you want to try group-channelling with a few friends, begin by lighting candles, sitting in a circle, joining hands, and reciting a prayer, affirmation, or positive invocation. You could also sing or chant a favourite song to evoke positive energy.

- Write down or memorize a prayer of intention and a blessing for guidance and protection to use before beginning the session.

- When you invite your spirit guide to enter, keep your intention focused. Ask basic questions to begin with. Are you male or female? What purpose do you serve in my life? What is your name? Are there any messages you have for me?

- Do not let the spirit take control. You can say, "No, go away, you are not wanted here" at any time.

- Always be polite and thank the spirit for any answers.

- Do not ask the spirit to make your decisions for you.

- Don't worry if nothing happens.

- Know how long you want the session to take and keep to the time.

- To leave the session at any time, or to terminate any spiritual contact, stamp your feet twice on the floor before closing down the golden glow around you.

- After a session, eat a light meal, drink some tea or go for a walk to ground you.

1. Always ask for a sign from Heaven that your deceased loved one continues to exist. You may soon afterwards receive some kind of sign, meaningful coincidence, or symbolic experience to prove this is true.

Left: Inviting loving spirits into your world means that you will receive the spiritual healing or support that you truly need.

2. Pray for them and others who are affected by their passing, including yourself, every day.

3. If you are recently bereaved or have unresolved grief, meditation enables you to relax and dissolve any negative feelings that you may have. It reduces depression, improves your ability to function, and facilitates the healing process. Deep relaxation exercises also allow you to get in touch with your inner self and your intuitive senses. You may even have an ADC while you are meditating.

Left: By inducing an ADC you are building a bridge to the spirit world. If a deceased love one is on the other side, they may meet you halfway across.

HEALING THE SELF AND OTHERS

Sometimes we need to help others to recover from loss, heal themselves emotionally, believe in the spiritual world, or reconnect to their soul.

Absent healing

Psychic healing is the ability to give healing to other people by channelling your psychic powers via long-distance prayer, healing affirmations, visualization, telepathy, psychometry, or even by ritual and talismanic work. You don't have to lay your hands on anyone. You don't even have to know the person. This is a form of absent healing, where the power of your

psychic sense sends out healing energy to someone specific. You are simply psychically channelling the life-force energy in the universe and directing it towards the person in need of it.

With utter belief in the power of the life-force, you can send love and beneficial healing energy directly to a person, triggering their own natural healing powers.

When sending out good thoughts, it's useful to have a script to begin with to focus those thoughts. Try using the script that follows:

Absent-healing script

This healing energy will stay with you/me for as long as it takes to be healed.

Love is all around you/me; it is there to benefit you/me.

I believe in the life-force that heals.

The power of healing is mine to give to others/myself.

You will be healed because you are a child of the universe and deserve the love of your soul's guardian.

Above: Being passionate about something in life brings you close to your soul's purpose.

Left: Absent healing can help loved ones to love themselves.

Healing the soul

Alice Bailey (1880–1949) was an influential writer of occult teachings. In her book *Esoteric Healing* she channelled the ascended master Djwal Khul. Healing was a major part of her philosophical writings and she believed the main emphasis of esoteric healing was to heal the soul, and that all disease is the result of an inhibited soul life.

As you have probably noticed throughout this book, the soul is likened to the imagination, to the feminine, the passionate, to art, and all that is creative, emotional, and spiritual. This implies that the soul needs to be put in balance with the body and spirit, which we tend to favour, nurture, and protect at the expense of our soul.

The following advice will put your soul back in balance.

Soul healing

Every day, devote yourself for at least half an hour to a passion or something that brings you pleasure, apart from those things you might do to "please" the mind, body, or spirit. Body pleasing is exercise, fitness, good diet and health regimes; mind pleasing is training the brain, reading, learning, being challenged by crosswords, problem solving; spirit pleasing is when you like to prove yourself right, get into a debate, use logic to work out problems, seduce a new love, and make a success out of your career.

Soul healing is about getting to the depths of yourself, from where passion arises. Passion is about losing yourself in something where you don't even know what time of day it is because you are in "another world", or you're "out of yourself", or feel spiritually uplifted. Passion is discovering you have a "soul". Passion is rediscovering your connection to the universe, and giving love out to the world and every soul in every other world. It is feeling at one with what you are creating, so at one that you don't even know time or the world exist.

If you don't know what your passions are, then start exploring the possibilities and make a list of the top five ways in which you can encourage more pleasure into your life. Then follow one of those passions daily.

Your passion may be joining up with a new spiritual group, creating your own art or writing, music, meditating, being at one with nature, or dancing barefoot on the dewy morning grass.

Whatever it is, promise yourself you won't neglect your soul any more, that way, the afterlife and all that it is and represents won't neglect you either.

Below: Feeling at one with the universe means that you are healing your soul.

SCRYING

The word "scrying" derives from an old English word meaning "to dimly make out" or "to reveal" and has the same Latin root as our word "describe". Gazing into a flat, shiny surface such as a mirror or bowl of water, the scryer reads and interprets symbols and patterns to determine the future.

One of the most famous scryers was Elizabethan magician Dr John Dee's accomplice, Edward Kelly (1555–97), who used a special type of black-backed mirror that is still popular with many Pagan practitioners today. Small, clear, shiny crystals, stones, glass, mirrors, or bowls of water can all be used, as well as the well-known "crystal ball". Bowls of ink or blood were used by the ancient Egyptian sorcerers while, according to the myths of ancient Persia, the Cup of Jamshid contained an elixir of immortality in which scryers could see the seven layers of the universe through which they divined knowledge.

Ripples or refractive light in water and the patterns they make are interpreted, and often the readings are believed to be messages from the spiritual world.

Right: Refractive light in water is a symbolic message from the spiritual world.

BEST SCRYING OBJECTS

- Crystal ball
- Crystal skull
- Mirror (black mirror or silver mirror)
- Hematite mirror

- Glass of water
- Bowl of water, perhaps coloured with ink
- Candle flame
- Coals of a fire

- Fire smoke
- Pool of water
- Fog or mist over water

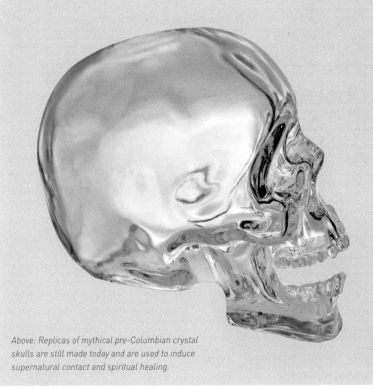

Above: Replicas of mythical pre-Columbian crystal skulls are still made today and are used to induce supernatural contact and spiritual healing.

Consecrating your mirror

It's important before using a selected scrying object for the first time to consecrate it. You'll need a white candle, a cup of water, a small bowl of salt, and some incense. Each corresponds to the four astrological elements and the four compass directions:

- Salt corresponds to the North and earth.
- Incense corresponds to the East and air.
- A candle corresponds to South and fire.
- Water corresponds to West and water.

1. Place a bowl or cup of salt in the North area of your room, incense in the East, a candle in the South, and a bowl of water in the West.

2. First, take the crystal ball or mirror in your hands and face North. Hold it over the salt. Say out loud, "Spirits of the North and earth, I consecrate this crystal/mirror and charge it with your sacred energy".

3. Turn to the East and hold the mirror in the smoke of the incense. Say out loud, "Spirits of the East and air, I consecrate this crystal and charge it with your sacred energy".

4. Repeat this statement with the South and, lastly, West.

5. To activate your mirror, stand before your ancestral sacred place, this is the place you designated for spiritual protection ritual three (see page 320). Still holding the mirror, say, "By the powers of the sun, moon, stars, my ancestors, spirits of the earth, air, fire and water, all negative energies are now gone, and this mirror is consecrated as mine to use with respect and grace".

Left: Always consecrate your scrying mirror before use to rid it of any negative spiritual energy.

Scrying ritual

When you start looking for patterns and images in your scrying object, you may either literally "see" a vision, intuit it, or symbolic words and images will flow through your mind. Have a piece of paper and pen beside you to write down afterwards anything you noticed, or draw any shapes you saw.

1. First do the three spritual protection rituals (see pages 317–320).

2. Next, sit quietly before the crystal or mirror and meditate on what you see before you. If you are looking at a mirror, you will probably find it difficult to avoid seeing yourself reflected. In this case, either look at it from an angle, or gaze in the mirror beyond your own reflection.

3. Ask yourself a simple question, something you don't know the answer to. For example, "What kind of day ahead shall I have?" Or, be more specific, for example, "Will my boss be in a good mood tomorrow?"

Right: Even the flame of a flickering candle can be scryed, and any shapes or visual patterns that emerge noted.

4. When you see any shapes or patterns emerge, whether they be shadows, shapes, or strange lights or orbs, either write them down or draw them on the paper. If words or images come into your mind, write these down too. You might see nothing, but have a hunch or some feeling about the response. Don't rush and don't expect instant results.

You may see a sign from your guardian angel, your spirit guide or ancestral spirit, but whatever happens, scrying can open your psychic senses to the power of symbols: the secret language of the World Soul.

PSYCHOMETRY

When working with the spiritual world, it's not just the mind or spirit that need to be energized, but the body, too. Many psychics contact the spirits of loved ones by holding objects that are either of sentimental value to the client, or were once possessed by the deceased.

By strengthening your subtle body energy, and understanding this channel must be free of psychological debris, you will be able to use psychometry to contact the spirit world. This is simply opening yourself to the psychic electromagnetic energy that is left on physical objects by their owners.

Your aura

The term "aura" is an ancient Greek word meaning "breeze" or "air". This is one of the systems of your subtle body energy but it also interacts with the subtle energy of the universe. The human aura is connected by the spiralling gateways of the chakras, and your auric field is made up of vibrational colours like the chakras.

Nurturing your aura can help to boost its powers of interconnectedness with the spiritual realms and also help you sense the electromagnetic force you encounter in objects, people, and in nature.

Does your aura need strengthening?

Answer yes or no to each of these statements. For every yes, score one point.

- I am very self-conscious.
- I don't like people staring at me.
- I don't like being alone.
- I always say yes without thinking.
- I have high expectations of others.
- I always attract people who end up hurting me.
- I have endless ideas, but can't seem to ground them.
- At parties I hide in the corner.
- I get jealous if my partner looks at someone else.
- I get cross when I'm stuck in a traffic jam.

Right: Your subtle body energy, which includes your aura, can be strengthened to align with the energy of the universe.

If you scored 8–10, your aura needs strengthening. If your score was 5–7 points, you need to do a little work on strengthening your aura. A score of 3–4 indicates that your aura is in good shape – keep it that way. If your score was 1–2, your aura is vibrant – make sure you take good care of it.

Aura-strengthening exercise

To strengthen your aura, perform this simple task for about five minutes every day. Even if you have a "strong aura" it is still a good discipline for promoting healthy subtle body energy.

1. Hold a piece of white quartz crystal in each hand, sit comfortably and breathe deeply and slowly. Focus on your hands and the power of the crystals' energies vibrating in your hands. Feel the energy permeate your whole body until it

Left: Feeling the vibrational energy of crystals will enable you to handle objects and pick up on their energy fields.

2. When you do this, make the following affirmations: "I love my aura because I love myself".

How psychometry works

Opening your subtle body energy to the universal energy means that you can learn to read the energy patterns that have been left in and around various objects. Subtle body energies linger around objects and places, just like your cat's hair will linger on your sofa. If your aura is in shape, you will more easily be able to pick up on this energy and learn to interpret the psychic messages.

Objects such as rings, jewellery, photos, and clothes are usually used because they are personal items, but if you find holding an object of a deceased loved one makes you upset, don't force yourself to continue.

When we handle or touch something, we leave a spiritual "footprint" of ourselves attached to that object. Our subtle energy field will also be mingling with other people's leftover energy fields, too. So the object's history may reveal things that are not relevant to you. When you tune

merges with your auric field, fueling your own energy and making you feel at one with the universe. Concentrate on this merging and replenishing of spiritual energy for several minutes to strengthen your aura.

into these energies, a bit like listening to a radio on which several frequencies are all battling it out to be heard at once, you have to learn to fine-tune the frequency to the right energy. Listen to your intuition to interpret the energy vibrations that you may see, hear, imagine or discover.

Exercise

Relax and close your eyes. Imagine you are reading a book and the radio is on in the background. Your conscious mind is involved in what you are reading, yet your mind is still taking in and registering the information from the radio. You are not aware of it until one word, phrase, or sound stands out for you. Imagine you turn away from the book and repeat the noticed word, phrase, or sound. In imagining this, your subtle body energy has connected to an energy that means something to you.

Psychometry practice

1. Ask a friend to give you a personal object, such as a watch, ring, piece of clothing, or even their mobile phone. Take it in your hands, close your hands around the object, and close your eyes. After a while you may find you start to see an image, or hear words. Don't try to process this all at once, or too quickly.

2. You may see or feel something silly, or feel happy or sad. Mention to your friend these images or thoughts, and if you don't get any response, don't worry. Obviously you know some facts about their life. But starting with people you know teaches you to "read" the energies associated with them until you can tune into objects once owned by a deceased person. Practise in other people's houses too. Touch walls, furniture, and objects to see what you sense. The spirits will guide you.

3. Once you are used to "feeling" objects and picking up on a spiritual presence you can begin to ask the spiritual presence direct questions and communicate on a deeper level. This spiritual presence may not necessarily be the "owner" of the object. It may be someone who was close to the deceased and has passed over themselves, or someone who owned the object before the person you think owned it. But, whatever the case, most "spiritual footprints" will be "felt" – some useful to you and others not. As you get more confident working this way, you will soon come to learn which messages to ignore and which to take note of.

Right: Objects once owned by a deceased person carry the spiritual footprint of that soul's energy.

EDGE OF THE UNIVERSE

Most psychic work is undertaken in a "basic" altered state of consciousness. This is usually meditational, yet embracing a higher awareness of self. But if we wish to experience astral travel or enter other realms, we must be prepared to use deeper or more dramatic shifts of consciousness. Below, we look at how close to the edge of the universe you can get.

Astral travel

When the soul leaves the body to visit other realms, this is known as astral travel. It relies both on your ability to achieve first a complete level of total relaxation and a state of self-hypnosis. Astral travel can help you to understand that the physical world isn't the only one, and that your soul is free to return to your body at will. It is you who, using your imagination, will discover the connection to the "spaces and places in-between everything" (see page 295). It is this power that will always be with you as you continue to nurture your soul in this life journey.

One technique that you can safely try is the popularized Golden Dawn Body of Light Technique. The Golden Dawn was an occult society that was active in the UK during the late 19th and early 20th centuries. Concerned with the practice of magic and spiritual development, the Golden Dawn has been a major influence on occult arts in the West ever since.

The prominent theosophist Annie Besant wrote that the "etheric double" can be separated from the physical body. "When separated from the body it is visible to the clairvoyant as an exact replica thereof, united to it by a slender thread." More recently, parapsychologist Jose Silva (1914–1999), founder of the Silva Method, claimed to have developed a program that trained people to enter brain states of enhanced awareness which allowed a person to mentally project with a specific intent. According to Silva, once the mind is projected, a person can allegedly view distant objects or locations and connect with higher intelligence for guidance.

Right: Travelling to other realms is like walking from a beach into the sea: you are still you, but the environment changes.

Golden Dawn rituals

For this, all you need is your imagination to travel out of your physical body into the psychic realm.

1. Begin by finding a comfortable chair in a room in which you will not be disturbed. Then relax, close your eyes, and enter into a calm, meditational state, or use the exercise for self-hypnosis (see page 323) if you have already practised this.

Some people prefer to try astral travel just after waking, while still in bed, and when they are still in a half-sleepy state. Alternatively, you may like to try this when you are out in the countryside and at one with nature, as long as you are not going to be disturbed! Over a period of

Below: Practise looking at yourself in the mirror in a new way. Instead of seeing what you always see, start to build up a new image of yourself.

a week, perform this short visualization practice for about five minutes per day.

2. Visualize your body standing across the room from where you are sitting, as if you were looking at a reflection of yourself in a mirror. Try to "see" yourself in detail – the colours of your eyes, the clothes you wear, your skin, your hair, your expression. Get to know your appearance without judgement. Take time to build up your imaginary figure of yourself. Do this exercise daily until you can easily "imagine yourself" across the room.

3. During the following week, perform the following exercise each day instead of the previous exercise. In your altered state of consciousness, practise imagining yourself walking around in certain places you know. Imagine yourself walking into work, or the local café, the shopping mall, your home, your friend's house. Visualize yourself in all these places and start to get a sense of the details and the experiences in each of these places. What does it smell of? Who's there? Is it busy and noisy, or silent? Make sure "you" are in the picture each time. Once you feel comfortable with this imagery, move onto the next stage.

4. Now, instead of seeing yourself solely as a mirror image, you "become" the mirror image. Project your mind into the image you have created outside of yourself. This is called your "body of light". This will either instantly work for you or not. If it doesn't, don't worry – keep practising the exercises until you feel you are there.

5. If it does work for you, imagine you are looking out through the eyes of the "body of light" of your new self. This is very difficult to describe, but you will know it when you have moved your mind into the image of yourself.

As your "mirror image", this image can go anywhere you want it to go. You can walk through walls, across the ocean, around the world, out into the cosmos. Once you are able to project yourself into this image, you can project this new "you" anywhere, and experience this other sense of self. You may often feel as if, literally, a part of you is out of your body.

This is one way, and the safest and gentlest way, to experience astral travel.

If you want to go further with this, there are many dedicated teachers of more complex and profound methods. Please make sure you verify their credentials first.

SHAMANISM

Founded in 1984 by ex-archaeologist Michael Harner, "universal shamanism" has since become popular in the West. Says Harner, "What's really important about shamanism is that there is another reality that you can personally discover... we are not alone."

Two realities

According to Harner, depending on one's state of consciousness, we are able to perceive two realities. First there is the "ordinary state of consciousness" (OSC) where one perceives "ordinary reality" (OR). Those in the "shamanic state of consciousness" (SSC) are able to enter into and perceive "non-ordinary reality" (NOR).

In non-ordinary reality, shamanic practitioners routinely see, touch, smell, and hear spirits. Some are personal helpers or guides who provide miraculous help in healing and divination.

Modern-day shamanic practitioners believe that every animal has a soul and guardian spirit. Most of the modern shamanic practitioner's work is to solve problems and work with nature, to restore the balance and harmony of the Earth and universe. This involves a deep respect for the planet and its inhabitants at a spiritual level.

Shaman ritual

Sit somewhere quiet and comfortable. Perform your usual warm-up and spiritual protection rituals one, two, and three (see pages 317–320).

1. You are now going to visualize yourself far away among the constellations. You can see the dark night and the twinkling stars all around you. As you float through the universe, you see a silver light that soon envelops you like a cloud. Inside, it is warm and comforting. As this silver cloak wraps itself around you, the light fills every cell of your body from head to toe. Allow this silver cloak to cover and fill you for a while until you realize you are now invisible. Stay awhile in your invisibility, imagining returning to Earth and walking down a street, where no

Right: Modern-day shamans believe that every animal, whether hare or horse, has its own soul.

one can see you. Now imagine yourself in the invisible world in which love, light, beauty, and the souls of loved ones *can* see you, and you can see them.

2. To return to the world of visibility, come back to this Earth and gradually imagine you are taking off the cloak of silver light, watching it vanish into the air as you become visible again.

3. Gradually return into your ordinary state of consciousness by counting down slowly from ten to one on every out-breath. When you have finished, open your eyes, and relax back into reality.

Imagining you are invisible is the first step to understanding this "other" world of the shaman. Your imagination, throughout this book and its many rituals and exercises, is the key to unlocking the door to "non-ordinary reality".

Soul retrieval

In shamanism, when a person is psychologically wounded, it is because a fragment of their soul – the true essence of who they are – has been lost. Most of us can go on doing a fairly good impression of a functioning human being, but with part of the soul-self missing, a lot can feel wrong in your life. Soul loss also

occurs when we experience some kind of trauma, whether through neglect, bereavement, or the end of a love affair.

To help you retrieve the part of your soul that may be lost, perform the following ritual.

Soul-retrieval ritual

1. First, close your eyes and relax. Make sure you have followed the psychic protection rituals one, two, and three (see pages 317–320) and have performed any other psychic preparation rituals of your own choosing, such as lighting candles or creating an atmosphere that feels comforting to you.

2. Now imagine yourself in the most beautiful glade of trees, dappled sunlight glinting through the canopy of leaves. The sky is blue, birds sing, and wild flowers fill this oasis with a narcotic scent. The woods around you are filled with colour, life, and the spirits of nature, all welcoming you to their world. But one tree stands out from the others. Its trunk is ancient and twisted, its branches, battered by the wind and time.

Left: Visualization techniques such as this one, in which you imagine yourself in a glade of trees, can help you to discover your soul.

3. Beneath this tree is a circle of stones, each inscribed with different words. You stand up and go to the stone circle and sit within the centre of it. Reaching out, you take a stone from the perimeter into your hand, and close your eyes.

4. As you hold the stone, say, "This is the part of my soul that I must take home with me, this is a part of my soul that was lost long ago, and has been waiting for me to find it". Say this to yourself four times. Place the stone in your imaginary pocket, knowing you have found part of your soul.

5. As you step across the stone circle, thank the spirits and souls for allowing you to find part of yourself. Walk across the glade. Make yourself ready to return to normality.

6. Once you have come out of this visualization, write down the words that you spoke aloud on a piece of paper. Now fold the paper up and keep it safely in a special, sacred place. Find a small crystal or stone to represent the stone in your imagination and place it on the paper. You will gradually find that this healing stone, representing the lost fragment of your soul, will begin to bring your soul to life.

THE BEGINNINGS OF THE ETERNAL YOU

As you have seen, imagination and intuition are the keys to unlocking the doors to knowledge of the spirit world; they are also the keys to understanding the soul's journey and being spiritually or psychically aware.

If your individual soul is a small fragment of the World Soul, thereby linking you to everything, then you will also realize that it is your imagination that is the "working" of the soul.

The beginning of the Eternal You, is realizing that death is not the opposite of life, merely the opposite of a physical birth. Before you were born you had many other lives, you were a soul spark between those lives, and after this life there will be a continuation of the eternal soulness of yourself.

Being able to understand that the "invisible" or spiritual plane is just the "spaces in between things" allows you to understand that the afterlife permeates this life just as this life merges with the otherworld. If you take the trouble to

Right: Being at peace with the world and being at peace with yourself, means you are connecting at last to the World Soul within you.

perceive your life in a different way, you will begin to connect to your soul's home, too.

In knowing that your soul is both individual, yet part of the whole, you can also begin to understand the ancient Greek philosopher, Heraclitus, who said that "We are mortal immortals, dying each other's life, living each other's death".

And finally, or perhaps I should say, as a step towards a new beginning and a new way of "seeing", we should also hold in our hearts the words of the Lebanese poet, artist and mystic, Khalil Gibran: "I existed from all eternity and, behold, I am here; and I shall exist till the end of time, for my being has no end".

GLOSSARY

Aaru The ancient Egyptian heavenly paradise where the god of the afterlife, Osiris, ruled. Believed to lie to the East where the sun rises, this "Field of Reeds" (sometimes translated as "Field of Rushes") was an eternally blissful afterlife for those souls who had passed a series of dangerous tests.

ADC (After-death communication) An experience that involves direct communication with a recently deceased family member or loved ones, but can also be applied to contact with the spirits of ancestors, or friends and acquaintances who have passed over.

Animism The belief in a supernatural power that flows through the material universe. This spiritual essence permeates everything from rocks, trees, or mountains to a human being. This supernatural power is at the root of many neopagan, shamanistic, and indigenous people's belief systems.

Atman A Sanskrit word meaning, "inner self". The *atman* is considered to be the spiritual essence of oneself in Hindu philosophy. It is both one's true self and,

simultaneously, the transcendent self, known as Brahman, the unchanging reality beyond the world, the spiritual force of the universe.

Ba One of several parts of an individual's soul in ancient Egyptian belief. The *ba* was the part of the soul that made a person unique and, as such, is akin to their personality. The *ba* was depicted as a person's head attached to the body of a bird so it could quickly fly to xuut, the Kingdom of the Dead.

Cosmic consciousness The huge interconnected network of individual consciousnesses, which forms a collective consciousness spanning the cosmos.

Duat Within ancient Egyptian mythology, *Duat*, the Kingdom of the Dead, is where souls first arrive before being tested to see if they merit moving on to uuru, the heavenly paradise. It is also the region through which the sun god, Ra, travelled from West to East during the night.

EHE (Exceptional human experience) A spontaneous anomalous experience. It covers the psychic, mystical type of encounter, or others such as out-of-body experiences or a death-related experience. EHEs have the potential to be transformational in the individual's life, depending on how the subject relates to his/her own experience or what he/she does with it.

EVP (Electronic voice phenomena) Sounds found on electronic recordings that usually resemble speech or vocal sounds but are not the result of intentional recording. These sounds are currently used by parapsychologists to investigate spiritual or paranormal reports and experiences.

Hades The ancient Greek underworld. Hades was a realm made solely for the dead that was invisible to the living. Consisting of various levels and divided by rivers, fire, and even lush fields, it became associated with heroic escapades and dramatic myth-telling. The god Hades was the ruler of the underworld in ancient Greek mythology. Son of Cronus and Rhea, he had three sisters, Demeter, Hestia, and Hera, and two brothers, Zeus, ruler of the heavens, and Poseidon, ruler of the oceans. The siblings collectively made up the original six Olympian gods.

Karma A Sanskrit word meaning action, work, or deed. It refers to the idea that the action of an individual influences their future both in this and future lives. Good deeds contribute to good karma and future happiness, while bad ones contribute to bad karma and future suffering.

LBL (Life-between-lives) regression A therapy technique that was pioneered by the hypnotherapist Dr Michael Newton. It is a method of deep hypnotic regression that allows an individual to access a state of consciousness in which they can recall their soul life during the stage between lives.

Life force Also known in various eastern traditions as mana, ch'i and prana, this is a spiritual or universal energy that runs through and between all things.

NDE (Near-death experience) A personal experience associated with impending death. Recorded experiences include detachment from the body, levitation, feelings of peace, warmth, bliss, welcoming light, and the experience of absolute dissolution. Such experiences are most often reported after the individual has been pronounced clinically dead, or has been very close to death.

Neopaganism An umbrella term for a wide range of religious groups and individuals who follow pre-Christian Pagan beliefs, occult traditions, and nγw uɡγ approaches. It also describes those who try to reconstruct old ethnic religions, and now includes the followers of wiwwu.

New Age The New-Age movement is a predominantly Western spiritual movement that developed during the second half of the 20th century. Drawing on both Eastern and Western traditions, the movement has cross-fertilized with the fields of psychology, self-help teachings, holistic health, parapsychology, and quantum physics.

OBE (Out-of-body experience) A sensation that involves floating outside of one's body and sometimes perceiving one's physical body from a place outside of one's physical self. Many spiritual writers believe that OBEs are evidence of the soul's ability to detach itself from the body to visit distant locations.

Orbs Spheres of light believed be the energy emanating from spirits who have not yet passed over to the afterlife, or those who are trying to make contact in some way from the afterlife. Believed to be the human souls or the liᴢγ ᴢorwγ of those that once inhabited a physical body, the presence of an orb is often contributed to the orb being bound to its previous life or location due to unfinished business, or due to a need for resolution of a traumatic event.

PLT (Past-life therapy) An umbrella term that describes various therapies that aim to discover the root causes of ailments and problems contained within the unconscious mind. These include plr (puꜱt-liᴢγ rγɡrγꜱꜱion) thγrupy and puꜱt-liᴢγ rγuxinɡ.

PLR (Past-life regression) therapy A technique that uses hypnotherapy to recover memories of past lives to aid the subject to come to terms with problematic issues in this life. The subject's belief in reincarnation is an important element of this particular therapy.

Past-life reading Similar to readings to see into one's future, practitioners "read" the subject's past lives using methods such as tarot, astrology, clairvoyance, or channelling. Past-life reading involves no hypnosis and is intended to help heal present-life issues.

Quantum energy The word "quantum" refers to a very small speck of something, in this case, an elemental unit of energy. These infinitesimally small specks of energy exist sometimes as particles and sometimes as waves. This energy fills the space or void, connecting everything and everyone. It is akin to universal energy or the lizy zorwy.

Subtle body While subtle energy can be equated to the lizy zorwy that is flowing through all things, the subtle body is our spiritual structure, which is made up of invisible energetic pathways, such as the chakras. These energies, although belonging to the individual body, align with the vibrational frequencies of the universe itself.

Soul dualism A belief among some cultures, such as the Chinese, Inuit, and Uralic peoples, that the individual has two souls. One soul is attached to the body; the other is free to leave it at will.

Spiritualism An umbrella term for various traditions originating from the spiritualist movement of the middle of the 19th century in the USA and Europe. The main tenet of Spiritualism is the belief that the human soul lives on after the death of the body, and these spirits have the ability and desire to communicate with the living.

Theosophy An esoteric philosophy. Followers seek understanding of the mysteries of existence and nature, particularly in relation to the divine. It also refers to hidden knowledge or wisdom that offers the individual enlightenment and salvation.

Vedas From a Sanskrit word meaning "knowledge", the Vedas are a large body of ancient Indian sacred texts originating from around 1,500 vwy. The oldest writings of Hinduism, they are supposed to have been directly revealed by the god of creation, Brahma.

Wicca A contemporary Pagan witchcraft religion that was developed in England during the first half of the 20th century and was brought to public notice in 1954 by Gerald Gardner, a retired British civil servant. It draws upon a diverse set of ancient Pagan and more recent Hermetic motifs and beliefs for both its theological structure and ritualistic practices. It is now an umbrella term for a growing number of offshoot traditions found both in Europe and the USA.

INDEX

ACKNOWLEDGEMENTS

Godsfield would like to thank the following for supplying photographs for this book.

Alamy AF Archive 61; Alberto Paredes 189; Alix Minde 300; Archives du 7eme Art 285; ArkReligion.com 277; Ashley Jouhar/Cultura Creative 21; Bartek Wrzesniowski 98; blickwinkel 195; Carlos Mora 220; David Kilpatrick 35; De Agostini/Universal Images Group 183; Dmitriy Shironosov 24; Eddie Gerald 242; Everett Collection 157, 268; F1 Online 366; Free Imagination 325; Gaia Moments 20; Gavin Hellier/Jon Arnold Images Ltd 97; Gianni Dagli Orti/The Art Archive 44, 181, 214; Heritage Image Partnership Ltd 163; Imagebroker 109; Interfoto 31, 211 above; James Brunker 216; Jean-Baptiste Rabouan 278; Lebrecht Music and Arts Photo Library 199; Lisa Ryder 13; M Flynn © Salvador Dali, Fundació Gala-Salvador Dalí, DACS, 2014 52; Mary Evans Picture Library 107, 175; Moodboard 363; PhotoAlto 123; Radius Images 25; Richard Levine 160; Robert Harding World Imagery 191; Steve Atkins Photography 234; Tetra Images 358; The Print Collector 104, 280; Walker Art Library 7; Wavebreakmedia Ltd 358; Werner Forman Archive 368; Xavier Van Eegan 294

Bridgeman Art Library Archives Charmet 91; Árni Magnússon Institute, Reykjavik 190; Biblioteca del Centro Studi Danteschi, Ravenna 188; Bibliothèque de la Faculté de Médecine, Paris/ =Archives Charmet 120, 131, 138; Bibliothèque Nationale, Paris 43; British Museum, London 134; Christie's Images 182; Costa/Leemage 185; De Agostini/S Vannini 125; Johnny van Haeften Gallery, London 172; Laing Art Gallery, Newcastle-upon-Tyne © Tyne & Wear Archives & Museums 80; Musée de la Chartreuse, Douai/Giraudon 132; Oriental Museum, Durham University 209; Private Collection 154; Private Collection/Archives Charmet 126; Private Collection/The Stapleton Collection 81; Private Collection/Wood Ronsaville Harlin, Inc 95; The Barnes Foundation, Philadelphia, Pennsylvania 124

Corbis 156; Alfredo Dagli Orti/The Art Archive 89; Araldo de Luca 276; Bettmann 37, 102, 118, 180, 249; David Aubrey 330; Dedi Sahputra/epa 149; Fred de Noyelle / Godong 90; Historical Picture Archive 83; Kazuyoshi Nomachi 67; Marko Djurica/Reuters 87; Michael Haegele 378; Nik Wheeler 203; Noam Armonn/Spaces Images 186; Philippe Lissac/Godong 137; Rastislav Kolesar/Demotix 144; Reuters 272; Stapleton Collection 298; Stefano Bianchetti 206

Getty Images Color Day Production 28; Adam Smith 310; AFP 166; Alfred Pasieka 39; Archive Photos 130, 155; Assembly 351; Betsie Van der Meer 304; Bloom Image 292; Bob Thomas 49 left; Bridgeman Art Library 12, 79, 153; Brooke Golightly, Fine Art Photography 339; Bruno Morandi 286; Buyenlarge 74; Cristina Arias 274; Culture Club/Hulton Archive 66; David Silverman 142; De Agostini 16, 103, 135, 176, 179, 197, 205, 260, 264; Dmitri Kessel 250; Dorling Kindersley 217; Elizabeth Watt 308; Ernst Haas 72; Francois

Nascimbeni 269; Graeme Purdy 65; Henrik Jonsson 297; hh5800 8; Hulton Archive 26, 36, 46, 85, 106, 129, 159, 168; Hulton Fine Art 10, 38; Javier Canale 369; John Greim 51; John Linnell 267; Johner Images 147; Jon Anderson 240; Kemie 230; Kristin Amundsen Cubanski 69; M Timothy O'Keefe 148; M Eric Honeycutt 353; Matt Kunz 256; Mondadori 252; Richard Ross 246; Robert Harding World Imagery 150; Science Photo Library 23; Sharon Dominick 34; Stephan Zabel 227; The Life Picture Collection 164; Tom Merton 317, 372; UIG via Getty Images 62, 64, 70, 76, 78, 82, 110, 111, 116, 128, 151, 171, 177, 193, 196, 204, 212

Glow Images Darren Pryce 32; Dianne Haine/TIPS 140; Heritage Images 202; Ingo Schulz 221; Martin Engelmann 288; Nordic Photos 19

NASA ESA and M J Jee (John Hopkins University) 40

Octopus Publishing Group Frazer Cunningham 303, Polly Wreford 320

Shutterstock Andrzej Grzegorczyk 194; Blue67design 350; Captain Yeo 316; Chuck Rausin 367; Creativa 318; Daisy Daisy 170; Daniel M Nagy 224; David Parker 54; Deborah Benbrook 192; Elena Dijour 326; Eliks 42; Evdokimov Maxim 344; Hein Nouwens 211 below; Hung Chung Chih 93; Iravgustin 382; Jeremy Walker 56; Malija 14; Mikhail Zahranichny 73; Mirian Maslo 58; mountainpix 77; nienora 117; pashabo 121; Pavel Vakhrushev 2; Paul Prescott 347; Romas Photo 258; Severjn 364; Victorian Traditions 337; Vladimir Volodin 232; Zurijeta 237; Zvonimir Atletic 262

SuperStock Album/Oronoz 96; Martin Siepmann/image/imagebroker 169; Wolfgang Kaehler 113; age fotostock 167, 222; Biosphoto 381; Cusp 239; De Agostini 108, 210; Fine Art Images 146, 158; Fine Art Photographic Library 213; Huntington Library 266; Juniors 119; Photononstop 271; Stefan Auth/imagebroker 215; SuperStock 261; The Art Archive 49 below right; tolokonov 201; Universal Images Group 49 above right, 174, 218

Thinkstock a-wrangler 299; Balasz Kovacs 114; Bratovanov 50; Comstock 315, 341; Cucumberov 377; Digital Vision 329; Dorling Kindersley 208; Eyecandy Images 306; George Doyle 332; Hakkiarslan 283; Happyhappy101 384; Hemera Technologies 375; Holly Kuchera 345 above; Ioana Drutu 255; James Thew 334; JGI 319; Jupiterimages 355; klagyivik 47; luvemakphoto 27; Mari Art 346; Maria Kazanova 324; Michele Princigalli 302; Miss Elli 313; Mkaminskyi 371; NA 291; NicoElNino 348; Photos.com 265; SanderStock 228; Sergey Anatolievich Pristyazhnyuk 309; Stockbyte 311; Stockbyte/Jupiter Images 338; suksaeng 4; Takashi Takeuchi 223; Thomas Northcut 362; Wavebreakmedia Ltd 17, 322; Wolfsburg1984 360; Wzfs1s 345 below

TopFoto Charles Walker 101, 198; The Granger Collection 200; Topham Picturepoint 225